DATE DUE

DEMCO 38-296

John Alden Carpenter

John Alden Carpenter. Used by Permission of G. Schirmer, Inc.

John Alden Carpenter
A Bio-Bibliography

Compiled by
Joan O'Connor

Bio-Bibliographies in Music, Number 54
Donald L. Hixon, *Series Adviser*

Greenwood Press
Westport, Connecticut • London

Library of Congress Cataloging-in-Publication Data

O'Connor, Joan.
  John Alden Carpenter : a bio-bibliography / compiled by Joan
O'Connor.
      p.   cm.—(Bio-bibliographies in music, ISSN 0742–6968 ; no.
54)
    Includes bibliographical references (p.   ) and index.
    Discography: p.
    ISBN 0–313–26430–9 (alk.   paper)
    1. Carpenter, John Alden, 1876–1951—Bibliography. 2. Carpenter,
John Alden, 1876–1951—Discography. I. Title. II. Series.
  ML134.C18O25 1994
  016.78′092—dc20   93–45943

British Library Cataloguing in Publication Data is available.

Library of Congress Catalog Card Number: 93–45943
ISBN: 0–313–26430–9
ISSN: 0742–6968

First published in 1994

Greenwood Press, 88 Post Road West, Westport, CT 06881
An imprint of Greenwood Publishing Group, Inc.

Printed in the United States of America

The paper used in this book complies with the
Permanent Paper Standard issued by the National
Information Standards Organization (Z39.48–1984).

10 9 8 7 6 5 4 3 2 1

Contents

Preface

This bio-bibliography on John Alden Carpenter consists of the
following sections: BIOGRAPHY — WORKS AND PER-
FORMANCES — DISCOGRAPHY — BIBLIOGRAPHY. Page
numbers refer to the PREFACE or BIOGRAPHY while numbers
preceded by the prefixes W, D, or B refer to entries in the
corresponding later sections. There are references in both the
WORKS AND PERFORMANCES and the DISCOGRAPHY
sections to reviews in the BIBLIOGRAPHY section, e.g., Premiere
(Review: B485).

WORKS are arranged chronologically by genre: orchestral
music, chamber music, piano music, songs, and music for plays.
Compositions completed or published in the same year are
arranged alphabetically. Undated works appear at the end of each
genre. A guide to the works precedes this section. Alphabetical
and chronological indexes precede the general index. In the
orchestral music section, instrumental doublings by one player
are indicated in parentheses.

The DISCOGRAPHY is arranged alphabetically. Complete
works precede selections from sets, e.g., the single movement
Dogs from the orchestral suite *Adventures in a Perambulator* will
follow in alphabetical order after all complete recordings of this
suite. When two or more Carpenter works appear on the same
label, the first entry is complete and others receive a brief listing
with a reference to the first entry. When more than four other
composers have works included on the album, only the first

three names arranged alphabetically are included with "et al" following these names. The names of these composers are listed in the index under "Recordings." Performances by the same performing group thought to be re-issues are included in the same D#. For non-commercially produced recordings, library call numbers and locations are given.

The BIBLIOGRAPHY is divided into the following genres: Bibliographies (Music Literature), Bibliographies (Music), Discographies, Yearbooks and Directories, Catalogs, Dissertations and Masters' Theses, Histories and Chronologies, Dictionaries and Encyclopedias, Music Theory, Dance, Journals, and Newspapers. Entries are arranged alphabetically within each genre. To preserve the writers' bias, quotations are used to retain the language and concerns of the time. When describing the ballets in particular, their length seems justified by their historic quality. The three-dot ellipsis is used consistently for all omissions in quotations, regardless of ending punctuation. All composition titles are italicized, including songs. In the WORKS section the composer's written comments are enclosed in quotations but the publisher's cover titles are not.

The APPENDIX gives Carpenter's program notes and musical analysis for *Adventures in a Perambulator*. They should be included in a work on Carpenter, but due to their length, neither the biography nor the works section seemed appropriate.

The CHRONOLOGICAL LIST OF WORKS gives date of completion, title, and date published or the abbreviation "n.p." meaning not published. Undated works appear at the end arranged alphabetically. The alphabetical index to the works attempts to give as many alternate spellings as possible, e.g., *Piano Concertino*, as well as *Concertino for Piano*. For the songs, it would be helpful to look at the guide to song order following the guide to works, p.33, for an explanation of cover titles on single songs.

It was necessary to limit INDEX entries for certain recurring items to a test of substance and, in the case of his compositions, to a ranking system: detailed description, informative description, and brief mention. All dedicatees are indicated in the index. Writers of program notes for the recordings are indicated by (PN) following the D#. In some instances the performer was also the program note author and that personal name receives two D#s, one indicating (PN). When appropriate, subdivisions and "see-references" are included. Titles of record albums are enclosed in parentheses.

Several scores were not found even though they are listed in major reference books. Only one, *Valse triste* for violin and piano, has been excluded from the works section. There was less information to justify its inclusion than for the others.

Therefore, it is included here in the preface. The song *Stars* is listed in the New York Public Library printed catalog as a composition by Carpenter, but this is incorrect. Several composers, including Carl Deis, Eric DeLamarter, and William Strasser, have made arrangements of Carpenter's works.

For a discussion of Carpenter's musical style, see Howard Pollack's book (forthcoming, Smithsonian Press).

Acknowledgments

I wish to express sincere appreciation to the staff and for the collection of the following libraries with special thanks to those people listed in parentheses: Chicago Public Library (Richard Schwegel), Newberry Library (Diana Haskell, Modern Mss.; and Carolyn Sheehy, Midwest Dance Collection), New York Public Library (Jean Bowen, Charles Eubanks, Music Division; Richard Jackson, Americana Collection; Don McCormick, Rodgers & Hammerstein Archives of Recorded Sound; Madeleine Nichols, Dance Collection; Dorothy Swerdlove, Richard Lynch, Billy Rose Theatre Collection), San Francisco Conservatory of Music (Allen Franzman, Valerie Gross, Frank Henry, Lucretia Wolfe), San Francisco Public Library (Mary Ashe, Art & Music Division), San Francisco State University (Richard Ross, Music Collection), San Jose State University (Jean Meyer, ILL), Stanford University (Aurora Perez, Archive of Recorded Sound), Tulane University, University of California, Berkeley (Ann Basart and Leah Emdy, Music Library), University of Minnesota (Katherine Holum, Music Library), University of San Francisco, University of Wisconsin, Madison, and the Washington D.C. Library of Congress (Charles Sens, Wayne D. Shirley, Music Division; Samuel Brylawski, Edwin M. Matthias, Motion Picture, Broadcasting and Recorded Sound Division).

For orchestral program notes and other materials I wish to thank the following individuals: Susan Wade (Chicago Symphony Orchestra), Michelle Feldman (Los Angeles

Philharmonic), Dennis McGovern and Robert Tuggle (Metropolitan Opera Archives), Paul B. Gunther (Minnesota Orchestra), Susan Feder (New Grove Dictionary of American Music), Marion R. Casey (New York Philharmonic Orchestra), Paul Orlando (The Philadelphia Orchestra), and Peter Herb (G. Schirmer).

For encouragement, proofreading, and suggestions I wish to express sincere appreciation to Tyler Abbott, Nell Boals, Scott Foglesong, Felder Graham, James Healey, Don Hixon, Wyatt Insko, Alden Jenks, Richard Koprowski, William Meredith, Jeffrey Miller, Howard Pollack, and Serena Stanford.

Abbreviations

acc.   accompaniment
arr.   arranged, or arrangement
ex.   example
L.H.   left hand
m.   measure
MM   metronome marking
ms.   manuscript
n.p.   no page number/not published
PN   program notes
port.   portrait, photograph
rev.   revised
t.p.   title page

LIBRARY LOCATIONS

DLC   Library of Congress, Washington, D.C.
Newberry   Newberry Library, Chicago
R&H ARS   Rodgers & Hammerstein Archive of Recorded
             Sound, New York Public Library

SOCIETIES

ASCAP   American Society of Composers, Authors, and
             Publishers

NEWSPAPERS

BET	Boston Evening Transcript
BG	Boston Globe
BH	Boston Herald
BP	Boston Post
CDN	Chicago Daily News
CDT	Chicago Daily Tribune
CST	Chicago Sun Times
CSM	Christian Science Monitor
NYEJ	New York Evening Journal
NYHT	New York Herald Tribune
NYS	New York Sun
NYT	New York Times
SFC	San Francisco Chronicle

Biography

To study John Alden Carpenter is to study the tastes and trends of the American people from 1912 through World War II. This bio-bibliography attempts to present his life and works, and the contemporary views, reviews, and criticisms which reveal historical attitudes and prejudices of American life in those troubled times. Looking back several decades, it is possible to discover what was enduring, what was transitory, and what elements would become important to our present state of musical composition.

Although he was an American with a Harvard education who quoted American popular tunes, Carpenter was also an eclectic. He wrote many works in a French impressionistic style, some with Germanic forms, and sometimes borrowing Spanish, Russian, and Oriental melodies, rhythms, and instruments. He was inspired by programmatic ideas and even wrote the program notes for his *Adventures in a Perambulator* suite. Humor and fantasy can be found in this suite which depicts a baby's stroll through the park with its nurse and in *Krazy Kat*, his jazz pantomime based on George Herriman's cartoon strip. Jazz first appeared at the Metropolitan Opera House in the 1926 production of *Skyscrapers*, his ballet of work and play.

John Alden Carpenter was born in Park Ridge, Illinois, on February 28, 1876. His mother, one of the founders of the Amateur Musician's Club of Chicago, began to teach John piano when he was five years old. Mrs. Elizabeth Curtis Greene

Carpenter, originally from Pittsfield, New Hampshire, studied voice with Salvatore Marchesi in Paris and with William Shakespeare in London. She shared her love of music with her four sons, Hubbard, Benjamin, John, and George Albert. The first three later worked in the family business while the fourth son became a federal judge in Chicago.

His father, George Benjamin Carpenter, came from Ohio to Chicago where he worked at Huginin & Pierce, a boat sails, ship chandlery, and grocery business founded in 1840. In 1857 the company became known as Gilbert Hubbard & Company with George Carpenter holding one-third interest in the firm. Hubbard died in 1881 and Carpenter took over. Incorporated in 1909, the George B. Carpenter Co. sold tents, camp bedsteads, flags, and banners. It remained in the family until John Alden Carpenter retired in 1936.

After studying piano with his mother, John continued lessons with Amy Fay from 1887 to 1891, then studied piano and theory with William Charles Ernest Seeboeck from 1891 to 1893. He attended Park Ridge Elementary School and University High School in Chicago. Report cards from University High School, 1891-1892, show classes taken in algebra, composition, declamation, German, Greek, gymnastics, history, Latin, military drill, reading, and spelling. After high school Carpenter went to Harvard where he studied composition with John Knowles Paine, the first professor of music there. Carpenter was active in student affairs as president of the Glee Club and as a member of the Institute of 1770, Zeta Psi, The Signet, and The Harvard Crimson. After graduation in 1897, Carpenter entered his father's business.

On November 20, 1900, John Alden Carpenter married Rue Winterbotham, daughter of Joseph and Genevieve Baldwin Winterbotham. Rue was a talented artist who illustrated her husband's songs for children, *Improving Songs for Anxious Children* (1902) and *When Little Boys Sing* (1904). Continuing her interest in art, Rue delivered several lectures on interior decoration in Chicago and the east, also superintended the art work for the Vanderbilt Suite at the Waldorf Astoria Hotel. Her only child, Genevieve, was born in 1904 and married Patrick Hill on December 21, 1931. Rue died of a cerebral hemorrhage on December 7, 1931, two weeks before her daughter's wedding.

John Alden Carpenter married his second wife, Ellen Waller Borden, on January 31, 1933 at the home of her aunt and uncle, Mr. and Mrs. Kingsley Porter of Cambridge, Massachusetts. The bride's two daughters, Mrs. Adlai E. Stevenson and Mrs. Robert C. Pirie, were present. Carpenter credited Ellen with finding pleasant places for them to visit while he composed. She died November 1, 1974.

Like Charles Ives, Carpenter combined the lives of a businessman and a composer. After Harvard, he continued to study composition. In 1906 Carpenter persuaded the English composer Edward Elgar to give him lessons for three months while they were both in Rome. Back in Chicago, Carpenter studied with Bernhard Ziehn, the German-American music theorist whom Carpenter regarded as the finest teacher he ever had. This instruction continued until Ziehn's death in 1912.

Carpenter traced his ancestry to determine if he was indeed a lineal descendant of the Pilgrim John Alden. A letter dated 29 August 1947 from Caroline Brewster traces the family tree:

ALDEN-CARPENTER LINES

(I)
JOHN & PRISCILLA ALDEN

(II)
JONATHAN

3rd son Capt.
Jonathan Alden
married Abigail
Hallett Dec.10, 1672

(III)
JONATHAN

Elder son Andrew   married Elizabeth
married Lydia   (Arnold) Waterman
Stamford Feb. 4, 1714   Jan. 17, 1717-18

(IV)
LYDIA   SETH

married Lydia Alden
(cousin)

(V)
JONATHAN

married Sarah Bartlett

(VI)
CHARLOTTE

Bartlett Alden
married Benjamin
Carpenter (John
Alden Carpenter's
(great?) grandfather)[1]

Carpenter's early works include the Harvard Hasty Pudding Plays, most of his piano music, and many songs. Carpenter's *Minuet for Orchestra* was performed by the Pierian Society for Harvard graduation services on December 18, 1894 and his *Piano Sonata* was performed at Harvard graduation exercises in 1897. His many songs are still heard at recitals. Two song cycles, *Gitanjali* (set to Rabindranath Tagore's text) and *Water Colors* (set to English translations of Chinese poetry) were later orchestrated as were the single songs *Blue Gal, Les silhouettes,* and *Slumber Song.* Carpenter was a master at setting words to music and his accompaniments keep interest through subtle shifts in rhythm and harmony.

Carpenter's *Violin Sonata,* dedicated to Bernhard Ziehn, is cyclic in form, reminding the listener of César Franck. Mischa Elman, the violinist, first performed it in New York on December 11, 1912, with the composer at the piano. David Ewen found it to be "without very much character or originality" in his book *Composers of Today*[2] but called it Carpenter's "first success" in *The World of Twentieth-Century Music.*[3]

Dedicated to Carpenter's first wife, the 1927 *String Quartet* is light, friendly, sometimes sensuous, and always pleasurable. One finds Spanish rhythms, jazz, and French impressionism. Quartal elements in both melody and harmony appear in the first movement.[4] First written in 1934, the *Piano Quintet* was revised in 1937 and also in 1946-1947. Later, parts of it were used in Carpenter's *Symphony no. 2.* Dedicated to Elizabeth Sprague Coolidge, the quintet seems better suited to a larger ensemble.

Adventures in a Perambulator, his first and most successful orchestral work, is a six-movement suite: En voiture — The Policeman — The Hurdy-Gurdy — The Lake — Dogs — Dreams. Carpenter's program notes and musical analysis can be found in the Appendix. This suite was first performed in Chicago March 19, 1915 and has been performed in places as far away as Mexico City, Stockholm, and London. Today it is most often heard at "Pops" concerts.

Percy Grainger introduced the *Piano Concertino* to Chicago on March 10, 1916. Carpenter described it as "a lighthearted conversation between two friends who have traveled different paths and become a little garrulous over their separate experiences. The conversation is mostly of rhythms—American, Oriental and otherwise."[5] Alfred Frankenstein found that the work "begins well, in a witty dialogue of piano and orchestra, which sounds like a bit of jazz by MacDowell, but before long the work bogs down in Carpenter's kind of banality."[6] Eric DeLamarter thought it was a "racy, barbarian fantasy of equally stunning rhythmic effects. It is involved, enigmatic, mesmeric...no end clever."[7]

Carpenter's *Symphony no. 1* (1917) or "Sermons in Stones" also has a cyclic form with an ostinato motif recurring in its first and third movements. The programmatic idea, from Act II, scene 1, of Shakespeare's *As You Like It*, is limited to a tendency toward optimism. The dramatic text follows:

Sweet are the uses of adversity;
Which, like the toad, ugly and venemous,
Wears yet a precious jewel in his head,
And this our life, exempt from public haunt,
Finds tongues in trees, books in the running brooks,
Sermons in stones and good in everything.[8]

Birthday of the Infanta, Carpenter's first ballet, is set to Oscar Wilde's short story about a young Spanish princess who is delighted when a dwarf dances at her surprise birthday party. She throws him her handkerchief and he falls in love with her. He follows the party into the castle where he enters a hall of mirrors. When he sees his grotesque image in the mirror he is horrified and realizes that the little princess cannot possibly love him. He dances until he falls dead from exhaustion.

Costumes and sets recall the seventeenth century of Velásquez. Vivid colors in the costumes and sunsets contrast with shaded hues and the pale costume of Pedro. Tall doors, ten-foot candle sticks, the hall of mirrors contrast with the little Infanta and her playmates. The characters include bandilleros, picadors, matadors, bullfighters, gardeners, foreign ambassadors, ministers, and cooks. They even have papier-mâché bulls! The girls are dressed in wide hooped skirts with matching sweeping hair-dos.[9]

Dedicated to his daughter Genevieve, the ballet was first performed in Chicago on December 23, 1919 with Adolf Bolm dancing the dwarf's part and Ruth Page as the Infanta. Carpenter made two orchestral suites from this ballet. Suite no. 1 consists of three movements: The Guests — The Infanta — Games. Suite no. 2 also has three movements: Gypsy Dance — Bull Fight — Finale tristo.

A Pilgrim Vision, written at the invitation of Leopold Stokowski in honor of the Tercentenary Mayflower program, was first performed in Philadelphia on November 26, 1920. Carpenter wrote these program notes:

In order that the purpose of the composer may be made clear, we are asked to imagine the grim little Pilgrim band in a last religious service in England, the march to the sea, the embarkation. We are asked to watch their ship as it sails away and disappears under the edge of the sky. Surely an extraordinary adventure! And surely, at the moment when the sea seems its most tremendous, and the Pilgrim ship its most forgotten, it is easy to think that in that moment the Eye of God rested upon them and smiled. For the sea speeds them on their way and they come at last to the Shore of their Hope. We can share in the exultation of their landing, in the joy of their discovery, and we can feel with them the thrill of the Future America.[10]

Carpenter's second ballet or jazz pantomime, *Krazy Kat*, was first performed as an orchestral suite December 23, 1921, in Chicago. The ballet version was first performed at Town Hall in New York on January 20, 1922. Based on George Herriman's cartoon strip of the same name, the ballet begins with Krazy Kat sleeping under a tree. Officer Pup passes swinging his club. Bill Postem pastes an announcement of the grand ball and departs. Upon awakening, Krazy sees the ad and prepares himself for the ball. He puts on a ballet skirt and finds some make-up which Old Joe Stork carelessly dropped. In the meantime Ignatz Mouse attempts to throw a brick at Krazy, but Officer Pup intervenes. Krazy is now practising a Spanish dance. As the dancing stops, the Mysterious Stranger appears with an enormous bouquet of catnip. Krazy inhales, and goes into a "Class-A Fit," the "Katnip Blues." At its climax, Ignatz casts off his disguise, throws the brick at Krazy who staggers, reels, and sleeps happily at the ballet's conclusion.

The ballet was performed in black and white costumes with grayish trees in the background. Cartoon images were drawn on backdrops which turned every 2-3 minutes from side to side just as one would read a cartoon strip. Besides the exotic rhythms, the Spanish dance with castanets, and the jazzy "Katnip Blues," Carpenter used trombone and clarinet glissandos, muted "wawa" trumpet, and syncopated rhythms.[11] For reviews of the 1922 performance see <u>B433</u> (Deems Taylor) and <u>B457</u> (Stark Young) in the Bibliography section. The ballet enjoyed several performances at the Greenwich Village Follies. Even with its technical and performing (two-piano version) inadequacies, a 1975 performance at the Newport Music Festival in Rhode Island showed that it was a "delightful period piece— fluffy, amusing, lightweight, and ever so much fun if it is approached for what it is."[12] Carpenter describes the principal characters:

To those who have not mastered Mr. Herriman's psychology it may be explained that Krazy Kat is the world's greatest optimist—Don Quixote and Parsifal rolled into one. It is therefore possible for him to maintain constantly at white heat a passionate affair with Ignatz Mouse, in which the gender of each remains ever a delightful mystery. Ignatz, on the other hand, condenses in his sexless self all the cardinal vices...In short, he is meaner than anything, and his complex is cats.[13]

Skyscrapers, Carpenter's last ballet, has an interesting history. Diaghilev heard of *Krazy Kat,* asked to see the score and photos of the dance, and then expressed interest in producing a ballet written by Carpenter. He asked Carpenter to write him a ballet about American life.

In 1924, Serge Diaghilev planned to tour the United States with his Ballet Russe de Monte Carlo. For this visit he commissioned Carpenter to create a ballet about American life. Carpenter completed his assignment in 1924, but the Ballet Russe tour did not materialize at this time. Nevertheless, Diaghilev was so interested in what Carpenter had done that he proposed mounting the ballet in Monte Carlo in March of 1925. However, as negotiations between Diaghilev and Carpenter dragged on, Carpenter responded to a request by the Metropolitan Opera Company that it be allowed to introduce the work.[14]

Although Diaghilev felt that scenes of "grèves" or strikes portray the American way of life, Carpenter wanted a certain element of Bolshevism.

After Giulio Gatti-Casazza of the Metropolitan Opera had persuaded Carpenter to let him produce *Skyscrapers*, Carpenter and Robert Edmond Jones spent six months in a Vermont farmhouse playing the music and developing the action. *Skyscrapers* was first produced February 19, 1926 at the Metropolitan Opera House with Albert Troy dancing "The Strutter," Rita de Leporte "Herself," and Roger Dodge "White-Wings," with choreography by Robert Edmond Jones, assisted by Sammy Lee; sets, scenery, and costumes by Robert Edmond Jones.

The ballet is in six scenes:

I. Symbols of restlessness
II. An abstraction of the skyscraper,
   the work that produces it—and the
   interminably passing crowd

III.   Transition from work to play
IV.   Any Coney Island and a reflection of a few of its activities, interrupted presently by a "throw-back" in the film sense, to the idea of work, and reverting with equal suddenness to play
V.   Return from play to work
VI.   Skyscrapers

Unusual features in this ballet include jagged steel outlines, Coney Island, a fantasy with merry-go-round, comic policemen, side-shows, flappers and sailors. Critics have varied in their response: from a "jazz-infected score"[15] to "unabashed tunefulness and brilliant orchestration"[16] to "devastating...despair."[17] In 1928 Heinrich Kröller produced the ballet in Munich under its German name, *Wolkenkratze*. The score was deposited in the cornerstone of Hampshire House, a 40-story New York skyscraper erected in 1931. The ballet was drastically changed for a 1933 Hollywood Bowl performance:

> Whereas in 1926 people ate hot dogs for diversion, in 1933 a hot dog constituted a full meal. For that, and similar reasons, the ballet was changed. Robots worked on the Skyscrapers and waited on table in the cabaret, while a bloated plutocrat known as The Boss had a dream in which angels sang, a seductive lady charmed him and demons pursued him. In the mêlée was thrown a prizefight. The new scenarists openly admitted that their "reasons" permitted them to retain the title of the ballet and eliminate the subtitles. Lo, the poor composer! Has he no jurisdiction over his brainchildren?[18]

Jazz Orchestra Pieces were written in 1925-1926. The first, *A Little Bit of Jazz*, was dedicated to Paul Whiteman. It is "an unimportant little thing which suffers from that musical politeness...that affects all Carpenter's jazz."[19] The second title is *Oil and Vinegar*.

Song of Faith, a cantata for chorus and orchestra on a text which the composer prepared from material by Walt Whitman and George Washington, was written for the Washington Bicentennial. The premiere was given February 23, 1932 with Clifton J. Furness as narrator; the Cecilia Society Chorus; Boston Symphony Orchestra; and Serge Koussevitzky conducting. First lines of each section follow:

CHILDREN AND MEN
Come now, hear our song!
CHILDREN
Comes to town young Doodle dandy!
MEN
Sounds the throb of the drum-beat
CHILDREN AND MEN
Sounds a sweet lullaby,
CHILDREN
Lead me to sleep where the still waters flow,
CHILDREN AND MEN
Oh, hear the band, the Yankee band!
NARRATOR
I close this last solemn act of my life by commending the interests of our dearest country to the protection of Almighty God.
CHILDREN
Comes a bright and shining day.
CHILDREN AND MEN
May the hand of God be our stay.[20]

Patterns, a one-movement symphonic work with piano obbligato written for the Boston Symphony Orchestra's fiftieth anniversary in 1930, had its premiere October 21, 1932 with the composer at the piano. The title has no literary or programmatic significance. Warren Storey Smith thought it should be called "Patchwork" because of its structural "hodgepodge."[21] Slonimsky calls it "eclectic hedonism, comprising waltzes, jazzy discursions and bits of Spanish dances."[22]

Sea Drift (1933) is a tone poem based on Walt Whitman's text. In the preface to the study score Carpenter explains how he came to compose it:

Away back around 1915, I experienced my first acute Whitman excitement, and for some time, then, I studied the problem of setting to music in vocal form excerpts from some of the *Sea-Drift* poems. These experiments I could not bring to any result that satisfied me, and I dropped the project.

In February of last year, under the influence of the blue Mediterranean at Eze Village, I took up the old problem again, and abandoned any attempt to make a literal setting of the Whitman verses in a vocal work. I tried to make a complete orchestral record of the imprint <u>upon me</u> of these poems. My hope is that the music makes sense, just as music, with perhaps a special meaning for those who love

Whitman. My work represents an effort to transcribe my impressions derived from these magnificent poems.[23]

This was Howard Hansen's favorite Carpenter work:

Here Carpenter reveals not only his descriptive powers...but an emotional depth of which we had not always been conscious...[There is] translucent sound at the end where muted horns, low strings, and vibraphone combine the sonorities of four keys with such delicate beauty that one strains one's powers of hearing to prolong the sheer ecstasy of the sound...[It is] more profound, more tragic and more mysterious [than Debussy's *La mer.*][24]

Dedicated to Carpenter's second wife, the *Violin Concerto* was first performed by Zlatko Balokovic in Chicago on November 18, 1937. Carpenter called it "moderately modern."[25] The concerto is "breezy rather than profound...too long to rivet attention."[26]

Symphony no. 1 (1940) is a revision of "Sermons in Stones," the 1917 symphony. Dedicated to the Chicago Symphony Orchestra and Frederic Stock on the occasion of the symphony's fiftieth anniversary, this one-movement work of four contrasting sections lasts eighteen minutes. Critics praised the tuneful themes and crystal clear orchestration. Carpenter called it "peaceful music, and in these days, perhaps that is something."[27]

Music from the *Piano Quintet* was reworked into the *Symphony no. 2* (1942), first performed October 22, 1942. Carpenter describes the derivation of the piece: "Some of the native tunes heard there [in Algiers] 'rubbed off' to some extent in the coloring of the last movement of my work, which is otherwise devoid of programmatic intent."[28] In a letter to Felix Borowski dated 2 March 1949 Carpenter explains the 1946 revised version:

In 1946 came a new version of the *Quintet* which resulted in a structural condensation in the first movement. This change seemed logical and sufficiently important to warrant a corresponding condensation in *Symphony II*, thus bringing the symphony to its final form, in which it is now being performed for the first time.[29]

Danza, a short work in simple two-part form, was first performed December 5, 1935 by the Chicago Symphony Orchestra. The opening theme is based on three notes: E, F, and G. Carpenter explains how it evolved:

> [*Danza* was an] offshoot from a larger work based on Oriental musical idioms on which I have been engaged ever since a visit to China last spring. In the course of the larger work I found myself toying with the following idea,...finally gave it its head and used it as the principal rhythmic germ of "Danza."[30]

Lesser well-known orchestral works include *Song of Freedom,* based on an M.H. Martin text for unison chorus and orchestra, and *Dance Suite* which is an arrangement of three works originally written for piano: *Polonaise américaine, Tango américain,* and *Danza.* The National Symphony gave the premiere performance of *Dance Suite* in Washington, D.C. on November 3, 1943 with Hans Kindler conducting.

The Anxious Bugler (1943), commissioned by the League of Composers to express an aspect of the war, was first performed on November 17, 1943. Carpenter said the work "may stand for any boy anywhere who finds himself a soldier. He works and sweats, and sometimes he fears. He also has his hopes, with home always in the back of his mind; and at times the stern voice of God is in his ears."

> [Olin Downes heard] confused sounds and rhythms and thoughts; the din of machines—the jog of drill; a musical reference to "Ein Feste Burg" and to the "V"- motive...from the Fifth Symphony; the chorus of "Old Folks at Home," the tune broken into bits...and toward the last the sounding of Taps.[31]

Seven Ages, from Act II, scene 7 of Shakespeare's *As You Like It,* depicts man from infancy to second "childishness." The seven musical episodes are:

I.	Vivace	"All the world's a stage"
	Andante amabile	"At first, the infant..."
II.	Animato gioco	"Then the whining schoolboy..."
III.	Andantino sentimentale	"And then the lover sighing like a furnace..."

IV. Allegro barbaro	"Then a soldier..."
V. Buffo-pomposo	"And then the justice, in fair round belly with good capon lin'd..."
VI. Lento dolente	"The lean and slippered pantaloon..."
VII. Adagio-agitato-placido	"Sans eyes, sans taste, sans everything."[32]

The symphonic suite was premiered at Carnegie Hall in New York on November 29, 1945 with Artur Rodzinski conducting the New York Philharmonic Symphony.

Carmel Concerto, first performed by the New York Philharmonic on November 20, 1949, is a one-movement work consisting of "a number of short sections of contrasting content, which seek to reflect the shifting atmosphere of that picturesque locale, in moods ranging from vigor to calm, with suggestions of Oriental or Spanish derivation, as well as bits of *America* unabashed."[33]

Carpenter, 5'11" tall and 156 lbs., had graying brown hair and blue eyes. He enjoyed reading, travel, and tennis. A member of the Cliff Dwellers, the University Club, and The Saddle and Cycle Club, all in Chicago, he also had memberships in the National Committee on Music in Army and Navy Camps during World War I, American Society of Composers, Authors and Publishers (1929), and the Manuscript Society of Chicago. During World War II Carpenter served as president of the Choral and Instrumental Music Association of Chicago which promoted free concerts in Chicago parks. He was director and past president of the Children's Home and Aid Society and director of the Chicago Allied Arts. He sat on the Honorary Board of Endorsers of the New Music Society Publisher and the Society for the Publication of American Music. He was an incorporator of the Illinois Composers' Guild.

Carpenter received an honorary Master of Arts degree from Harvard in 1922 and two honorary doctorate degrees: one from the University of Wisconsin in 1935 and one from Northwestern in 1941. A letter dated 16 June 1936 from the American Conservatory of Music to Carpenter expresses interest in giving him an honorary Doctor of Music degree and a letter dated 19 April 1943 from Alan Valentine, University of Rochester, to Carpenter acknowledges the verdict of Carpenter's doctor against travel to Rochester to receive an honorary degree.

Carpenter became a Chevalier of the French Legion of Honor in 1921. He was decorated by the Yugoslav government in 1938. A member of the National Institute of Arts and Letters

(1918) and the American Academy of Arts and Letters (1942), Carpenter received a gold medal for distinguished achievement in music from the Institute of Arts and Letters in 1947. This medal was the third such given in the Institute's history.

Carpenter died April 26, 1951 in Chicago. His widow dedicated a concert hall in Ipswich, Massachusetts in his memory. His music has been the subject of several masters' theses and doctoral dissertations. The Library of Congress in Washington, D.C. and Newberry Library in Chicago have extensive collections of his works and correspondence. For a time his music was out of favor with the public but new recordings have recently been issued in LP and CD formats, and some of his works may again be performed in the concert hall or on the ballet stage or in the school auditorium.

NOTES

1. Caroline Brewster to John Alden Carpenter (29 Aug. 1947) letter, Music Division, Library of Congress.

2. David Ewen, *Composers of Today*, New York: H.W. Wilson, 1934, p. 37.

3. _____. *The World of Twentieth-Century Music*, Englewood Cliffs, NJ: Prentice Hall, 1968, p. 140.

4. Felix Borowski, "John Alden Carpenter," *Musical Quarterly* 16 (1930): 233.

5. Philo Adams Otis, *The Chicago Symphony Orchestra, 1891-1924*, Freeport, NY: Books for Libraries, 1924, p. 277.

6. Alfred Frankenstein, "Records in Review," *High Fidelity* 14 (June 1964): 75.

7. Eric Delamarter, "Percy Grainger at Orchestra Hall," *Chicago Daily Tribune* (11 Mar. 1916): 14.

8. *Boston Symphony Program Notes* (19 Apr. 1918): 1331.

9. René Devries, "Chicago Opera Association Reviews 'Don Pasquale' Starring Galli-Curci," *Musical Courrier* 112 (8 Jan. 1920): 14.

10. *The Philadelphia Orchestra Program Notes* (26 Nov. 1920): 223.

11. Charles Hamm, *Music in the New World*, New York: W.W. Norton, 1983, p. 423.

12. Harold C. Schoenberg, "Music: Fry's Challenge," *New York Times* (30 July 1975): D4.

13. John Alden Carpenter, *Krazy Kat*, New York: G. Schirmer, 1922, p. [ii]

14. David Ewen, *The World of Twentieth Century Music*, p. 142-43.

15. Arthur Cohn, "Skyscrapers," *American Record Guide* 31 (May 1965): 838.

16. Oscar Thompson, "Koussevitzky's Bostonians Give Second American Program," *Musical America* 59 (10 Dec. 1939): 27.

17. Alice Holdship Ware, "Skyscrapers," *Survey* 56 (1 Apr. 1926): 35.

18. Verna Arvey, *Choreographic Music*, New York: Dutton, 1941, p. 291.

19. Henry O. Osgood, *So This Is Jazz*, Boston: Little, Brown, 1926, p. 156.

20. Lawrence Gilman, "An American Song of Faith," *New York Herald Tribune* (1 May 1932): VII: 6.

21. Warren Storey Smith, "Symphony Performs New Music," *Boston Post* (22 Oct. 1932): 12.

22. Nicholas Slonimsky, *Music Since 1900*, 4th ed., New York: Charles Scribner's Sons, 1971, p. 554.

23. John Alden Carpenter, *Sea Drift*, New York: G. Schirmer, 1934, p. 4.

24. Howard Hanson, "John Alden Carpenter," *Saturday Review* (24 Feb. 1951): 50-51.

25. "Carpenter Concerto Played in Chicago," *Musical America* 57 (25 Nov. 1937): 26.

26. "Carpenter Violin Concerto Played by Balokovic," *Musical America* 59 (25 Mar. 1939): 10.

27. "Peaceful Music," *Time* 36 (4 Nov. 1940): 58.

28. David Ewen, *The World of Twentieth-Century Music*, p.144.

29. John Alden Carpenter to Felix Borowski (2 Mar. 1949) letter, Music Division, Library of Congress.

30. *Boston Symphony Program Notes* (17 Jan. 1936): 561.

31. Olin Downes, "'Anxious Bugler' by Philharmonic," *New York Times* (18 Nov. 1943): 28.

32. *The Philadelphia Orchestra Program Notes* (15 Nov. 1946): 139.

33. Cecil Smith, "Carmel Concerto," *The Philharmonic-Symphony Society of New York Program Notes* (20 Nov. 1949): [n.p.]

Works and Performances

GUIDE TO THE WORKS

EXAMPLE

1.   **W5.**
2.   **Gitanjali; arr.**
3.   Completed 1914; revised 1934.
4.   For mezzo soprano and orchestra (1914: 2 flutes ...)(1934: 2 flutes...)
5.   Song cycle; acc. originally for piano.
6.   Words by Rabindranath Tagore.
7.   [Dedicated...]
8.   [Commissioned...]
9.   Contents: When I Bring You Coloured Toys — On the Day...
10. Score & parts available for rent from G. Schirmer.
11. [Published:...]
12. Holograph of score...
13. Premiere
     1914 (Apr. 27) Chicago; Orchestra Hall; Lucille Stevenson, soprano; Chicago Symphony Orchestra; Glenn Dillard Gunn, conductor.

KEY FOR EXAMPLE

1. "W" number of composition in the works section, arranged chronologically by genre, undated works at end arranged alphabetically by title.

2. Title of work in most common usage, with alternate inverted forms and subtitles appearing in alphabetical index to works.

3. Dates of completion and revision taken from holographs; *National Union Catalog*, the *New Grove Dictionary of American Music*, the 1930 Borowski *Musical Quarterly* article, and the Pierson dissertation.

4. Instrumentation (piano music refers to solo piano music; songs and plays are for voice and piano unless otherwise indicated). This example gives original and revised orchestration, taken from the music, when available, and from program notes.

5. Form.

6. Literary reference.

7. Dedication, if any.

8. Commission, if any.

9. Contents of separate movements or titles.

10. Availability of score & parts for rental.

11. Publication information includes format (e.g., piano, 4 hands), number of pages, publisher, date, plate number, series, and cover titles.

12. Holograph information lists number of pages, in ink or pencil with corrections, deletions, and emendations, any written material (e.g., begun [date]), and library location.

13. Premiere information gives year, date, place, performers, and reviews.

GUIDE TO SONG ORDER

Chronological arrangement is by year of publication if published, else by year of completion if given, undated works are arranged alphabetically at the end. Preceding "W" numbered entries for certain years are bold face titles which appear on the cover of individual songs indicating that the publisher intended them to be a set or series. After the bold face series title, the contents are listed in the order they appear on the cover with "W" numbers following the titles. Since the series titles do not receive "W" numbers, references in the alphabetical index to the works are to the preceding "W" number followed by "a" or, when two series titles appear alphabetically preceding that year's "W" number, W#a, W#b, etc.

Songs with translations have translation following title and 1st line. Language and translator's name follow the author's name.

ORCHESTRAL MUSIC

W1.   **Minuet.**
   Completed 1894.
   For orchestra.
   Premiere
      1894 (Dec. 18) Harvard; Graduation
      Exercise; Pierian Sodality Orchestra.

W2.   **Berceuse.**
   Completed Mar. 1908.
   For small orchestra (2 flutes, 2 oboes, 4 clarinets,
      2 bassoons, 2 horns & strings).
   Holograph of score (32 p.) in ink at DLC.

W3.   **Suite.**
   Completed 1909.
   For small orchestra (flute, oboe, 2 clarinets, 2
      bassoons, horn, timpani & strings).
   Contents: Andantino — Allegro.
   Holograph of score (28, 51 p.) in ink with
      corrections in pencil at DLC.

W4.   **Adventures in a Perambulator.**
   Completed 1914; revised 1941.
   For orchestra (1914: 3 flutes (piccolo), 2 oboes,
      English horn, 2 clarinets, bass clarinet, 2
      bassoons, 4 horns, 2 trumpets, 3 trombones,

tuba, timpani, bass drum, cymbals, triangle,
tambourine, 2 xylophones, Glockenspiel,
bells, harp, celesta, piano & strings) (1941:
piccolo, 2 flutes, 2 oboes, English horn, 2
clarinets, bass clarinet, 2 bassoons, 4 horns, 2
trumpets, 3 trombones, tuba, cymbals, bass
drum, snare drum, timpani, triangle, Glockenspiel, cylinder bells, celesta, piano, harp &
strings).

Orchestral suite; story by John Alden Carpenter.
Dedicated "To my friend Joseph Winterbotham."
Contents: En voiture! — The Policeman — The
Hurdy-Gurdy — The Lake — Dogs — Dreams.
Score & parts available for rent from G.
Schirmer.
Published: score (117 p.) G. Schirmer, c1917
(pl.no. 26122)
Holograph of revised score (105 p.) in ink at
DLC; at end: "Chicago. March-May '41."
Premiere (Reviews: B338, B511)
1915 (Mar. 19) Chicago; Orchestra Hall;
Chicago Symphony Orchestra;
Frederick Stock, conductor.

W5.   **Gitanjali; arr.**
Completed 1914; revised 1934.
For mezzo soprano and orchestra (1914: 2 flutes,
2 oboes, English horn, 2 clarinets, bass clarinet, 4 horns, 2 trumpets, 3 trombones, tuba,
timpani, harp, triangle & strings) (1934: 2
flutes, 2 oboes, English horn, 2 clarinets, 2
bassoons, 2 horns, timpani, bass drum,
cymbals, gong, Glockenspiel, celesta, vibra-
phone, harp, piano & strings).
Song cycle; acc. originally for piano.
Words by Rabindranath Tagore.
Contents: When I Bring You Coloured Toys —
On the Day When Death Will Knock at Thy
Door — The Sleep That Flits on Baby's Eyes
— I Am Like a Remnant of a Cloud of Au-
tumn — On the Seashore of Endless Worlds
— Light, My Light.
Score & parts available for rent from G.
Schirmer.
Holograph of earlier version (37, 21, 14 p.) in
pencil at DLC; copyist's ms. of earlier version
(12, 7, 7, 12, 22, 22 p.) in ink with emendations

in the composer's hand at DLC; holograph
of revised version (84 p.) in ink at DLC; at
end: "Aug. 15th '34. Chicago, Pride's Crossing."
Premiere
    1914 (Apr. 27) Chicago; Orchestra Hall;
        Lucille Stevenson, soprano; Chicago
        Symphony Orchestra; Glenn Dillard
        Gunn, conductor.

W6.   **Piano Concertino.**
      Completed 1915; revised 1947.
      For piano and orchestra (1915: 3 flutes (piccolo),
        2 oboes, English horn, 2 clarinets, bass clari-
        net, 2 bassoons, contrabassoon, 4 horns, 2
        trumpets, 3 trombones, tuba, timpani, bass
        drum, cymbals, tambourine, castanets,
        Glockenspiel, harp, piano & strings).
      Contents: Allegro con moto — Lento grazioso —
        Allegro risoluto
      Score & parts available for rent from G.
        Schirmer.
      Published: score (80 p.) G. Schirmer, c1920 (pl.no.
        27854); 2 piano, 4 hand arr. (65 p.) G. Schirmer,
        c1920 (pl.no. 27853)
      Holograph of score (80 p.) in ink with blue and
        red pencil additions and corrections at DLC;
        holograph of cadenza (4 p.) in ink at DLC.
      Premiere
        1916 (Mar. 10) Chicago; Orchestra Hall;
          Percy Grainger, piano; Chicago Sym-
          phony Orchestra; Frederick Stock, con-
          ductor.

W7.   **Symphony no. 1 (1917).**
      Completed 1917; revised 1940.
      For orchestra (piccolo, 2 flutes, 2 oboes, English
        horn, 2 clarinets, bass clarinet, 2 bassoons, con-
        trabassoon, 4 horns, 3 trumpets, 3 trombones,
        tuba, timpani, side, bass, & tenor drums,
        cymbals, triangle, Glockenspiel, celesta, tam-
        tam, gong, tambourine, 2 harps & strings).
      Subtitled: "Sermons in Stones" from Shake-
        speare's *As You Like It*, Act II, scene 5.
      Contents. Largo — Scherzo — Moderato.
      Holograph of score (167 p.) in ink at DLC; on
        verso of t.p.: "Sermons in Stones;" at head

of p.1: "Begun July 31–16;" at end: "Finished
March 6th–17. Corrections and changes in
piano part (46 p.); at end: "To Ellen, Èze
Village & Beverly, March to September 1936."
Premiere (Review: B485)
  1917 (Jun. 5) Norfolk, CT; Carl Stoeckel's
    Music Shed; Litchfield County Choral
    Union Festival; Frederick Stock, conductor.

W8.   Birthday of the Infanta.
Completed 1918; revised 1938; suite no. 1: 1932;
  revised 1940; suite no. 2: 1949.
Ballet pantomime (1918: 3 flutes, 3 oboes, 3
  clarinets, 2 bassoons, contrabassoon, 4 horns, 3
  trumpets, 3 trombones, tuba, harp, piano,
  celesta, xylophone, Glockenspiel, cylinder
  bells, timpani, bass drum, cymbals, snare
  drum, oriental drum, gong, castanets, wood
  block, mezzo soprano & strings) (suite no. 1: 3
  flutes (piccolo), 3 oboes (English horn), 3 clarinets (bass clarinet), 2 bassoons, contrabassoon,
  4 horns, 3 trumpets, 3 trombones, tuba, harp,
  piano, celesta, xylophone, Glockenspiel, cylinder bells, timpani, bass drum, cymbals, snare
  drum, oriental drum, gong, castanets, wood
  block, mezzo soprano & strings).
Story by Oscar Wilde.
Dedicated to daughter Genevieve.
Commissioned by Cleofonte Campanini,
  director of the Chicago Opera Company (who
  died before the premiere)
Score & parts of suite available for rent from G.
  Schirmer.
Holograph of original sketch of ballet (20, 44, 6
  p.) in pencil at DLC; at end of p.44: "Finished
  8/20/18;" holograph of ballet score (184 p.) in
  ink with additions, corrections and deletions
  in red and blue pencil with stage directions in
  red ink at DLC (with portfolio consisting of
  photographs, magazine clippings, costume
  sketches and stage designs in water colors, and
  several letters); holograph of piano arr. (45 p.)
  in ink with stage directions in red ink at DLC;
  holograph of piano, 4 hand arr. (44 p.) in ink,
  in part, photocopy (positive) at DLC; at end:
  "This revision 1938."
Suite no. 1; Published: score (127 p.) G. Schirmer,

c1932 (pl.no. 35100)
Contents: The Guests — The Infanta —
Games.
Suite no. 2; Holograph of score (60 p.) in ink, in
part, photocopy (positive) at DLC; at end:
"This arrangement 1949. Chicago and Carmel,
Calif.;" includes two copies of the composer's
reduction of the vocalise in the first move-
ment, with harp and piano acc. (4 p. each).
Contents: Gypsy Dance — Bull Fight — Finale
tristo.
Premiere of ballet (Reviews: B309, B319, B479)
1919 (Dec. 23) Chicago; Auditorium; Adolf
Bolm "Pedro;" Ruth Page "The Infanta;"
Margit Leeraas "A Gypsy;" Caird Leslie "A
Juggler;" Alexander Oumansky "A Tight-
Rope Walker;" Paul Oscardier "A
Matador;" Vincenzo Ioucelli "The Bull;"
Adolf Bolm, scenes and action; Robert
Edmond Jones, sets and costumes; [orches-
tra] Louis Hasselmans, conductor.
Premiere of suite no. 1
1920 (Dec. 3) Chicago; Orchestra Hall; Chi-
cago Symphony Orchestra; Frederick Stock,
conductor.

W9.   **Water Colors; arr.**
Completed 1918?
For mezzo soprano and chamber orchestra (2
flutes, oboe, clarinet, bassoon, 2 horns, 2
trumpets, percussion (I: triangle, Glocken-
spiel; II: cymbals, timpani, bass drum,
Glockenspiel, small oriental drum; III: tam-
tam, bass drum, cymbals, timpani; IV:
Glockenspiel, cymbals, celesta) piano &
strings).
Song cycle; acc. originally for piano.
Words from Chinese poems by Li-Po, Yü-hsi, Li-
Shê, and *National Odes of China* (collected by
Confucius); translated by Herbert Allen Giles.
Contents: On a Screen — The Odalisque — The
Highwaymen — To a Young Gentleman.
Score & parts available for rent from G.
Schirmer.
Holograph of score (26 p.) in ink with red &
blue pencil additions at DLC.
First Minneapolis Performance

> 1920 (Nov. 21) Minneapolis; Mina Hager,
> contralto; Minneapolis Symphony
> Orchestra; Emil Oberhoffer, conductor.

W10.   **A Pilgrim Vision.**
> Completed Sept. 1920.
> For orchestra (3 flutes (piccolo), 2 oboes, English
> horn, 2 clarinets, bass clarinet, 2 bassoons,
> contrabassoon, 6 horns, 4 trumpets, 3 trom-
> bones, tuba, bells,harp, organ & strings).
> Commissioned by Leopold Stokowski for the
> Tercentenary of the Pilgrims' Landing.
> Holograph of score (35 p.) in ink at DLC; on p.1:
> "September 1920."
> <u>Premiere</u>
>> 1920 (Nov. 26) Philadelphia; Mayflower
>> Celebration; Philadelphia Orchestra;
>> Leopold Stokowski, conductor.

W11.   **Krazy Kat.**
> Completed Sept. 1921; revised 1940, 1948.
> Ballet, or jazz pantomime (<u>1921</u>: flute (piccolo),
> oboe, clarinet, tenor saxophone, bassoon, 2
> horns, 2 trumpets, tenor trombone, timpani,
> "traps," harp, piano & strings) (<u>1940</u>: flute
> (piccolo), oboe, 2 clarinets (Bb soprano saxo-
> phone), bassoon, 2 horns, 2 trumpets, tenor
> trombone, bass drum, cymbals, timpani, snare
> drum, wood blocks, Glockenspiel, harp, piano
> & strings) (<u>1948</u>: 2 flutes, oboe, 2 clarinets,
> saxophone, bassoon, 2 horns, 2 trumpets,
> trombone, timpani, percussion, Glockenspiel,
> xylophone, piano & strings; may be reduced
> to: flute, oboe, 2 clarinets, bassoon, 2 horns, 2
> trumpets, trombone, timpani, percussion,
> Glockenspiel, piano & strings).
> Story by George Herriman.
> Score & parts available for rent from G.
> Schirmer.
> Published: piano arr. (39 p.) G. Schirmer, c1922
> (pl.no. 30760); revised piano arr. (39 p.) G.
> Schirmer, c1948 (pl.no. 41938); dated: "Jan. 2-
> 12, '40."
> Holograph of score (58 p.) at Newberry; at end:
> "8/23/21;" includes "Suggestions for
> conductor" and composer's letter to C.J.
> Hambleton, dated 18 December 1934

commenting on "another arrangement for concert performance, which is the one now used whenever it is played."

Holograph of revised score (58 p.) in ink with stage directions in red ink at DLC; at end: "Dec. '39;" includes composer's letter to the choreographer Leonide Massine and composer's sketch of scenery mounted on flyleaf.

Holograph of piano arr. (15 p.) in ink, prepared for publisher at DLC; on p.1: "May-Sept. 1921."

Holograph of piano arr. of revised version (15 p.) in ink with stage directions in red ink at DLC; at end: "Jan. 2nd-12th-'40."

Premiere of orchestral suite (Review: B486)
   1921 (Dec. 23) Chicago; Orchestra Hall; Chicago Symphony Orchestra; Frederick Stock, conductor.

Premiere of ballet (Review: B316)
   1922 (Jan. 20) New York; Town Hall; Adolf Bolm "Krazy Kat;" Ulysses Graham "Officer Pup;" Ledru Stiffler "Bill Postem;" Olin Howland "Joe Stork;" Bella Kelmans "Ignatz Mouse;" George Herriman, scenario, scenery and costumes; Adolf Bolm, staging; [orchestra] George Barrère, conductor.

W12.   Skyscrapers.
   Completed 1924.
   Ballet of modern American life (3 flutes (piccolo), 3 oboes (English horn), 3 clarinets (bass clarinet), 3 bassoons (contrabassoon), 3 saxophones (soprano, alto, tenor), 4 horns, 4 trumpets, 3 trombones, tuba, compressed air whistle, tenor banjo, 2 pianos, celesta, xylophone, timpani, cymbals, bass drum, oriental drum, snare drum, tambourine, Glockenspiel, cylinder bells, anvils, tam-tam, wood block, "thunder" machine (offstage) & strings with chorus (6 tenors and 6 sopranos)).
   Story by Robert Edmond Jones and John Alden Carpenter.
   Contents: Allegro molto (SYMBOLS OF RESTLESSNESS) — Tempo I° (ABSTRACTION OF SKYSCRAPER: WORK) — Moderato (TRANSITION FROM WORK TO PLAY) — Modera-

to (CONEY ISLAND: PLAY, WORK, PLAY) —
Molto più moderato (RETURN FROM PLAY
TO WORK) — A tempo (SKYSCRAPERS)

Score & parts of concert version available for
rent from G. Schirmer.

Published: score (136 p.) G. Schirmer, c1927
(pl.no. 32858); piano arr. (55 p.) G. Schirmer,
c1926 (pl. no. 32722)

Holograph of score (92 p.) in ink at DLC; on t.p.:
"1923-24;" photocopy (negative) from a ms.
copy (92 p.) at Newberry; 10 soprano-tenor
scores & 19 parts in ms. (some photocopy) at
Newberry; reproduction from holograph of 2
piano, 4 hand arr. (54 p.) with composer's ms.
additions, corrections and emendations at
DLC.

Premiere (Reviews: B272, B422, B474, B512)
1926 (Feb. 19) New York; Metropolitan
Opera House; Albert Troy "The Strutter;"
Rita de Leporte "Herself;" Roger Dodge
"White-Wings;" Robert Edmond Jones,
choreography, scenery and costumes;
Sammy Lee, choreography; John Alden
Carpenter and Robert Edmond Jones,
scenario; Giulio Gatti-Casazza, producer;
Negro group organized by Frank Wilson;
[orchestra] Louis Hasselmans, conductor.

W13.   **A Little Bit of Jazz.**
Completed June 1925.
For orchestra (3 saxophones (soprano, alto,
tenor), oboe, 2 horns, 2 trumpets, trombone,
tuba, cymbal, bass drum, wood block, timpani,
banjo, 2 pianos (celesta) & strings).
Dedicated to Paul Whiteman.
Photocopy (negative) of holograph (18 p.) at
NYPL.

W14.   **Oil and Vinegar.**
Completed June 25, 1926.
For jazz orchestra (3 clarinets, 3 saxophones
(soprano, alto, tenor), 4 trumpets, 2 trombones, tuba, cymbals, bass drum, tenor banjo,
2 pianos & strings).
Holograph of score (29 p.) in ink at DLC; at end:
"6/25/26."

W15.   **Song of Faith.**
Completed 1931; revised 1936, 1937.
For narrator, 4-part chorus of children's (or women's) and men's voices, and orchestra (1936:
2 flutes (piccolo), 2 oboes (English horn), 2
clarinets, 2 bassoons, 2 horns, 3 trumpets, 2
tenor trombones, bass trombone, tuba, tenor
drum, snare drum, bass drum, cymbals, timpani*, oriental drum, xylophone*, Glockenspiel, strings, organ* & piano; * = if available)
(1937: 2 flutes (piccolo), 2 oboes (English
horn), 2 clarinets, 2 bassoons, 4 horns, 3 trumpets, 2 tenor trombones, bass trombone, tuba,
snare drum, bass drum, cymbals, timpani,
oriental drum, strings, organ & gong).
Words by the composer based on texts by Walt
Whitman and George Washington.
Dedicated to Rue Carpenter.
Commissioned by the United States George
Washington Bicentennial Commission.
Score & parts available for rent from G.
Schirmer.
Published: score (39 p.) G. Schirmer, c1932 (pl.no.
35686)(G.S. 8vo choruses, no. 7595); revised
piano-vocal score (23 p.) G. Schirmer, c1939
(pl.no. 35660)
Reproduction of holograph, 1st revision of score
(39 p.) in ink with composer's ms. revisions
and additions written or pasted in, at DLC; at
end: "Revised Feb. '36."
Holograph, 1937 revision of score (40 p.) in ink
with revisions written or pasted in, at DLC.
Premiere
1932 (Feb. 23) Boston; Clifton J. Furness, narrator; Cecilia Society Chorus; Boston Symphony Orchestra; Serge Koussevitzky, conductor.

W16.   **Patterns.**
Completed July 1932.
For orchestra with piano obbligato (2 flutes
(piccolo), 2 oboes, English horn, 2 clarinets, 2
bassoons, 4 horns, 3 trumpets, 2 tenor trombones, bass trombone, tuba, bass drum, cymbals, timpani, Glockenspiel, cylinder bells,
piano, strings & solo piano).
Written for the Boston Symphony Orchestra.

Score & parts available for rent from G.
Schirmer.
Holograph of score (41 p.) in ink at DLC; at end:
"Begun Mar.-April 1930. Completed May-July
1932."
Premiere (Reviews: B340, B432, B475, B478,
B502)
1932 (Oct. 21) Boston; John Alden Carpenter,
piano; Boston Symphony Orchestra; Serge
Koussevitzky, conductor.

W17.   Sea Drift.
Completed 1933; revised 1944.
Symphonic poem (1933: 2 flutes, 2 oboes (English horn), 2 clarinets (bass clarinet), 2 bassoons, 4 horns, 3 trumpets, 2 trombones, bass
trombone, tuba, timpani, cymbals, bass drum,
gong, cylinder bell, Glockenspiel, celesta,
vibraphone (Deagan—no. 145), harp, piano &
strings).
Based on sea poems of Walt Whitman.
Score & parts available for rent from G.
Schirmer.
Published: study score (36 p.) G. Schirmer, c1936
(pl.no. 36769)(G. Schirmer's edition of study
scores of orchestral works & chamber music,
no. 9)
Holograph of original sketch (condensed score)
(12 p.) in ink and pencil at DLC; at end: "Éze-
Prides' '33;" holograph of score (30 p.) in ink
at DLC; at end: "Éze-Pride's Crossing. Feb.-Sep.
1933;" another holograph of score (32 p.) at
DLC; on cover: "Do not use this score. See
later version JAC."
Premiere (Review: B487)
1933 (Nov. 30) Chicago; Orchestra Hall; Chicago Symphony Orchestra; Frederick Stock,
conductor.

W18.   Danza; arr.
Completed 1935.
For orchestra (2 flutes, piccolo, 2 oboes, English
horn, 2 clarinets, 2 bassoons, 4 horns, 3 trumpets, 3 trombones, tuba, timpani, bass drum,
cymbals, side drum, castanets, tambourine,
Glockenspiel, xylophone, harp, piano &
strings).

Originally for piano.

Score & parts available for rent from G.
Schirmer.

Holograph of score (5 p.) in ink with emendations at DLC; at end: "August '35. Pride's
Crossing."

Premiere

1935 (Dec. 5) Chicago; Orchestra Hall; Chicago Symphony Orchestra; Frederick
Stock, conductor.

W19.   **Violin Concerto.**

Completed 1936.

For violin and orchestra (2 flutes, piccolo, 2
oboes, English horn, 2 clarinets, 2 bassoons, 4
horns, 3 trumpets, 3 trombones, tuba, celesta,
harp, Glockenspiel, cylinder bells, piano, vibraphone, timpani, snare drum, oriental
drum, bass drum, cymbals, gong, wood block
(small) & strings).

Dedicated to Ellen.

Published: violin-piano arr. (46 p.) & part G.
Schirmer, c1939 (pl.no. 38046); at end: "Éze
Village and Beverly March to Sept. 1936."

Holograph of score (52 p.) in ink at DLC; at end:
"Eze-Beverly, March-September '36;" holograph of violin-piano arr. (23 p.) in ink with
corrections pasted in, at DLC; at end: "Eze-
Beverly, March-Sept. 1936."

Premiere (Reviews: B282, B285, B460)

1937 (Nov. 18) Chicago; Orchestra Hall;
Zlatko Balokovic, violin; Chicago
Symphony Orchestra; Frederick Stock,
conductor.

W20.   **Symphony no. 1 (1940).**

Completed 1940.

For orchestra (3 flutes (piccolo), 2 oboes, English
horn, 2 clarinets, bass clarinet, 2 bassoons,
contrabassoon, 4 horns, 3 trumpets, 2 tenor
trombones, bass trombone, tuba, timpani,
cymbals, bass drum, snare drum, tenor drum,
wood block, Glockenspiel, gong, cylinder bells,
celesta, harp, piano & strings).

Revision of "Sermons in Stones" (1917).

Dedicated "To Frederick A. Stock for the 50th
anniversary ('40-'41) of the Chicago

Symphony Orchestra."
Score & parts available for rent from G.
Schirmer.
Holograph of revised version of 1917 symphony
score (72 p.) in ink at DLC; on t.p.: "To
Frederick A. Stock for the 50th anniversary
('40-'41) of the Chicago Symphony Orchestra;"
on p.1: "Begun 1/18/40;" at end: "Santa
Barbara—Chicago. Jan-April '40."
Premiere (Reviews: B402, B461, B493)
1940 (Oct. 24) Chicago; Orchestra Hall; Chi-
cago Symphony Orchestra; Frederick
Stock, conductor.

W21.   A Song for Illinois.
Completed Jan. 17, 1941.
Variation for orchestra (piccolo, 2 flutes, 2 oboes,
2 clarinets, 2 bassoons, contrabassoon, 4 horns,
3 trumpets, 3 trombones, tuba, cymbal, bass
drum, timpani, harp & strings).
Subtitled: "El-A-Noy."
Holograph of score (12 p.) in ink at DLC; at end:
"Jan. 8-17, 1941."
Premiere
1941 (Apr. 17) Chicago; Orchestra Hall; Chicago Symphony Orchestra; Frederick Stock,
conductor.

W22.   Song of Freedom.
Completed 1941.
March for orchestra with ad lib. unison chorus
at end (piccolo, 2 flutes, 2 oboes, 2 clarinets,
bass clarinet, 2 bassoons, contrabassoon, 4
horns, 3 trumpets, 2 tenor trombones, bass
trombone, tuba, timpani, cymbals, bass drum,
snare drum, Glockenspiel, bells, xylophone,
piano, harp, organ, chorus & strings) (band: 2
piccolos, 2 flutes, 2 oboes, 7 clarinets (Eb, 4
regular, alto, bass), 2 bassoons, 5 saxophones (2
alto, tenor, baritone, bass), 3 cornets, 3 trumpets, 4 horns, 3 trombones, euphonium,
baritone, basses & tuba, string bass, piano (ad
lib.) & percussion).
Words by Morris H. Martin.
Published: conductor's condensed (band) score
(19 p.) G. Schirmer, c1943 (pl.no. 40077) (Band
series, no.140); piano-vocal score (4 p.) G.

Schirmer, c1942 (pl.no. 39712)(choral version;
to be used with band)
Holograph sketches of condensed score (7 p.) in
pencil at DLC; at end: "Beverly Oct- '41;"
holograph of score (35 p.) in ink at DLC; at end:
"Oct.-Dec. '41. Beverly-Chicago;" holograph of
vocal score (2 p.) in ink, originally included as an
ad lib. final section in the orchestral version of
the composer's march.

W23. **Symphony no. 2 (1942).**
Completed 1941; revised 1947.
For orchestra (<u>1941</u>: piccolo, 2 flutes, 2 oboes,
English horn, 2 clarinets, bass clarinet, 2 bassoons, 4 horns, 3 trumpets, 3 trombones, tuba,
timpani, cymbals, bass drum, snare drum,
Glockenspiel, wood blocks, harp, piano,
xylophone & strings) (<u>1947</u>: piccolo, 2 flutes, 2
oboes, English horn, 2 clarinets, bass clarinet,
2 bassoons, contrabassoon, 4 horns, 3 trum-
pets, 3 trombones, tuba, timpani, cymbals, bass
drum, snare drum, gong, Glockenspiel, wood
blocks, celesta, harp, piano, xylophone &
strings).
Based on material from the Piano Quintet.
Contents: Moderato: Allegro — Andante —
Allegro.
Score & parts available for rent from G.
Schirmer.
Holograph of first movement (46 p.) in ink at
DLC; holograph of revised score (86 p.) in ink
with composer's emendations pasted in, at
DLC; on t.p. "Revised version 1947;" at end:
"Sunset Hill, Beverly, Mass. July-October '41."
<u>Premiere</u> (Reviews: B473, B506)
1942 (Oct. 22) New York; Carnegie Hall;
New York Philharmonic Symphony;
Bruno Walter, conductor.

W24. **The Anxious Bugler.**
Completed 1943.
Symphonic poem (piccolo, 2 flutes, oboe,
English horn, 2 clarinets, bass clarinet, 2
bassoons, contrabassoon, 4 horns, 3 trumpets,
2 trombones, bass trombone, tuba, timpani,
cymbals, bass drum, snare drum, gong, xylophone, piano & strings).

Commissioned by the League of Composers.
Score & parts available for rent from G.
Schirmer.
Holograph of score (26 p.) in ink at DLC; at end:
"Beverly, Aug. '43;" includes introductory
notes by the composer.
<u>Premiere</u> (Review: B470)
1943 (Nov. 17) New York; Carnegie Hall;
New York Philharmonic; Artur
Rodzinski, conductor.

W25.   **Blue Gal; arr.**
Completed May 1943.
For mezzo soprano and orchestra (2 flutes, 2
oboes, 2 clarinets, 2 bassoons, 2 horns, trum-
pet, 2 trombones, cymbals, bass drum, snare
drum, piano & strings).
Acc. originally for piano.
Words by John Alden Carpenter.
Holograph of score (16 p.) in ink at DLC; at
end: "May '43."

W26.   **Dance Suite.**
Completed 1943.
For orchestra (piccolo, 2 flutes, 2 oboes, English
horn, 2 clarinets, bass clarinet, 2 bassoons, 4
horns, 3 trumpets, 3 trombones, tuba, timpani, cymbals, bass drum, snare drum, wood
block, castanets, Glockenspiel, harp, xylophone, piano & strings).
Originally for piano.
Contents: Polonaise — Tango — Danza.
Score & parts available for rent from G.
Schirmer.
Holograph of score (13, 18, 28 p.) in ink at DLC; at
end of 1st movement: "Feb. '43;" 2nd movement: "March '43."
<u>Premiere</u>
1943 (Nov. 3) Washington, D.C.; National
Symphony; Hans Kindler, conductor.

W27.   **Les silhouettes; arr.**
Completed May 1943.
For mezzo soprano and small orchestra (2 flutes,
2 oboes, 2 clarinets, 2 bassoons, Glockenspiel,
celesta, harp & strings).
Acc. originally for piano.

Words by Oscar Wilde.
Holograph of score (11 p.) in ink at DLC; at end:
"May '43."

W28.   Slumber Song; arr.
Completed May 1943.
For voice and orchestra (2 flutes, 2 oboes, 2
    clarinets, 2 bassoons, 2 horns, Glockenspiel,
    celesta, harp & strings).
Acc. originally for piano.
Words by Siegfried Sassoon.
Holograph of score (13 p.) in ink at DLC; at end:
"May '43."

W29.   The Seven Ages.
Completed 1945.
Symphonic suite (piccolo, 2 flutes, 2 oboes,
    English horn, 2 clarinets, bass clarinet, 2 bas-
    soons, contrabassoon, 4 horns, 3 trumpets, 2
    trombones, bass trombone, tuba, timpani, bass
    drum, snare drum, cymbals, gong, wood
    blocks, cylinder bells, Glockenspiel,
    xylophone, celesta, harp, piano & strings).
From Shakespeare's *As You Like It*, Act II, scene
    7.
Dedicated:"For Ellen."
Contents: All the World's a Stage; At First, the
    Infant — Then the Whining School Boy —
    And Then the Lover, Sighing Like a Furnace
    — Then a Soldier —And Then the Justice, in
    Fair Round Belly, with Good Capon Lin'd —
    The Lean and Slipper'd Pantaloon — Last
    Scene of All, sans Teeth, sans Eye, sans Taste,
    sans Everything.
Score & parts available for rent from G.
    Schirmer.
Holograph of score (74 p.) in ink with emenda-
    tions and Monteux cuts at DLC; at end: "Hobe
    Sound, Chicago, Beverly, Feb.-July 1945. 'Haec
    dim memmeuisse juvabit'."
Premiere
    1945 (Nov. 29) New York; Carnegie Hall;
    New York Philharmonic Symphony
    Orchestra; Artur Rodzinski, conductor.

W30.   **Carmel Concerto.**
    Completed 1948.
    For orchestra (piccolo, 2 flutes, 2 oboes, English horn, 2 clarinets, bass clarinet, 2 bassoons, contrabassoon, 4 horns, 3 trumpets, 3 trombones, tuba, timpani, cymbals, bass drum, snare drum, oriental drum, Glockenspiel, gong, harp, piano & strings).
    Holograph of score (45 p.) in ink with corrections in pencil and Stokowski tempi changes listed on a separate page, at DLC; at end: "Jan. to June '43. Carmel. Chicago. Beverly."
    Premiere (Review: B423)
        1949 (Nov. 20) New York; Carnegie Hall; New York Philharmonic; Leopold Stokowski, conductor (Radio broadcast performance)

W31.   **War Lullaby.**
    Completed date unknown.
    For orchestra (3 flutes, 3 oboes, 2 clarinets, 2 bassoons, 4 horns, trumpet, 2 trombones, timpani, percussion, harp, celesta, Glockenspiel, piano & strings).
    Score & parts available for rent from G. Schirmer.

CHAMBER MUSIC

W32.   **Violin Sonata.**
    Completed 1911.
    For violin and piano.
    Dedicated to Bernhard Ziehn.
    Contents: Larghetto — Allegro — Largo mistico — Presto giocoso.
    Published: score (35 p.) & part, G. Schirmer, c1913 (pl.no. 23703)
    Holograph of score (39 p.) in ink at DLC; holograph of score (35 p.) in pencil at DLC; copyist's ms. of score (44 p.) in ink, L.H. of piano part in pencil, at DLC; holograph of part (14 p.) in ink at DLC; copyist's ms. of violin part in ink with composer's pencilled corrections at DLC.
    Premiere
        1912 (Dec. 11) New York; Aeolian Hall;

Mischa Elman, violin; John Alden Carpenter, piano.

W33. **Minuet.**
Completed June 1923.
For flute, violin, violoncello & piano.
Dedicated "To Monsieur A. Bartholemy."
Holograph of score (4 p.) & parts in ink at DLC.

W34. **The Wrigley Wriggle.**
Completed Nov. 20, 1924.
For violin and piano.
Holograph of score (2 p.) in pencil with name
"Thury" written on cover, at DLC; holograph
of part (2 p.) in ink with name "Jerome Levy"
written on cover, at DLC.

W35. **String Quartet.**
Completed 1927.
For 2 violins, viola & violoncello.
Contents: Allegro — Adagio — Moderato.
Published: study score (36 p.) G. Schirmer, c1928
(pl.no. 34143)(G. Schirmer's edition of study
scores of orchestral works and chamber music,
no.2) & parts (pl.no. 34144); at end: "April-July
1927."
Premiere
1928 (Apr. 28) Washington, D.C.; Library of
Congress; Rosé String Quartet at the
Chamber Music Festival of the Elizabeth
Sprague Coolidge Foundation.

W36. **The Music Doctor's Blues.**
Completed June 14, 1928.
For violin and piano.
Holograph of score (3 p.) in ink and 2
photocopies (one positive, one negative) at
DLC; at end: "We thank you!;" on cover: "Nr
II TWO LITTLE PIECES" crossed out.

W37. **Piano Quintet.**
Completed 1934; revised 1937, 1946-47.
For piano, 2 violins, viola & violoncello.
Dedicated "To Elizabeth Sprague Coolidge."
Published: score (60 p.) G. Schirmer, c1937 (pl.no.
37144) & parts (pl.no. 37145); at end: "Algiers.
Pride's Crossing. 1934."

> Holograph of the 1934 score (43 p.) in pencil at
> DLC; on t.p.: "To Elizabeth Sprague Coolidge.
> Algiers 2/8/34.;" at end of 1st movement:
> "2/8/34-2/26/34;" 2nd movement: "3/4/34;"
> 3rd movement: "3/24/34;" holograph of 1946-
> 47 score (33 p.) in ink at DLC; at end: "Beverly,
> Chicago, Carmel, 46-'47;" copyist's reproduced
> ms. of parts at DLC.
>
> Premiere
> > 1934 (Sept. 19) Pittsfield, MA; Coolidge
> > Festival; South Mountain Quartet; John
> > Alden Carpenter, piano.

W38. **Fanfarette-Berceuse for Richard.**
> Completed Feb. 1945.
> For voice, 3 trumpets, 3 trombones & per-
> cussion.
> Contents: La mere qui chant — Le pere puissent
> — Les anges — Le peuple — L'auteur.
> Holograph of score (1 p.) in ink at DLC; at end:
> "For Halina, Artur and Richard. God bless
> you all. J.A.C. Hobe Sound, Fla. Feb. '45."

W39. **Impromptu.**
> Completed date unknown.
> For violin and piano.
> Holograph of score (9 p.) in ink at DLC.

W40. **Miniature.**
> Completed date unknown.
> For violin and piano.
> Holograph of score (3 p.) in pencil at DLC.

W41. **Two Little Pieces Nr. I.**
> Completed date unknown.
> For violin and piano.
> Holograph of score (7 p.) in ink at DLC.

PIANO MUSIC

W42. **Minuet.**
> Completed 1894.
> Published: score (3 p.) Miles & Thompson, c1894
> (pl.no. M. & T. 571-2)

W43.   **Twilight reverie.**
> Completed 1894.
> Published: score (7 p.) Miles & Thompson, c1894
> (pl.no. M. & T. 572–5)
> Holograph of score (4 p.) in ink at DLC; section
> endings differ from published version.

W44.   **Piano Sonata in G minor.**
> Completed 1897.
> Contents: Allegro ma non troppo — Adagio con
> moto — Allegro con brio. Rondo.
> Holograph of score (9, 4, 6 p.) in ink at DLC;
> holograph of earlier version (11, 4, 7 p.) in ink
> with corrections at DLC; holograph of score
> (14 p.) and sketches (4 p.) in ink and pencil at
> DLC.
> <u>Premiere</u>
> 1897 (n.d.) Harvard; Music Dept.;
> Graduation Exercise.

W45.   **Nocturne.**
> Completed 1898.
> Published: score (7 p.) H.B. Stevens, c1898   (pl.no.
> H.B.S.Co. 801–5); Theodore Presser,   c1906
> (Pianoforte compositions by American
> composers, 5738)

W46.   **Polonaise américaine.**
> Completed Dec. 1912; arranged for orchestra,
> 1943.
> Published: score (7 p.) G. Schirmer, c1915 (pl.no.
> 25596); on cover: Two Piano Pieces.
> Holograph of score (3 p.) in ink at DLC.

W47.   **Impromptu.**
> Completed July 1913.
> Published: score (7 p.) G. Schirmer, c1915 (pl.no.
> 25597); on cover: Two Piano Pieces.
> Holograph of score (3 p.) in ink at DLC.

W48.   **Little Indian.**
> Completed April 1916.
> Published: score (5 p.) G. Schirmer, c1918 (pl.no.
> 28364); on cover: Two Pieces for Piano I;
> (Piano music for recital)

W49. **Little Dancer.**
> Completed March 1917.
> Published: score (7 p.) G. Schirmer, c1918 (pl.no.
> 28365); on cover: Two Pieces for Piano I; (Piano
> music for recital)(Schirmer's Galaxy, 345)

W50. **Tango américain.**
> Completed Aug. 1920; arranged for orchestra,
> 1943.
> Published: score (9 p.) G. Schirmer, c1921 (pl.no.
> 30015)

W51. **Diversions.**
> Completed 1923.
> Contents: Lento — Allegretto con moto —
> Animato. Più lento — Moderato — Adagio.
> Published: score (25 p.) G. Schirmer, c1923 (pl.no.
> 31645)

W52. **Danza.**
> Completed Aug. 1935; arranged for orchestra,
> 1935.
> Published: score (14 p.) G. Schirmer, c1947 (pl.no.
> 41670)
> Holograph of score (5 p.) in ink with emenda-
> tions at DLC; at end: "August '35. Pride's
> Crossing."
> Premiere
> > 1946 (Nov. 15) New York; Helmut Baer-
> > wald, piano.

W53. **Animato.**
> Completed date unknown.
> Holograph of score (3 p.) in ink at DLC.

W54. **Dutch Dance.**
> Completed date unknown.
> Holograph of score (4 p.) in ink with No. 2 Polka
> (2 p.) in ink at DLC.

W55. **Largo.**
> Completed date unknown.
> Holograph of score (2 p.) in ink with
> emendations at DLC.

W56. **Petite Suite.**
> Completed date unknown.
> Contents: Moderato con grazia à la minuet —

Cantando — Molto vivace.
Reproduction of score (2, 3, 2 p.) at DLC;
Carpenter's name does not appear on score.

W57. Prelude and Fugue.
Completed date unknown.
Holograph of prelude (3 p.) in ink at DLC; no
fugue.

W58. Sehnsucht.
Completed date unknown.
Holograph of score (1 p.) in ink at DLC.

W59. Serenade.
Completed date unknown.
Reproduction of score (4 p.) at DLC.

SONGS

W60. Love Whom I Have Never Seen.
Completed 1894.
Words by John Alden Carpenter.
1st line: "Oh, Love, whom I have never seen."
Published: score (5 p.) Miles & Thompson, c1894
(pl.no. M. & T. 574-4)
For baritone voice.

W61. My Sweetheart.
Completed 1894.
Words by Griffith Alexander.
1st line: "She's neither scholarly nor wise."
Published: score (3 p.) Miles & Thompson, c1894
(pl.no. M. & T. 573-2)

W62. Alas, How Easily Things Go Wrong.
Completed 1896.
Words by George McDonald.
1st line: "Alas, how easily things go wrong."
Dedicated to Miss Marguerite Hill.
Published: score (6 p.) H.B. Stevens, c1896 (pl.no.
H.B.S.Co. 638)

W63. In Spring.
Completed 1896.
Words by William Shakespeare.
1st line: "It was a lover and his lass."

Dedicated to Francis Fisher Powers.
Published: score (5 p.) H.B. Stevens, c1896 (pl.no.
H.B.S.Co. 636)

W64.   Memory.
Completed 1896.
Words from the London *Atheneum*.
1st line: "As a perfume doth remain."
Dedicated to Miss Marguerite Hill.
Published: score (5 p.) H.B. Stevens, c1896 (pl.no.
H.B.S.Co. 637)

W65.   Norse Lullaby
Completed 1896.
Words by Eugene Field.
1st line: "The sky is dark and the hills are
white."
Dedicated to Miss Amy Fay.
Published: score (5 p.) H.B. Stevens, c1896   (pl.no.
H.B.S.Co. 639); Theodore Presser, c1903.
Holograph of score (3 p.) in ink with numbering
in blue pencil at DLC.

W66.   Little John's Song.
Completed 1897.
Words by Nora Hopper.
1st line: "It's oh, and oh, 'tis merry to go."
Published: score (7 p.) H.B. Stevens, c1897 (pl.no.
H.B.S.Co. 683)

W67.   Mistress Mine.
Completed 1897.
Words by William Shakespeare.
1st line: "Mistress mine, where are you
roaming?"
Published: score (5 p.) H.B. Stevens, c1897 (pl.no.
H.B.S.Co. 682)
Reproduction of score (2 p.) at DLC.

W68.   Sicilian Lullaby.
Completed 1897.
Words by Eugene Field.
1st line: "Hush my little one, fold your hands."
Published: score (5 p.) H.B. Stevens, c1897 (pl.no.
H.B.S.Co. 684)

W69.   **Improving Songs for Anxious Children.**
Completed 1901-02.
Words, music and pictures by John and Rue
   Carpenter.
Published: score (50 p.) G. Schirmer, c1904, c1907,
   c1913 (pl.no. 24045); score (35 p.) A.C. McClurg,
   c1907 (1st twelve titles)
Contents:
For Careless Children.
   1st line: "Oh! children only think of it."
Stout.
   1st line: "Alas, I am a heavy child."
The Liar.
   1st line: "I've done a very frightful thing."
A Reproach.
   1st line: "Oh, small and gaily frisking lambs."
Humility.
   1st line: "My nature it is very wild."
A Wicked Child.
   1st line: "My parents say that dancing."
Vanity.
   1st line: "In evenings of the summer days."
Maria, — Glutton.
   1st line: "Maria sits in her high chair."
Good Ellen.
   1st line: "Oh, little Ellen never did."
War.
   1st line: "When I hear the blare of trumpet."
Spring.
   1st line: "I wander far and unrestrained."
Lullaby.
   1st line: "The lady lily nods her head."
   Holograph of "The Lady Lily Nods Her Head"
      (2 p.) at Newberry.
Practising.
   1st line: "What's the use of practising?"
Red Hair.
   1st line: "I wish I knew a sea of ink."
   Holograph of "My Red Hair" (2 p.) in pencil at
      DLC.
A Plan.
   1st line: "When I'm a big man."
   Holograph of "My Play" (3 p.) in ink at DLC.
Brother.
   1st line: "My brother he's a funny one."
   Holograph of "Brother" (3 p.) in pencil at DLC.

Making Calls.
1st line: "The most unpleasant thing to do."
Contemplation.
1st line: "For days and days I've climbed a
tree."
When the Night Comes.
1st line: "When the night comes."

W70.   **When Little Boys Sing.**
Completed 1904.
Words, music and pictures by John and Rue
Carpenter.
Published: score (39 p.) A.C. McClurg, c1904,
c1905.
Holograph of score (39 p.) with composer's letter
to Herbert Stone, Jr., dated 1 May 1948, at
Newberry.
Contents:
About My Garden.
1st line: "Out in the sun my garden stands."
Holograph of "About my garden" (2 p.) at DLC.
Red Hair.
1st line: "I wish I knew a sea of ink."
Holograph of "My Red Hair" (2 p.) in pencil at
DLC.
Aspiration.
1st line: "Oh what I give, to be able to live."
The Thunderstorm.
1st line: "I wonder if God thinks of me."
Holograph of "The Thunderstorm" (1 p.) in
ink at DLC.
A Plan.
1st line: 'When I'm a big man."
Holograph of "My Play" (3 p.) in ink and pencil
at DLC.
Practising.
1st line: "What's the use of practising?"
Brother.
1st line: "My brother he's a funny one."
Holograph of "Brother" (3 p.) in pencil at DLC.
Contemplation.
1st line: "For days and days I've climbed a
tree."
Happy Heathen.
1st line: "Just think of little heathen boys!"
To Cross the Street.
1st line: "Tell me why do wagons frown?"

Making Calls.
1st line: "The most unpleasant thing to do."
When the Night Comes.
1st line: "When the night comes."

W71.   **The Debutante.**
Completed 1908.
Words by John T. McCutcheon.
1st line: "She lays away her favorite book."
Dedicated: "To the Debutantes of 1908 (A Co-
Coon Song), song for baritone, opus 1."
Subtitled: "A Ka-koon song."
Holograph of score (3 p.) at Newberry.
Premiere
1908 (n.d.) Harry Harvey, soloist.

Eight Songs for a Medium Voice.
Contents:
The Green River (W81)
Don't ceäre (W78)
Looking-Glass River (W85)
Bid Me to Live (W72)
Go, Lovely Rose (W80)
The Cock Shall Crow (W75)
Little Fly (W84)
A Cradle Song (W76)

Four Poems for a Solo Voice with Piano Accompaniment.
Contents:
Chanson d'automne (W73)
Le ciel (W74)
Dansons la gigue! (W77)
Il pleure dans mon coeur (W83)

W72.   **Bid Me to Live. (Dis-moi d'aimer)**
Completed 1911.
Words by Robert Herrick (French: Maurice
Maeterlinck)
1st line: "Bid me to live and I will live."
1st line: "Dis-moi de vivre, et je vivrai."
Published: score (5 p.) G. Schirmer, c1912
(pl.no. 23650)(On cover: Eight songs for a
medium voice)

W73.   **Chanson d'automne. (Song of Autumn)**
Completed 1910.
Words by Paul Verlaine (English: Henry G.

Chapman)

1st line: "Les sanglots longs des violons de l'autumne."

1st line: "Autumnal sobs, viol throbs monotoning."

Published: score (3 p.) G. Schirmer, c1912 (pl.no. 23647)(On cover: Four poems for a solo voice with piano accompaniment)

W74.   Le ciel. (The Sky)

Completed 1910.

Words by Paul Verlaine (English: Henry G. Chapman)

1st line: "Le ciel est pardessus le toit."

1st line: "The sky hangs far above the roof."

Published: score (5 p.) G. Schirmer, c1912 (pl.no. 23649)(On cover: Four poems for a solo voice with piano accompaniment)

W75.   The Cock Shall Crow.

Completed 1908.

Words by Robert Louis Stevenson.

1st line: "The cock shall crow in the morning grey."

Published: score (4 p.) G. Schirmer, c1912 (pl.no. 23568)(On cover: Eight songs for a medium voice)

Holograph of score (2 p. + 1 m.) in ink at DLC.

W76.   A Cradle Song.

Completed 1911.

Words by William Blake.

1st line: "Sleep, sleep, beauty bright."

Published: score (4 p.) G. Schirmer, c1912 (pl. no. 23569)(On cover: Eight songs for a medium voice)

W77.   Dansons la gigue! (Come Dance the Jig)

Completed 1910.

Words by Paul Verlaine (English: Helen Dudley)

1st line: "Dansons la gigue!"

1st line: "Come dance the jig!"

Published: score (7 p.) G. Schirmer, c1912 (pl.no. 23651)(On cover: Four poems for a solo voice with piano accompaniment)

W78. **Don't ceäre.**
Completed 1911.
Words by William Barnes.
1st line: "At the feäst, I do mind very well."
Published: score (7 p.) G. Schirmer, c1912 (pl.no. 23570) (On cover: Eight songs for a medium voice)
Holograph of score (7 p.) in ink at DLC; in G major, published version in F major.

W79. **En sourdine. (When the Misty Shadows Glide)**
Completed 1910.
Words by Paul Verlaine (English: John Alden Carpenter)
1st line: "Calmes dans le demi-jour."
1st line: "When the misty shadows glide."
Published: score (5 p.) O. Ditson, c1912 (pl .no. 5-83-68910-4, low)(pl.no. 5-87-691900-4, med.) (On cover: Songs by John Alden Carpenter)
Holograph of score (4 p.) in ink with corrections in pencil at DLC.

W80. **Go, Lovely Rose.**
Completed 1908.
Words by Edmund Waller.
1st line: "Go, lovely rose!"
Published: score (5 p.) G. Schirmer, c1912 (pl.no. 23571)(On cover: Eight songs for a medium voice)
Holograph of score (4 p.) in ink at DLC.

W81. **The Green River.**
Completed 1909 .
Words by Lord Alfred Douglas.
1st line: "I know a green grass path. "
Dedicated to Mrs. Samuel Wright.
Published: score (5 p.) G . Schirmer, c1912 (pl . no. 23572)(On cover: Eight songs for a medium voice)
Holograph of score (5 p.) in ink with newspaper clippings of poem at DLC.

W82. **The Heart's Country.**
Completed 1909.
Words by Florence Wilkinson.
1st line: "Hill-people long for their hills."
Published: score (5 p.) O. Ditson, c1912 (pl.no. 5-

83-68909-3, med.)(pl.no. 5-85-69044-3, high)(On
cover: Songs by John Alden Carpenter)

Holograph of score (2 p.) in pencil at DLC; in E
minor, published version (med.) in F minor,
(high) in A minor.

W83. **Il pleure dans mon coeur. (The Tears Fall in My
Heart)**

Completed 1910.

Words by Paul Verlaine (English: Henry G.
Chapman)

1st line: "Il pleure dans mon coeur."

1st line: "The tears fall in my heart."

Published: score (5 p.) G. Schirmer, c1912 (pl.no.
23648)(On cover: Four poems for a solo voice
with piano accompaniment)

Holograph of score (5 p.) in ink at DLC; in D
minor, published version in E minor, with
different MM.

W84. **Little Fly.**

Completed 1909.

Words by William Blake.

1st line: "Little fly, thy summer's play."

Dedicated to Kurt Schindler.

Published: score (4 p.) G. Schirmer, c1912 (pl.no.
23573)(On cover: Eight songs for a medium
voice)

Holograph of score (4 p.) in ink at DLC.

W85. **Looking-Glass River.**

Completed 1909.

Words by Robert Louis Stevenson.

1st line: "Smooth it slides upon its travel."

Published: score (4 p.) G. Schirmer, c1912 (pl.no.
23574)(On cover: Eight songs for a medium
voice)

W86. **May, the Maiden.**

Completed 1908.

Words by Sidney Lanier.

1st line: "May, the maiden, violet laden."

Published: score (5 p.) O. Ditson, c1912 (pl.no. 5-
83-68908-3, low)(pl.no. 5-85-69043-3, high)(On
cover: Songs by John A. Carpenter)

Four Songs for a Medium Voice.
Contents:
Les silhouettes (W89)
Her Voice (W88)
To One Unknown (W91)
Fog Wraiths (W87)

W87. **Fog Wraiths.**
Completed 1912.
Words by Mildred Howells.
1st line: "In from the ocean the white fog creeps."
Published: score (5 p.) G. Schirmer, c1913 (pl.no. 23866)(On cover: Four songs for a medium voice)
Holograph of score (3 p.) in ink at DLC; in Eb minor, published version in E minor.

W88. **Her Voice.**
Completed Sept. 6, 1912.
Words by Oscar Wilde.
1st line: "The wild bee reels from bough to bough."
Published: score (7 p.) G. Schirmer, c1913 (pl.no. 23859)(On cover: Four songs for a medium voice)
Holograph of score (5 p.) in ink at DLC.

W89. **Les silhouettes.**
Completed 1912; acc. arranged for orchestra, 1943.
Words by Oscar Wilde.
1st line: "The sea is fleck'd with bars of gray."
Published: score (5 p.) G. Schirmer, c1913 (pl.no. 23858)(On cover: Four songs for a medium voice)

W90. **Terre Promise.**
Completed June 1913.
Words by Ernest Dowson.
1st line: "Even now the fragrant darkness of her hair."
Holograph of score (3 p.) in ink at DLC.

W91. **To One Unknown.**
Completed 1912.
Words by Helen Dudley.

1st line: "I have seen the proudest stars."
Published: score (7 p.) G. Schirmer, c1913 (pl.no.
  23865)(On cover: Four songs for a medium
  voice)
Holograph of score (4 p.) in ink at DLC; in Bb
  minor, published version in B minor.

W92.   **Gitanjali. (Song Offerings)**
Completed Sept. 1913; revised 1934; acc. arranged
  for orchestra, 1914.
Words by Rabindranath Tagore.
Song cycle; 1st lines are the same as titles.
Published: score (42 p.) G. Schirmer, c1914 (pl.no.
  24609); The Boston Music Company, c1914.
  Contents:
When I Bring to You Colour'd Toys.
  also published separately: score (7 p.) G.
    Schirmer, c1914 (pl.no. 33219, low)(pl.no.
    24610, med. or high)(On cover: Three songs
    from the cycle: Gitanjali)
**On the Day When Death Will Knock at Thy
  Door.**
The Sleep That Flits on Baby's Eyes.
  also published separately: score (5 p.) G.
    Schirmer, c1914 (pl.no. 24612, med.)(On
    cover: Three songs from the cycle: Gitanjali)
I Am Like a Remnant of a Cloud of Autumn.
On the Seashore of Endless Worlds.
  also published separately: score (13 p.) G.
    Schirmer, c1914 (pl.no. 24614)(On cover:
    Three songs from the cycle: Gitanjali)
Light, My Light.

W93.   **The Little Prayer of I.**
Completed 1914.
Words by Archibald Sullivan.
Two settings:
1st line (I): "I think of all the nicest things."
1st line (II): "When you unfold the red red rose."
Published: score ([1, 2] p., i.e. p. 35, 36-37) in *Kitty
  Cheatham, Her Book,* G. Schirmer, c1915
  (pl.no. 26158)
Holograph of score (II)(2 p.) in pencil at DLC;
  holograph of "When You Unfold the Red
  Red Rose" (2 p.) in ink at DLC.

W94. **Aged Woman.**
Completed Feb. 7, 1915.
Words by R.W.C.
1st line: "Aged woman though I be."
Holograph of score (2 p.) in ink at DLC.

W95. **The Day Is No More.**
Completed Sept. 1914.
Words by Rabindranath Tagore.
1st line: "The day is no more."
Published: score (5 p.) G. Schirmer, c1915 (pl.no.
25327)

W96. **The Player Queen.**
Completed 1914.
Words by William Butler Yeats.
1st line: "My mother dandled me and sang."
Published: score (7 p.) G. Schirmer, c1915 (pl.no.
25335)

W97. **Spring Joys.**
Completed March 1916.
Words from the Chinese of Wei Hing-Wu.
1st line: "When fresh-ets cease in early spring."
Holograph of score (3 p.) in ink at DLC.

W98. **Water Colors.**
Completed 1916; acc. arranged for orchestra,
1918.
Chinese poems translated by Herbert Allen
Giles.
Song cycle.
Published: score (23 p.) G. Schirmer, c1916 (pl.no.
26879)
Contents:
On a Screen.
Words by Li-Po.
1st line: "A tortoise I see on a lotus flower
resting."
Holograph of score (2 p.) in ink at DLC; at
beginning: "April 30th '16."
The Odalisque.
Words by Yü-hsi.
1st line: "A gaily dressed damsel steps forth."
The Highwaymen.
Words by Li-Shê.
1st line: "The rainy mist sweeps gently."

Dedicated to Tom Dobson.
To a Young Gentleman.
Words from *National Odes of China*
(Confucius, collector)
1st line: "Don't come in, sir, please!"
Dedicated to Maggie Teyte.
Holograph of score (4 p.) in ink at DLC.

W99.   The Home Road.
Completed July 1917.
Words by John Alden Carpenter.
1st line: "Sing a hymn of freedom."
Published: score (3 p.) G. Schirmer, c1917 (pl.no.
28343); piano-vocal score (3 p.) for chorus of
mixed voices or unison chorus with piano
accompaniment, G. Schirmer, c1917 (pl.no.
27876)(G, Schirmer's secular choruses, no.
6687)
Reproduction of "The Road That Leads Me
Home", verse 1 (1 p.) at DLC.

W100.   Khaki Sammy.
Completed Aug. 20, 1917.
Words by John Alden Carpenter.
1st line: "All the way from Illinois."
Dedicated to Miss Nora Bayes.
Published: score (5 p.) G. Schirmer, c1917 (pl.no.
27852)
Holograph of score (3 p.) in ink at DLC.

W101.   Land of Mine.
Completed Aug. 4, 1917.
Words (author unknown)
1st line: "Sing a song of freedom!"
Holograph of score (1 p.) in ink and pencil at
DLC.

Three Songs for a Medium Voice.
Contents:
The Lawd Is Smilin' Through the Do' (W103)
Wull ye come in eärly spring (W105)
Treat Me Nice (W104)

W102.   Berceuse de guerre.   (A War Lullaby)
Completed July 1918.
Words by Émile Cammaerts (English: Tita
Brand-Cammaerts on p.1)

1st line: "Do-do, l'enfant do."
Published: score (7 p.) G. Schirmer, c1918 (pl.no.
28618); John Lane, c1918.

W103. **The Lawd Is Smilin' Through the Do'.**
Completed Jan. 20, 1918.
Words: traditional.
1st line: "Sleep, my honey, sleep."
Published: score (5 p.) G. Schirmer, c1918 (pl.no.
28454)(On cover:Three songs for a medium
voice)

W104. **Treat Me Nice.**
Completed 1905.
Words by Paul Laurence Dunbar.
1st line: "Treat me nice, Miss Mandy Jane."
Dedicated to and sung by Mrs. Kitty Cheatham
Thompson.
Published: score (5 p.) G. Schirmer, c1918 (pl.no.
28453)(On cover: Three songs for a medium
voice); Frank Root, c1905.

W105. **Wull ye come in eärly spring.**
Completed June 1914.
Words by William Barnes.
1st line: "Wull ye come in eärly spring."
Published: score (6 p.) G. Schirmer, c1918 (pl.no.
28452)(On cover: Three songs for a medium
voice)
Holograph of "Come" (6 p.) in ink at DLC.

W106. **Thoughts.**
Completed May 1920.
Words by Sara Teasdale.
1st line: "When I can make my thoughts come
forth."
Holograph of score (2 p.) in ink at DLC.

**Two Night Songs for Low or Medium Voice with Piano
Accompaniment.**
Contents:
Serenade (W107)
Slumber-Song (W108)

W107. **Serenade.**
Completed Apr. 1920.
Words by Siegfried Sassoon.

1st line: "You were glad tonight."
Dedicated to Mina Hager.
Published: score (11 p.) G. Schirmer, c1921 (pl.no.
30001)(On cover: Two night songs for low or
medium voice with piano accompaniment)

W108.   Slumber-Song.

Completed May 1920; acc. arranged for orchestra,
1943.
Words by Siegfried Sassoon.
1st line: "Sleep; and my song shall build about
your bed."
Published: score (7 p.) G. Schirmer, c1921 (pl.no.
30000)(On cover: Two night songs for low or
medium voice with piano accompaniment)

W109.   Les cheminées rouges. (Red Chimneys)

Completed Feb. 1922; revised Nov. 14, 1934.
Words by Mireille Havet (English: Lorraine
Noel Finley)
1st line: "Vingt-huit cheminées rouges."
1st line: "Chimneys, twenty-eight red ones."
Subtitled: "La Maison dans l'Oeil du Chat."
Dedicated to Miss Eva Gauthier.
Holograph of 1922 version (10 p.) in ink in D
major at DLC; holograph of 1934 holograph
(6 p.) in ink with different MM, at DLC.

W110.   Le petit cimetière. (The Little Graveyard)

Completed 1923; revised 1934.
Words by Mireille Havet (English: Lorraine
Noel Finley)
1st line: "Derrière le mur du petit cimetière."
1st line: "Behind the wall that guards the little
graveyard."
Dedicated to Eva Gauthier.
Holograph of 1923 version (3 p.) in ink at DLC;
holograph of 1934 version (3 p.) in ink with
red ink corrections and English words pen-
cilled in, at DLC; at end: "11/14/34."

W111.   O! Soeur divine.

Completed Oct. 1923.
Words by Emma Calvé.
1st line: music not found.

W112.   **The Little Turtle.**
Completed Nov. 1926.
Words by Vachel Lindsay.
1st line: "There was a little turtle."
Holograph of score (2 p.) in ink at DLC.

W113.   **Mountain, Mountain.**
Completed Nov. 1926.
Words by John and Rue Carpenter.
1st line: "Mountain, mountain, mountain
wild."
Holograph of score (2 p.) in ink at DLC.

W114.   **Four Negro Songs for Medium Voice and Piano.**
Completed March 1926.
Words by Langston Hughes.
Published: score (18 p.) G. Schirmer, c1927 (pl.no.
33481)
Holograph of 2nd version (4, 2, 3, 2 p.) same as
published version, at DLC.
Contents:
Shake Your Brown Feet, Honey.
1st line: "Shake your brown feet, honey."
Reproduction of holograph, 1st version (4 p.)
at DLC.
The Cryin' Blues.
1st line: "Hey! Hey! That's what the blues
singers say."
Reproduction of holograph, 1st version (2 p.)
at DLC.
Jazz-Boys.
1st line: "Sleek black boys in a cabaret."
Reproduction of holograph, 1st version (3 p.)
at DLC.
That Soothin' Song.
1st line: "Play de blues for me."
Bennington performance
1941 (Aug. 10 & 17) Bennington College; Ethel
Luening, soprano; Lionel Nowak, piano.

W115.   **America, the Beautiful.**
Completed March 27, 1928.
Words: traditional.
1st line: "O beautiful for spacious skies."
Holograph of score (1 p.) in ink at DLC.

W116. **The Hermit Crab.**
>> Completed Jan. 1929.
>> Words by Robert Hyde.
>> 1st line: "With the sound of the sea."
>> Holograph of score (2 p.) in ink at DLC; 2 photocopies (one positive, one negative) at DLC.

W117. **Young Man, Chieftain!**
>> Completed Jan. 1929.
>> Words by Mary Austin.
>> 1st line: "Lord of the mountain."
>> Subtitled: "An Indian Prayer."
>> Published: score (7 p.) G. Schirmer, c1930 (pl.no. 34796)
>> Holograph of score (8 p.) in ink at DLC; photocopy (negative) at DLC.

W118. **Gentle Jesus, Meek and Mild.**
>> Completed Dec. 21, 1931.
>> Words by John Alden Carpenter.
>> 1st line: "Gentle Jesus, meek and mild."
>> Dedicated to Ginny (for his daughter's wedding)
>> Holograph of score (2 p.) at Newberry; holograph of score (2 p.) in ink and two photocopies (one positive, one negative) at DLC.

Songs of Silence.
>> Contents:
>> **Rest** (W120)
>> **The Past Walks Here** (W119)

W119. **The Past Walks Here.**
>> Completed Aug. 23, 1934.
>> Words by Virginia Woodward Cloud.
>> 1st line: "The past walks here, noiseless."
>> Holograph of score (3 p.) in ink at DLC; at end: "Pride's Crossing, Aug. '34." (On cover: Songs of Silence, II)

W120. **Rest.**
>> Completed Aug. 1934.
>> Words by Mabel Simpson.
>> 1st line: "No song, no song, from far or near."
>> Published: score (5 p.) G. Schirmer, c1934, c1936 (pl.no. 36798)(On cover: Songs of Silence, I; Two songs for high voice and piano)

Two Songs for High Voice and Piano.
Contents:
Rest (W120)
Morning Fair (W121)

W121.   Morning Fair.
Completed Jan. 1935.
Words by James Agee.
1st line: "Now stands our love on that still verge of day."
Published: score (7 p.) G. Schirmer, c1936 (pl.no. 36797)(On cover: Two songs for high voice and piano)
Holograph of score (5 p.) in ink at DLC; at end: "Jan.'35;" reproduction of holograph at DLC.

Three Songs for Medium Voice and Piano.
Contents:
If (W122)
Worlds (W124)
The Pools of Peace (W123)

W122.   If.
Completed Dec. 1934.
Words by Mabel Livingston.
1st line: "Oh, would not it be funny."
Published: score (3 p.) G. Schirmer, c1938 (pl.no. 37056)(On cover: Three songs for medium voice and piano); Ginn & Co., c1936.
Holograph of score (2 p.) in ink with different MM, at DLC.

W123.   The Pools of Peace.
Completed Dec. 1934.
Words by Joan Campbell.
1st line: "The quiet pools of peace."
Published: score (5 p.) G. Schirmer, c1938 (pl.no. 37055)(On cover: Three songs for medium voice and piano); Ginn & Co., c1938.
Holograph of score (3 p.) in ink with words in red ink at DLC; holograph of score (3 p.) in ink with deletions and blue pencil additions at DLC; at end: "Dec. 1934."

W124.   Worlds.
Completed Dec. 1934.
Words by Aileen Fisher.

1st line: "The world is high as a bird can fly."
Published: score (5 p.) G. Schirmer, c1938 (pl.no.
37057)(On cover: Three songs for medium
voice and piano); Ginn & Co., c1938.
Holograph of score (2 p.) in ink with different
MM at DLC; at end: "Dec. 1934."

W125.   Blue Gal.
Completed Nov. 1941; acc. arranged for
orchestra, 1943.
Words by John Alden Carpenter.
1st line: "When a gal is breathin' sorrow."
Holograph of score (3 p.) in ink with pencil
sketch (1 p.), text written in ink, at DLC; at
end: "Chicago. Nov. '41."

W126.   Bright Truth Is Still Our Leader.
Completed date unknown.
Words (author unknown)
1st line: "As now our eyes turn forward."
Holograph of score (1 p.) in ink at DLC.
Harvard song.

W127.   Canterbury Bells.
Completed date unknown.
Words (author unknown)
1st line: "Oh, the swinging and the ringing."
"Music by Uncle John" for 3 treble voices and
piano.
Holograph of score (1 p.) in ink at DLC.

W128.   Dawn in India.
Completed date unknown.
Words by Lawrence Hope.
1st line: "Just in the hush before the dawn."
Holograph of score (2 p.) & two copies (clean
copy, and one with corrections and deletions)
at DLC.

W129.   Endlose Liebe.
Completed date unknown.
Words by Karl Florenz.
1st line: "Wo ich ferne des Mikane."
Holograph of score (2 p.) in ink at DLC; another
holograph of score in pencil with faster MM
at DLC; another holograph in ink at DLC.

W130. **How to Dance.**
Completed date unknown.
Words (author unknown)
1st line: "There's a tickle in my feet."
Holograph of score (3 p.) in pencil at DLC.

W131. **The Marshes of Glynn.**
Completed date unknown.
Words by Sidney Lanier.
1st line: "Glooms of the live oaks."
Holograph of score (2 p.) in ink with sketches
(2 p.) in ink and pencil at DLC.

W132. **Midnight Nan.**
Completed date unknown.
Words by Langston Hughes.
1st line: "Strut and wiggle, shameless gal."
Holograph of score (3 p.) in ink at DLC;
reproduction of holograph at DLC.

W133. **Schifferlied.**
Completed date unknown.
Words by Karl Florenz.
1st line: "Das Steuer des Botes."
Holograph of score (3 p.) in ink at DLC.

W134. **Triste était mon âme.**
Completed date unknown.
Words by Paul Verlaine.
1st line: "Oh, triste, triste, était mon âme."
Holograph of score (3 p.) in ink at DLC;
holograph sketch (4 p.) in pencil at DLC;
holograph of clean copy (5 p.) at DLC.

W135. **Die vier Jahreszeiten.**
Completed date unknown.
Words by Karl Florenz.
Holograph of score (9 p.) in ink at DLC; holo-
graph of score (8 p.) in pencil with metric
changes suggested by J.A. West, at DLC.
Contents:
Frühling.
1st line: "Wenn in Morgengraun des
Frühlingstages."
Sommer.
1st line: "Lieblich düften die Orangen-
blühten."

Herbst.
1st line: "Nun ist schon der Herbst ins Land gekommen."
Winter.
1st line: "Morgengraun nach kalter Winternacht."

PLAYS

W136. **Branglebrink.**
Completed 1896.
1896 Hasty Pudding Play.
Words by R.M. Townsend and E.G., Knoblauch.
Music by J.A. Carpenter, F.B. Whittemore, and R.G. Morse.
Published: score (101 p.) Miles & Thompson, c1896.
Contents (Carpenter music):
ACT I
no. 1 Opening Chorus (Monks)
1st line: "Lo, yonder in the heavens."
no. 3 Tramp Duet (Tatters & Robert)
1st line: "We are two tramps of high degree."
no. 6 "Jimmy Jinks" (Robert)
1st line: "Oh, Jimmy Jinks was an organist."
no. 7 Shout Chorus (Princess, Tatters, Brother John)
1st line: "Oh, didn't you notice that dreadful shout?"
no. 8 Duet (Tatters & Mirabelle)
1st line: "She's the neatest little girl I ever saw."
ACT II Entr'acte
no.10 Opening Chorus "In May"
1st line: "Oh, around the gay Maypole."
no.11 Could You But Tell
1st line: "Pansies, with your faces smiling."
no.13 Dreaming Song
1st line: "As I lay a dreaming, dreaming, dreaming."
no.14 "Jones" (Tatters & Chorus)
1st line: "I had a friend I loved so fond and truly."
no.15 Serenada
1st line: "Open wide the lattice."
no.16 Duet (Mirabelle & Robert)

1st line: "Most lovers sing in lofty way."
no.17 Drinking Song & Chorus (Brother John &
Chorus of Monks)
1st line: "When the harvest moon has
ripened."
no.18 Love Is Love Anyway (Mirabelle's song)
1st line: "She was a silly little schoolgirl."
no.19 Duet (Robert & Dan de Lion)
1st line: "Oh, what can't be done with
money."
no.20 Cold Song (Bishop)
1st line: "A sitting id that irod box."
Holograph (3 p.) in ink, red ink, and pencil, at
DLC.
no.21 Chorus
1st line: "Mercy on us, tell us all."
no.22 Topical Song (Tatters)
1st line: "Some people think it very hard."
no.24 Finale
1st line: "We admire your majesty's
clemency."
Premiere
1896 (Apr. xx) Cambridge & Boston; James
Gilbert, stage manager.

W137. **Strawberry Night Festival Music.**
Completed 1896.
Harvard.
Music not found.

W138. **The Flying Dutchmen.**
Completed 1897.
1897 Hasty Pudding Play.
Words by M.E. Stone, Jr.; lyrics by H.T. Nichols.
Published: score (95 p.) H.B. Stevens, c1897
(H.B.S.Co. 688)
Contents:
ACT I
no. 1 Opening Chorus
1st line: "Long may our cheers ring in his
ears."
no. 2 I'm as mean as mean can be
1st line: "You may roam the whole world."
no. 3 On the Bouwerie
1st line: "As we wander up and down the
Bouwerie."
no. 4 Conspirator's Trio

1st line: "Well, here we are at last."
no. 5 Sextette
    1st line: "It's dreadfully discouraging."
no. 6   The Graminivorous Goat
    1st line: "High on a mountain."
no. 7   Slumber Song
    1st line: "Faintly, drowsily, murmuring low."
ACT II
no. 8   Opening Chorus
    1st line: "Hail our joyous shouts in rapture
    blend."
no. 9   Faculty Song
    1st line: "To create 'sensations' requires some
    'nerve'."
no.10   Memories
    1st line: "Peace, peace, vague haunting
    memories."
no.11   Dance (no words)
no.12   Don't Tell It to Tom, Dick, and Harry
    1st line: "If you should hear a bind."
no.13   Farewell, Fair Harvard
    1st line: "Farewell, farewell, fair Harvard."
ACT III
no.14   Wooden Shoe Dance
    1st line: "Dancing, prancing, merry folk are
    we."
no.15   The Little Soldier
    1st line: "There was once a little soldier."
no.16   Duet "Flutter at Will, My Heart"
    1st line: "Oh, how rapturous! Love is sweet!"
no.17   The Breeze and the Violet
    1st line: "A roving breeze of perfumed sweet-
    ness."
no.18   Dance (no words)
no.19   Topical Song
    1st line: "I've come here to sing you some
    topical verses."
no.20   Finale
    1st line: "We've certainly done our best."
    Premiere
    1897 (Apr.29, 30 & May 1) Cambridge; (May 3
    & 4) Boston; James Gilbert, stage manager.

Selections from The Flying Dutchmen.
    Published: score (1 v.) H.B. Stevens, 1897.
    Contents:
    1. On the Bouwerie

2. Memories
3. Farewell, Fair Harvard
4. The Little Soldier
5. Flutter at Will, My Heart
6. The Breeze and the Violet

W139. **A Little Dutch Girl.**
Completed 1900.
Pastoral play in three acts.
Words by Melville E. Stone, Jr.
Published: score (28 p.) Clayton F. Summy, 1900,
c1901.
Contents:
Dream Song
1st line: "Ah me, if it were only true."
Thou Wilt Surely Know
1st line: "I cannot find the words to tell thee
dear."
I'll Be Waiting for Your Coming
1st line: "I'll be waiting for your coming."
In Gay Bohemia
1st line: "It's here and there and ev'rywhere."
Prayer
Drinking Song
Duet

Lyrics from A Little Dutch Girl.
Published: score (1 v.) C.F. Summy, c1901.
Contents:
Dream Song
Thou Wilt Surely Know
I'll Be Waiting for Your Coming
In Gay Bohemia

Discography

GUIDE TO THE DISCOGRAPHY

EXAMPLE 1
1.   **Adventures in a Perambulator.**
2.   D1. Eastman-Rochester Orchestra; Howard Hanson,
3.   conductor.
4.   <u>Mercury MG-50136</u>/<u>SR-90136</u>/<u>AMS 16015</u>/<u>MRL 2542</u>.
5.   Recorded 10/28/56.
6.   Rel 1957/1959; del 1964.
7.   Program notes by Harold Lawrence.
8.   With: Selections from..., by Phillips.
9.   Olympian series.
10.   Reviews: B268 (MG-50136); B347 (MRL 2542).

EXAMPLE 2
4.   <u>Mercury SRI-75095</u>.
6.   Rel 1977; previously rel as SR 90136.
8.   With: [different]

EXAMPLE 3
1.   **Adventures in a Perambulator. En voiture.**
3.   NBC Orchestra; Frank Black, conductor.
4.   <u>LWO 9670 R6Bl</u>.
11.   See D5.

KEY FOR EXAMPLES

1. Title precedes all numbered entries for that work; complete work precedes part or movements which are arranged alphabetically after title of complete work.

2. "D" number indicates release or issue; many label numbers can have the same "D" number if re-issued with the same accompanying works.

3. Performing group; arranged alphabetically following title.

4. Label numbers; if library call no., location given. When questionable, rpms are indicated, e.g. (33) or (78).

5. Recorded dates (mo/da/yr)

6. Release and delete dates, taken from Oja book.

7. Author(s) of program notes.

8. Accompanying selections; if there are other Carpenter works, the first one cited contains complete information, later entries include title, performer, label, and "see reference." For those non-Carpenter accompanying selections, the first three composers (alphabetical arrangement) are listed followed by "et al."

9. Series.

10. Reviews in bibliography section.

11. "See-ref" to first complete citation for recording.

RECORD ARCHIVES ABBREVIATIONS

DLC   Library of Congress Archive of Recorded Sound

R&H ARS   New York Public Library: Rodgers & Hammerstein Archive of Recorded Sound

Adventures in a Perambulator.

D1. Eastman-Rochester Orchestra; Howard Hanson, con-
ductor.
Mercury MG-50136/SR-90136/AMS 16015/MRL 2542.
Recorded 10/28/56.
Rel 1957/1959; del 1964.
Program notes by Harold Lawrence.
With: *Selections from McGuffey's Reader*, by Phillips.
Olympian series.
Reviews: B268, B293, B328, B359, B364, B388, B407 (MG-
50136); B347 (MRL 2542).

Mercury SRI-75095.
Rel 1977; previously rel as SR 90136.
Program notes by Eric Kisch.
With: *The Pageant of P.T. Barnum*, by Moore;
and *Savannah River Holiday*, by Nelson.
Golden Import series.
Reviews: B297, B312, B361, B508.

Eastman Rochester Archives ERA-1009.
Rel 1976.
Program notes by Harold Lawrence.
With: *Selections from McGuffey's Reader*, by Phillips.
Reviews: B297, B341, B467.

D2. Minneapolis Symphony; Eugene Ormandy, conductor.
Victor 8455-58/8459-62 (in set M-238). (78)
Rel 1934.
Program notes unsigned.
With: *The Marriage of Figaro Overture*, by Mozart.
Musical Masterpiece series.

D3. NBC Symphony; Frank Black, conductor.
ncp 919/920. (DLC)
With: *Symphony no. 2*, by Carpenter.
U.S. Composers series.

D4. Vienna State Opera Orchestra; Henry Swoboda,
conductor.
Concert Hall Society H-1640.
Rel 1952, del 1957.
Concert Hall Society CHS-1140.
Rel 1957; del 1959.
Program notes unsigned.
With: Contemporary American Violin Music

(works by Copland, McBride, and Still).
Reviews: B275, B321, B382, B408, B415.

Adventures in a Perambulator. Dogs.

D5. NBC Orchestra; Frank Black, conductor.
<u>LWO 9670 R6B1</u>. (DLC)
Office of War Information OWI 16" disc. (33)
With: *En Voiture,* and *The Policeman,* from
Adventures in a Perambulator, by Carpenter.

Adventures in a Perambulator. En Voiture.

NBC Orchestra; Frank Black, conductor.
<u>LWO 9670 R6B1</u>.
See D5.

Adventures in a Perambulator. The Hurdy-Gurdy.

D6. Los Angeles Philharmonic Symphony Orchestra; Alfred
Wallenstein, conductor.
<u>ncp 1232/33</u>. (DLC)
<u>QND6-MM-4059</u> (R&H ARS); Master no. 17-3660 <u>16-P-461</u>
16" disc. (33)
Department of State, program no. 22.
With: *The Policeman,* from *Adventures in a Perambulator,* by Carpenter.

D7. Minneapolis Symphony; Eugene Ormandy, conductor.
<u>Victor 11-9231</u> (in set <u>M-1063</u>). (78)
Rel pre-1948.

Adventures in a Perambulator. The Policeman.

Los Angeles Philharmonic Symphony Orchestra; Alfred
Wallenstein, conductor.
<u>ncp 1232/33</u>/<u>QND6-MM-4059</u>/<u>16-P-461</u>.
See D6.

NBC Orchestra; Frank Black, conductor.
<u>LW0 9670 R6B1</u>.
See D5.

Berceuse de guerre.

D8. Mina Hager, mezzo-soprano; Celius Dougherty, piano.
<u>Musicraft 1016</u>. (78); Matrix no. GM 36A.
Rel 1937.
With: *The Odalisque*, and *On a Screen*, from *Water Colors*, by
Carpenter.

Bid Me to Live.

D9. May (Mrs. Charles E.) Winters, soprano; Edwin Earle
Ferguson, piano.
<u>T8018 LWO 8018</u>. (DLC)
With: *Le ciel; Dansons la gigue!; Fog wraiths; Go, Lovely Rose;
Green River; The Heart's Country; Her Voice; Il pleure dans
mon coeur; In Spring; Love Whom I Have Never Seen; May
the Maiden; Mistress Mine; My Sweetheart; Norse Lullaby;
Player Queen; Sicilian Lullaby; Les silhouettes; To One
Unknown; Water Colors;* and *When the Misty Shadows
Glide;* by Carpenter; and two songs by Ruggles.

Carmel Concerto.

D10. New York Philharmonic; Leopold Stokowski, conductor.
<u>LWO 6359, r70A4-71A2</u>. (DLC)(tape)
Recorded 11/20/49; Carnegie Hall Sunday afternoon
broadcasts.
With: works by Handel, Mozart, and Poulenc.

Le ciel.

May (Mrs. Charles E.) Winters, soprano; Edwin Earle
Ferguson, piano.
<u>T8018 LWO 8018</u>.
See D9.

Dansons la gigue!

May (Mrs. Charles E.) Winters, soprano; Edwin Earle
Ferguson, piano.
<u>T8018 LWO 8018</u>.
See D9.

Danza.

D11. Denver Oldham, piano.
 <u>New World Records NW 328/329</u>.
 Rel 1986.
 Program notes by Thomas C. Pierson.
 Album title: "Collected Piano Works."
 With: *Diversions; Impromptu; Little Dancer; Little Indian; Minuet; Nocturne; Polonaise américaine; Sonata in G minor; Tango américain;* and *Twilight Reverie;* by Carpenter.
 Recorded Anthology of American Music series.
 Reviews: B334, B335, B430.

The Day Is No More.

D12. Carol Brice, contralto; Jonathan Brice, piano.
 <u>Columbia 17608-10D</u> (in set <u>MM-910</u>). (78)
 Rel 1950.
 Program notes by Morris Hastings.
 Album title: "A Carol Brice Recital."
 With: songs by Beethoven, Berger, Falla et al.

 <u>Columbia ML 2108</u>; Matrix no. LP 2336.
 Rel 1950; del 1956.
 Reviews: B344, B358, B380, B385, B414, B426.

Diversions.

D13. Jeanne Behrend, piano.
 <u>Victor 17911</u> (in set <u>M-764</u>). (78)
 Recorded 2/10/39.
 Rel 1941.
 Album title: "Piano Music by American Composers."
 With: works by Guion, MacDowell, and Mason.
 Behrend American Piano Music series.

 <u>Curtis Institute disc 1314</u>.
 <u>LWO 8575, R42 B2</u>. (DLC)

 Denver Oldham, piano.
 <u>New World Records NW 328/329</u>.
  See D11.

Diversions. I & II.

D14. Anne McClenny, piano.
T5050. (DLC)

Fog Wraiths.

May (Mrs. Charles E.) Winters, soprano; Edwin Earle
   Ferguson, piano.
T8018 LWO 8018.
   See D9.

Gitanjali.

D15. Alexandra Hunt, soprano; Regis Benoit, piano.
Orion ORS-77272.
Rel 1978.
Program notes by E. McArthur.
With: songs by Griffes and MacDowell.
Reviews: B277, B368, B381.

D16. Alice Mock, soprano; Shibley Boyes, piano.
Claremont Records 1206.
Rel 1952; del 1965.
Program notes unsigned.
With: *Water Colors*, by Carpenter; and songs, by Loeffler.

Gitanjali. Light, My Light.

D17. Rose Bampton, contralto; Wilfred Pelletier, piano.
Victor 1628. (78)
Recorded 7/8/32 and 9/29/32.
Rel pre-1936.
With: *When I Bring You Colour'd Toys*, by Carpenter.

New World Records NW 247.
Rel 1976.
Program notes by Philip L. Miller.
Album title: "When I Have Sung My Songs: The
   American Art Song (1900-1940)."
With: songs by Beach, Burleigh, Cadman et al.
Recorded Anthology of American Music series.
Reviews: B332, B443.

Gitanjali. The Sleep That Flits on Baby's Eyes.

D18. Rose Bampton, soprano; Wilfred Pelletier, piano.
RCA Victor 10-1118 (in set 1607). (78)
Recorded 12/__/44.
Rel pre-1948.
With: songs by Hageman.

Gramophone DA-1855. (78)
Rel pre-1952.

D19. Kirsten Flagstad, soprano; Edwin McArthur, piano.
RCA Victor LM-2825.
Recorded 3/18/52 and 4/19/52.
Rel 1965; del 1967.
Program notes by Edwin McArthur.
Album title: "Songs by Brahms, Strauss, Kramer,
    Carpenter."
With: songs by Brahms, Kramer, and Strauss; *When I
    Bring You Colour'd Toys,* from *Gitanjali,* by Car-
    penter; and *Haugtussa,* by Grieg.
Treasury of Immortal Performances.
Reviews: B353, B366, B384.

D20. Vera Nesnikoff, soprano; Eugene Hellmer, piano.
Curtis Institute disc 1449.
LW0 8575 R53B2. (DLC)
Recorded 4/10/39.

Gitanjali. When I Bring You Colour'd Toys.

Rose Bampton, contralto; Wilfred Pelletier, piano.
Victor 1628.
    See D17.

D21. Glenn Darwin, bass-baritone; Elsa Fiedler, piano.
Victor 36224. (78)
Rel 1939.
With: songs by Griffes and Tchaikovsky.

Kirsten Flagstad, soprano; Edwin McArthur, piano.
RCA Victor LM-2825.
    See D19.

D22. John Kennedy Hanks, tenor; Ruth Friedberg, piano.
Duke University Press DWR 6417/18/DWRM 7501.
Rel 1966; del 1975.

Program notes unsigned.
Album title: "The Art Song in America."
With: songs by Chadwick, Loeffler, MacDowell et al.
Reviews: B318, B323, B330, B332, B379, B437, B480.

D23. Conchita Supervia, mezzo-soprano; Ivor Newton, piano.
<u>Historic Masters HMA-1</u>. (78)
Recorded 3/17/32 by Parlophone-odeon.
Rel 1971: re-pressing from original metal parts of un-
    published   matrix no. LWO 3006-2; issued by the
    British Institute of Recorded Sound in collabora-
    tion with EMI.
With: *Lullaby*, op. 57, no. 2, by Cyril Scott.
Review: B288.

    <u>2119</u> (R&H ARS)(tape)

D24. Camilla Williams, soprano; Borislav Bazala, piano.
<u>MGM E-140</u>.
Rel 1952; del 1957.
Album title: "A Camilla Williams Recital."
With: songs by Debussy, Delibes, Dougherty et al.

Go, Lovely Rose.

    May (Mrs. Charles E.) Winters, soprano; Edwin Earle
      Ferguson, piano.
    <u>T8018 LWO 8018</u>.
      See D9.

Green River.
    May (Mrs. Charles E.) Winters, soprano; Edwin Earle
      Ferguson, piano.
    <u>T8018 LWO 8018</u>.
      See D9.

The Heart's Country.

    May (Mrs. Charles E.) Winters, soprano; Edwin Earle
      Ferguson, piano.
    <u>T8018 LWO 8018</u>.
      See D9.

Her Voice.

> May (Mrs. Charles E.) Winters, soprano; Edwin Earle
>   Ferguson, piano.
> T8018 LWO 8018.
>   See D9.

The Home Road.

D25. Ralph Crane, baritone; and orchestra.
     RCA Victor 22616-A. (78)
     Rel pre-1936.
     Album title: "Familiar Songs."
     With: songs by Foster, Pitts, and Thümmel; and two
          Scotch folk songs.

D26. Ernestine Schumann-Heink, contralto; and orchestra.
     Victor 831. (78)
     Rel 1917-25.

     Victor 87320. (78)
     Rel 1917-25.

D27. Illegible listing for performers.
     Follett Educational Record 2102/21 (in Album 21). (78)
     Album title: "Together We Sing."
     With: *Hymn for the Nations,* by Beethoven-Bacon.

Il pleure dans mon coeur.

> May (Mrs. Charles E.) Winters, soprano; Edwin Earle
>   Ferguson, piano.
> T8018 LWO 8018.
>   See D9.

Impromptu.

D28. Grant Johannesen, piano.
     Golden Crest CR-4065/CRS 4065.
     Rel 1963-66.
     Program notes by Jon Morton.
     Album title: "American Encores from a Russian Tour."
     With: piano music by Barber, Bowles, Farwell et al.
     Reviews: B269, B494.

Denver Oldham, piano.
New World Records NW 328/329.
    See D11.

D29.   Roger Shields, piano.
Vox SVBX 5303.
Rel 1977 (p1976).
Program notes by Lejaren Hiller.
Album title: "Piano Music in America, v.2: 1900-45."
With: piano music by Antheil, Barber, Copland et al.
Reviews: B336, B371, B448, B507.

Improving Songs for Anxious Children. Red Hair.

D30.   Ada Lattimer Stillman, singer; Frank Bibb, piano.
Columbia 91374. (78)
With: *When the Night Comes,* from *Improving Songs for Anxious Children* and from *When Little Boys Sing,* by Carpenter.

Improving Songs for Anxious Children. When the Night Comes.

Ada Lattimer Stillman, singer; Frank Bibb, piano.
Columbia 91374.
    See D30.

In Spring.

May (Mrs. Charles E.) Winters, soprano; Edwin Earle Ferguson, piano.
T8018 LWO 8018.
    See D9.

Khaki Sammy.

D31.   Mabel Garrison, soprano; and orchestra.
Victor 64783. (78)

D32.   Percy Hemus, baritone; and orchestra.
Pathé B25016. (78); M..mx 25016B.
With: *There's a long long trail,* by Elliott.

Krazy Kat.

D33.   The Hamburg Philharmonia Orchestra; Richard Korn,
           conductor.
           <u>Allegro ALG-3150</u>/<u>Allegro Elite 3150</u>/<u>Allegro Royale 3150</u>.
           Rel 1955.
           Album title: "A Panorama of American Orchestral
               Music."
           With: works by Chadwick, Griffes, Hadley et al.

D34.   Los Angeles Philharmonic Orchestra; Calvin Simmons,
           conductor.
           <u>New World Records NW 228</u>.
           Recorded 8/__/77.
           Rel 1978.
           Program notes by R.D. Darrell and David Baker.
           With: works by Gilbert, Powell, and Weiss.
           Recorded Anthology of American Music series.
           Reviews: B362, B424, B444.

D35.   Orchestra of America; Richard Korn, conductor.
           <u>LT-10 3038</u>. (R&H ARS)(tape)
           Recorded 10/14/59.
           With: works by Barber, MacDowell, Sokoloff, and Watts.

           <u>LT-10 3060</u>. (R&H ARS)(tape)
           Recorded 11/14/62.
           With: *Dance Rhythms*, by Riegger.

Little Dancer.

D36.   Antonini Orchestra.
           <u>ncp 1348</u>. (DLC)

           Denver Oldham, piano.
           <u>New World Records NW 328/329</u>.
               See D11.

Little Indian.

           Denver Oldham, piano.
           <u>New World Records NW 328/329</u>.
               See D11.

Little Turtle.

D37. Ann Howard, soprano; and piano.
Victor 36033. (78)
Rel pre-1936.

Looking Glass River.

D38. Donald Gramm, baritone; Richard Cumming, piano.
St/And SPL 411/12.
Rel 1963; del 1964.
Desto D411/12/DST6411/12.
Rel 1964.
Program notes by Jack Beeson.
Album title: "Songs by American Composers."
With: *Jazz-Boys,* from *Negro Songs,* by Carpenter; and
songs by Beeson, Bowles, Edmunds et al.
Reviews: B303, B378, B383, B393, B410, B503.

Love Whom I Have Never Seen.

May (Mrs. Charles E.) Winters, soprano; Edwin Earle
Ferguson, piano.
T8018 LWO 8018.
See D9.

May the Maiden.

May (Mrs. Charles E.) Winters, soprano; Edwin Earle
Ferguson, piano.
T8018 LWO 8018.
See D9.

Minuet.

Denver Oldham, piano.
New World Records NW 328/329.
See D11.

Mistress Mine.

May (Mrs. Charles E.) Winters, soprano; Edwin Earle
Ferguson, piano.
T8018 LWO 8018.
See D9.

My Sweetheart.

> May (Mrs. Charles E.) Winters, soprano; Edwin Earle
> Ferguson, piano.
> T8018 LWO 8018.
>> See D9.

Negro Songs. Cryin' Blues.

D39.   Jean-Emile Vanni-Marcoux, baritone; Piero Coppola,
       piano.
       Gramophone DA-988. (78); mx BT 4145.
       Rel pre-1936.
       With: *Jazz-Boys,* from *Negro Songs,* by Carpenter

Negro Songs. Jazz-Boys.

> Donald Gramm, baritone; Richard Cumming, piano.
> St/And SPL 411/12/Desto D411/12/DST6411/12.
>> See D38.

> Jean-Emile Vanni-Marcoux, baritone; Piero Coppola,
> piano.
> Gramophone DA-988.
>> See D39.

Night Songs. Serenade.

D40.   Ethel Casey, soprano; Bill Siddell, piano; or orchestra;
       Wallace Grieves, concertmaster.
       Carolina 712C-1713.
       Rel 1965.
       Album title: "Classic and Rare Songs and Arias."
       With: songs by Ardite, Auber, Benedict et al.

D41.   James Melton, tenor; Robert Hill, piano.
       Victor 10-1051 (in set M-947). (78)
       Rel pre-1948.
       Album title: "A Song Program by James Melton."
       With: songs by Hageman, Hughes, Lover et al.

D42. Gladys Swarthout, mezzo-soprano; Lester Hodges, piano.
Victor 16780 (in set M-679). (78)
Rel pre-1942.
Program notes unsigned.
Album title: "Gladys Swarthout in Song."
With: songs by Chausson, Dowland, Granados et al.
Musical Masterpiece series.

Nocturne.

Denver Oldham, piano.
New World Records NW 328/329.
See D11.

Norse Lullaby.
May (Mrs. Charles E.) Winters, soprano; Edwin Earle
Ferguson, piano.
T8018 LWO 8018.
See D9.

Piano Concertino.

D43. Marjorie Mitchell, piano; Göteborg Symphony Orchestra;
William Strickland, conductor.
Composers Recordings CRI-180.
Rel 1964-73.
Program notes by D.H.
With: *Piano Concertino*, by Piston; and *The Fourth of
July*, from *Holidays*, by Ives.
Reviews: B271, B290, B324, B329, B360, B377, B421.

LT-10 3072. (R&H ARS)(tape)
LRX 3711. (R&H ARS)(33)

Piano Sonata.

Denver Oldham, piano.
New World Records NW 328/329.
See D11.

The Player Queen.

D44. Elizabeth Suderburg, soprano; Robert Suderburg, piano.
University of Washington Press OLY-104.
Rel 1976.
With: songs by Benshoof, Bond, Dett et al.
Reviews: B270, B331.

May (Mrs. Charles E.) Winters, soprano; Edwin Earle
   Ferguson, piano.
   <u>T8018 LWO 8018</u>.
      See D9.

Polonaise américaine.

Denver Oldham, piano.
   <u>New World Records NW 328/329</u>.
      See D11.

D45.   Lee Pattison, piano.
       <u>Piano roll Ampico AMP 58714-H</u>. (DLC)

Sea Drift.

D46.   Albany Symphony Orchestra; Julius Hegyi, conductor.
       <u>New World Records NW 321</u>.
       Recorded 12/11/83.
       Rel 1984.
       Program notes by Nicolas Tawa.
       With: works by Hadley, Mason, and Porter.
       Recorded Anthology of American Music series.
       Reviews: B298, B425, B441.

D47.   Eastman School Students.
       <u>LW0 9324, R18 B2</u>. (DLC); VOA(Voice of America) disc,
          unnumbered part 5 of 8.
       Recorded 5/10/51 at Eastman Festival.

D48.   Orchestra of America; Richard Korn, conductor.
       <u>LT-10 3066</u>. (R&H ARS)(tape)
       Recorded 1/17/65.
       With: *Violoncello Concerto*, by Kleinsinger.

D49.   Royal Philharmonic Orchestra (London); Karl Krüger,
          conductor.
       <u>SPAMH MIA-142</u>. (Society for the Preservation of the
          American Musical Heritage; Music in America)
       Rel 1969.
       Program notes by Karl Krüger.
       Album title: "Instrumental Music in the 20th Century."
       With: *Stevensoniana Suite I*, by Hill.

Seven Ages.

D50. New York Philharmonic; Artur Rodzinski, conductor.
ncp 1131/33. (DLC)
Carnegie Hall broadcast.

D51. Orquesta Filarmonica de Nueva York; Artur Rodzinski,
conductor.
YTNY 5214/15. (R&H ARS)(16" disc)(33)
Radio Transcription 16-P-261/262.

Sicilian Lullaby.

May (Mrs. Charles E.) Winters, soprano; Edwin Earle
Ferguson, piano.
T8018 LWO 8018.
See D9.

Les silhouettes.

May (Mrs. Charles E.) Winters, soprano; Edwin Earle
Ferguson, piano.
T8018 LWO 8018.
See D9.

Skyscrapers.

D52. American Recording Society Symphony; Meinhard von
Zallinger, conductor.
American Recording Society ARS-37; Matrix no. E3KP-
4201.
Rel 1953.
Program notes unsigned.
Album title: "200 Years of American Music."
With: *The Happy Hypocrite*, by Elwell.
Reviews: B327, B497.

D53. London Symphony Orchestra; Kenneth Klein, conductor.
EMI Angel CDC-7 49263 2 (CD); EMI Angel DS-49263 (LP).
Rel 1988.
Program notes by Gerald Fox, Anne Fullam, and Lewis
Smoley.

Album title: "John Alden Carpenter: Skyscrapers and
Other Music of the American East Coast School by
John Knowles Paine, Edward MacDowell, Arthur
Foote [and] Dudley Buck."
With: works by Buck, Foote, MacDowell, and Paine.
Reviews: B311, B429.

D54. National Symphony Orchestra; Howard Mitchell, conductor.
T5353, r1. (DLC)(tape)

D55. Victor Symphony Orchestra; Nathaniel Shilkret, conductor.
Victor 11250/52 (in set M-130); serial 72607/8. (78)
Victor ND-313/15; serial 72610/11 (Japanese). (78)
Victor 13227/29 (in set DM-130); serial 72613/14. (78)
Rel 1932.
Program notes unsigned.
Musical Masterpiece series.

D56. Vienna Symphony Orchestra; Meinhard von Zallinger,
conductor.
Desto D-407/DST-6407.
Rel 1964; del 1976.
Program notes unsigned.
With: *The Mystic Trumpeter*, by Converse.
The American Composer series.
Reviews: B291, B302, B325, B409, B504.

Song of Faith.

D57. John Alden Carpenter, narrator; Chicago A Cappella
Chorus and Orchestra; Nobel Cain, organ and
conductor.
Victor 1559/60. (78)
Rel pre-1936.
Victor 26529/30. (78)
Rel pre-1942.
Review: B477.

String Quartet.

D58. Gordon String Quartet.
Schirmer 2513/15 (in set SCH-4). (78)
Rel pre-1942.

Symphony no. 2.

> Chicago Symphony Orchestra; Frank Black, conductor.
> ncp 919/920. (DLC)
>> See D3.

Tango américain.

D59. Ruth Bradley, piano.
Piano roll Solo Carola SC 75906. (DLC)

> Denver Oldham, piano.
> New World Records NW 328/329.
>> See D11.

To One Unknown.

> May (Mrs. Charles E.) Winters, soprano; Edwin Earle
>   Ferguson, piano.
> T8018 LWO 8018.
>> See D9.

Twilight Reverie.

> Denver Oldham, piano.
> New World Records NW 328/329.
>> See D11.

Violin Sonata.

D60. Eugene Gratovich, violin; Regis Benoit, piano.
Orion ORS-76243.
Rel 1977.
Program notes by Eugene Gratovich.
With: *Violin Sonata*, by Foote.
Reviews: B372, B442, B447, B449, B468.

Water Colors.

D61. Mina Hager, contralto; John Alden Carpenter, piano.
Chicago Gramophone Society CGS 50019P. (78)
Rel pre-1936.

> Alice Mock, soprano; Shibley Boyes, piano.
> Claremont 1206.
>> See D16.

May (Mrs. Charles E.) Winters, soprano; Edwin Earle
Ferguson, piano.
<u>T8018 LWO 8018</u>.
See D9.

Water Colors. The Odalisque.

Mina Hager, mezzo-soprano; Celius Dougherty, piano.
<u>Musicraft 1016</u>, Matrix no. GM 35A.
See D8.

Water Colors. On a Screen.

Mina Hager, mezzo-soprano; Celius Dougherty, piano.
<u>Musicraft 1016</u>; Matrix no. GM 35A.
See D8.

When Little Boys Sing. Red Hair.

Ada Lattimer Stillman, singer; Frank Bibb, piano.
<u>Columbia 91374</u>.
See D30.

When Little Boys Sing. When the Night Comes.

Ada Lattimer Stillman, singer; Frank Bibb, piano.
<u>Columbia 91374</u>.
See D30.

When the Misty Shadows Glide.

May (Mrs. Charles E.) Winters, soprano; Edwin Earle
Ferguson, piano.
<u>T8018 LWO 8018</u>.
See D9.

Bibliography

BIBLIOGRAPHIES (MUSIC LITERATURE)

B1. Bull, Storm. *Index to Biographies of Contemporary Composers.* New York: Scarecrow, 1964.
Cites ten books which have biographies on Carpenter. Includes "NDM," an unidentified source not listed in the abbreviation index.

B2. Gleason, Harold and Becker, Warren. *20th-Century American Composers.* Music Literature Outline, 4. 2nd ed. Bloomington: Frangipani Press, 1980.
In outline form, lists chronologically the main points of Carpenter's life, his published compositions arranged by genre, his style (techniques and devices) divided into: general characteristics, melodic line, harmony, counterpoint, rhythm, form, and orchestration; the bibliography is divided into articles by Carpenter, references to him in books and articles, references to his works, and the Pierson dissertation.

B3. Greene, Frank. *Composers on Record.* Metuchen, NJ: Scarecrow, 1985.
Lists sixteen discographies for Carpenter.

B4.   Heintze, James R. *American Music Studies*. Detroit:
Information Coordinators, 1984.
Lists eight masters' theses on Carpenter, giving
author, title, academic institution, degree, date, and
annotation.

B5.   *RILM Abstracts of Music Literature*. Flushing, NY:
International RILM Center, 1967-
Abstracts to two dissertations on Carpenter,
another on Rabindranath Tagore, on ragtime, and
on song cycles by Carpenter and other composers.

B6.   U.S. Works Projects Administration. *Bio-Bibliographical
Index of Musicians in the U.S.A. since Colonial Times*.
Washington, D.C.: Pan Am, 1956.
Includes seventeen citations for books including
page numbers (except for the first three) and two
citations for journals.

BIBLIOGRAPHIES (MUSIC)

B7.   Altmann, Wilhelm. *Kammermusik-Katalog*. 6th ed.
Hofheim am Taunus: Friedrich Hofmeister, 1944.
Lists the *String Quartet*, *Piano Quintet*, and the *Violin
Sonata*. Includes date of composition and/or
publication, and publisher. The quartet is available in
score and parts. The quintet is in "D, bzw. polyton."
[p.124]

B8.   _____. *Orchester-Literatur-Katalog*. 2nd ed. Wiesbaden:
Martin Saendig, 1972; Leipzig: F.E.C. Leuckart, 1926.
Lists *Adventures in a Perambulator*, *Skyscrapers*, and
the *Piano Concertino*. Includes date of composition
and/or publication, publisher, form available, e.g.,
Adventures in a Perambulator (score & parts), *Skyscrapers*
(score and parts), and the *Piano Concertino* (score and
parts; and, 2 pianos, 4 hands). Lists durations and
instrumentations for *Skyscrapers*, *Adventures in a
Perambulator*, and *Birthday of the Infanta*.

B9.   American Society of Composers, Authors, and Publishers.
ASCAP Symphonic Catalog. 2nd ed. New York: The
American Society of Composers, Authors, and
Publishers, 1959.
Lists seventeen works giving instrumentation,
duration, and publisher.

B10. _____. *ASCAP Symphonic Catalog.* 3rd ed. New York: R.R.
Bowker, 1977.
Adds *War Lullaby* to the list of works.

B11. *Band Music Guide.* 4th ed. Evanston: Instrumentalist, 1964.
Lists Carpenter's *Song of Freedom* and *You Can
Depend* (song) arranged for band, includes the
publisher and date.

B12. Coffin, Berton. *Singer's Repertoire.* 2nd ed. New York:
Scarecrow, 1960.
Each of five volumes is for a different voice type;
songs are listed by title, difficulty, range, publisher,
and description (e.g., American recital songs, American songs employing spirited singing, ...limited
range, atmospheric songs, etc.).

B13. Daniels, David. *Orchestral Music: A Source Book.* Metuchen,
NJ: Scarecrow, 1972.
Arranged by composer-title, this book gives
durations, instrumentations, and publishers for
Carpenter's *Adventures in a Perambulator* and
Skyscrapers.

B14. _____. *Orchestral Music: A Handbook.* 2nd ed. Metuchen,
NJ: Scarecrow, 1982.
Adds *Sea Drift* to the 1972 ed.

B15. DeCharms, Desiree and Breed, Paul F. *Songs in Collections.*
Detroit: Information Service, 1966.
Lists four songs by Carpenter and indicates in
which song collection they can be found.

B16. Engel, Carl. "Carpenter, John Alden." *Cobbett's Cyclopedic
Survey of Chamber Music.* Edited by Walter Willson
Cobbett. London: Oxford University Press, 1929.
Carpenter's *Violin Sonata* is "less original or
personal than his other and later compositions. It is,
however, well written for both instruments, without
excessive difficulties." Gives descriptions of moods
and themes. [p.227]

B17. Espina, Noni. *Repertoire for the Solo Voice.* Metuchen, NJ:
Scarecrow, 1977.
Gives Carpenter's dates. Discusses his songs; then
lists by title *Gitanjali, Watercolors,* and fifteen single
songs, giving suitable voice and specific range (e.g.,

b2-f#4), mood or character of song, level of difficulty of accompaniment, poet and publisher.

"His songs are charming, very singable, and not overburdened with too much accompaniment. His style, although American, shows some of his European influences—especially that of Elgar and Debussy."[p.141]

B18.   Farish, Margaret K., ed. *Orchestral Music in Print.* Philadelphia: Musicdata, 1979.

Arranged by composer. Lists sixteen orchestral works with durations, instrumentations, availability of score and parts, publisher, all rental information, and unique catalog number.

B19.   _____. *String Music in Print.* 2nd ed. New York: R.R. Bowker, 1973.

Lists Carpenter's *String Quartet*: sc, GS2 [G. Schirmer].

B20.   Faurot, Albert. *Concert Piano Repertoire.* Metuchen, NJ: Scarecrow, 1974.

Only *Skyscrapers* and *Gitanjali* are still "in the recorded repertoire. His Concertino...deserves an occasional hearing." [p.71]

Discusses six piano pieces, describing musical content and pianistic demands, and rating the difficulty.

B21.   Friskin, James and Freundlich, Irwin. *Music for the Piano.* New York: Rinehart, 1954.

Describes the rhythm, orchestration, and difficulty of the *Piano Concertino.* Lists six solo piano pieces.

B22.   Fromm Music Foundation (Harvard). *Music of the Last Forty Years Not Yet Established in the Repertoire, 1974-75 Survey.* Boston: Harvard University Press, 1975.

Skyscrapers, Symphony no. 2, Piano Concertino, and *Adventures in a Perambulator* were performed from one to four times.

B23.   Gillespie, John and Gillespie, Anna G. *A Bibliography of Nineteenth-Century American Piano Music.* Westport, CT: Greenwood Press, 1984.

Lists nine solo piano works giving publisher, date, number of pages, and which libraries own them.

B24. Goleeke, Thomas. *Literature for Voice.* Metuchen, NJ: Scarecrow, 1984.
>   Lists four songs, giving key signature (e.g., 2#s), vocal range, and song collection in which they can be found.

B25. Hinson, Maurice. *Guide to the Pianist's Repertoire.* Bloomington: Indiana University Press, 1973.
>   Includes Carpenter's dates. Lists seven solo piano pieces, giving two dates, publisher, description of style, and grade of difficulty. Refers to Pierson dissertation.

B26. _____. *Guide to the Pianist's Repertoire.* 2nd, rev. & enl. ed. Bloomington: Indiana University Press, 1987.
>   Adds two lines about Carpenter, the businessman-composer, and omits the *Sonata in g* and the Pierson dissertation.

B27. _____. *Music for Piano and Orchestra.* Bloomington: Indiana University Press, 1981.
>   Gives dates, publishers, and duration for the *Piano Concertino* and *Patterns.* "Much of Carpenter's music might be termed American Impressionism, with an always discernible sentiment and charm allied with a fluent mastery of form and melody. Carpenter combined Impressionistic and conservatively modern compositional techniques with elements of jazz."[p.818]

B28. _____. *The Piano in Chamber Ensemble.* Bloomington: Indiana University Press, 1978.
>   Musical descriptions of Carpenter's *Violin Sonata* and *Piano Quintet*, give date, publisher, and length, movement titles, and grade of difficulty.

B29. Horn, David. *Literature of American Music.* Metuchen, NJ: Scarecrow, 1977.
>   Gives annotations to three books on Carpenter.

B30. Institute of American Music of the University of Rochester. *American Composers' Concerts and Festivals of American Music, 1925-1971, Cumulative Repertoire.* Rochester: Institute of American Music, 1972.
>   Gives seven entries of four titles, forms (e.g Ballet, Suite), seasons performed, and one recording.

B31.   Kagen, Sergius. *Music for the Voice.* Rev. ed. Bloomington: Indiana University Press, 1968.

"The songs of John Alden Carpenter are too well known to need any introduction. With the exception of the *Gitanjali* cycle, however, few of his songs seem to have attained the popularity they deserve." [p.471]

Songs are listed by composer giving titles, ranges, tessitura, voice type, and remarks.

B32.   Lahee, Henry Charles. *Annals of Music in America.* Freeport, NY: Books for Libraries, 1922.

Gives dates, titles, places and performers for five works.

B33.   Lockwood, Albert. *Notes on the Literature of the Piano.* New York: Da Capo, 1968.

Lists five solo piano works and the *Piano Concertino.* Gives publisher. Refers to Rosenfeld book.

B34.   Mueller, Kate Hevner. *Twenty-Seven Major American Symphony Orchestras.* Bloomington: Indiana University Press, 1973.

Gives a history and analysis of the repertoire for these orchestras during the seasons 1842-43 through 1969-70. Carpenter has twenty-one entries, but five are movements from larger works.

B35.   Nardone, Thomas R. *Classical Vocal Music in Print.* Philadelphia: Musicdata, 1976.

Gives nine songs with voice range (e.g., med-high voice), publisher, price, and key.

B36.   Pedigo, Alan. *International Encyclopedia of Violin-Keyboard Sonatas.* Booneville, AR: Arriaga, 1979.

Includes birth and death dates and places. Lists Harvard and Paine, Elgar, honors, and father's business.

"Spasmodically he studied music...[Carpenter] wrote a great variety of music compositions, including...[the] *Violin Sonata* of 1912 (G.S.)."[p.47]

B37.   Phemister, William. *American Piano Concertos: A Bibliography.* Detroit: Information Coordinators, 1985.

Includes Carpenter's *Piano Concertino* and *Patterns.* Gives music titles, movements, publishers, dates, dates of revisions, durations, instrumentations, premiere dates, places and performers; record labels and performers, and reviews of premieres.

B38. *Resources of American Music History.* Urbana: University of Illinois Press, 1981.
A directory of source materials from Colonial times to World War II. Lists materials and fifteen locations of letters, holographs, scrapbooks, and presentation copies held by libraries and private individuals.

B39. Rezits, Joseph and Deatsman, Gerald. *The Pianist's Resource Guide.* Park Ridge, IL: Pallma Music, 1978.
Lists eight titles for solo piano including the *Concertino* and *Skyscrapers*, and two versions of the *Concertino* for 2 pianos, 4 hands. Gives publisher.

B40. Sears, Minnie Earl. *Sears Song Index...and Supplement.* [n.p.] Shoe String Press, 1966.
The *Home Road* is included in three collections indexed in this book.

DISCOGRAPHIES

B41. *American Music on Records.* New York: American Music Center, 1956.
Lists four labels for Carpenter giving title, size (e.g., 10" disk), label, performers, contents, and availability of music.

B42. Clough, Francis F. and Cuming, G.J. *The World's Encyclopedia of Recorded Music.* London: Sidgwick & Jackson, 1952.
Cites eighteen recorded performances of works by Carpenter listing title, genre, date of composition, contents, performers, label; 2nd and 3rd supplements (1951-52; 1953-55) add five titles.

B43. Cohn, Arthur. *Recorded Classical Music: A Critical Guide to Compositions and Performances.* New York: Schirmer, 1981.
Gives nine Carpenter recordings with title and date of composition, performers and label, and a short review of the work and the performance.

B44. Darrell, Robert D. *Good Listening.* New York: Alfred A. Knopf, 1953.
Written in narrative format, gives historical perspective but no recording information. Indexed. Gives one reference to Carpenter and one to his *Adventures in a Perambulator.*

B45. Davis, Elizabeth A. *Index to the New World Recorded Anthology of American Music: A User's Guide to the Initial One Hundred Records.* New York: W.W. Norton, 1981.
Lists two issues of New World Records containing Carpenter works with album title, program notes and their author(s), titles of works, performers, and durations included.

B46. *The Gramophone Shop Encyclopedia of Recorded Music.* Edited by Robert D. Darrell. New York: Gramophone Shop, 1936.
Lists five labels for Carpenter in addition to three withdrawn labels with title, contents, performers, size, label, and cost. Carpenter is "one of the most skillful conservatively modern American composers. His technique and idiom are derived almost entirely from the French schools, but many of his works display genuine and unmistakable native qualities." [p.87]

B47. *The Gramophone Shop.* Edited by George Leslie. New York: Simon & Schuster, 1942.
Lists twelve labels for Carpenter which include short descriptions. "This Chicago businessman has produced a considerable body of music attractive for its sense of style, lack of pomposity, and pervasive vitality. Modern without self-consciousness, Carpenter belongs to no school."[p.95]

B48. *The Gramophone Shop Encyclopedia of Recorded Music.* 3rd ed., rev. & enl. by Robert H. Reid. New York: Crown Publishers, 1948.
Lists six labels including title, performers, size, and other works on record or album.

B49. *The Gramophone Shop Record Supplement.* v.1:1 (Jan. 1938)- v.17:2 (Feb. 1954).
Twenty-one citations for Carpenter works.

B50.   Greenfield, Edward. *The Stereo Record Guide, v. 2*. London:
Long Playing Record Library; New York: Taplinger,
1961.
Arranged by composer, this book gives title, label,
performers, other contents, and a review which includes historical perspective of the composer, the
work, and the quality of the recording.

B51.   Hall, David. *The Record Book: A Music Lover's Guide to the
World of the Phonograph*. New York: The Citadel Press,
1946.
Arranged by genre, then composer (or album title);
lists title, performers, label, cost and brief description
of the music. There are seven entries for Carpenter.

B52.   Halsey, Richard Sweeney. *Classical Music Recordings for
Home and Library*. Chicago: American Library
Association, 1976.
Listed by composer-title, this book gives genre, date
of composition, duration, label, and three sets of
criteria: 1) age minima, 2) aesthetic significance, and
3) accessibility rating. Carpenter's *Skyscrapers* was
given a secondary age minima, a nondescript
aesthetic significance, and a "may require 2nd or 3rd
hearing but...easily comprehended" accessibility
rating.

B53.   Kolodin, Irving. *The Guide to Long Playing Records,
v.1: Orchestral Music*. New York: Alfred A. Knopf, 1955.
Two references to *Adventures in a Perambulator*;
gives performers, label, and a one-sentence review.

B54.   _____. *A Guide to Recorded Music*. Garden City, NY:
Doubleday, Doran, 1941.
Arranged by composer, this book gives title,
performers, label, cost, rating, and a brief review.
There are six citations for Carpenter.

B55.   _____. *The New Guide to Recorded Music*. Garden City, NY:
Doubleday, 1950.
Four references to Carpenter's music giving title,
performers, label, rating, and brief reviews.

B56.   Maleady, Antoinette O. *Index to Record and Tape Reviews: A
Classical Music Buying Guide*. San Anselmo: Chulainn
Press, 1971-82.
Lists by date the composer-title, performers, label,

rating, and locations of reviews. Carpenter has four citations.

B57.   Miller, Philip L. *The Guide to Long-Playing Records, v.2: Vocal Music.* New York: Alfred A. Knopf, 1955.
Lists by performer the contents, other performers, size and label. Gives one-paragraph review. Includes two song albums which contain songs by Carpenter and other composers.

B58.   Myers, Kurtz. *Index to Record Reviews Based on Material Originally Published in "Notes, the Quarterly Journal of the Music Library Association" between 1949 and 1977.* Boston: G.K. Hall, 1980.
Gives title, page reference, label, cost, rating and location of reviews. Carpenter receives eighteen entries.

B59.   Oja, Carol J. *American Music Recordings: A Discography of 20th Century U.S. Composers.* New York: Institute for Studies in American Music, Conservatory of Music, Brooklyn College of the City University of New York, 1982.
Lists by composer the title, performers, label, dates recorded, released, and deleted, and if currently in print. Includes forty numbered references to Carpenter.

B60.   *Polart Index to Record Reviews.* Detroit: Polart, 1964, 1965.
Two Carpenter citations give title, performers, and location of reviews (journals and newspapers).

B61.   *Records In Review.* Great Barrington, MA: Wyeth Press, 1955-
Arranged by composer-title, lists performers, label, and locations of reviews (includes symbols for rating the music and the performance). Six references to Carpenter.

B62.   Stahl, Dorothy. *A Selected Discography of Solo Song.* Detroit Studies in Music Bibliography, 13. Detroit: Information Coordinators, 1968.
Arranged by composer, gives title, performers, album title, and label. Three references to Carpenter in 1st and 2nd supplements (1972, 1984).

B63. *Who Is Who in Music.* Chicago: Lee Stern Press, 1941.
This master record catalog gives title and label.
Seven Carpenter titles on five labels.

YEARBOOKS AND DIRECTORIES

B64. Bloom, Julius, ed. *The Year in American Music, 1946-1947.*
New York: Allen, Town & Heath, 1948.
Douglas Moore, president of the National Institute
of Arts and Letters, announced that Carpenter's gold
medal would be presented formally May 22, 1947 at
the annual joint meeting of the American Academy
and the Institute. This is the third time the award
was presented.
Briefly describes four of Carpenter's compositions
and also some of his songs. Lists first performance of
Danza for piano.

B65. *Directory of American Contemporary Operas.* New York:
Central Opera Service, 1967.
Includes *Krazy Kat*, a children's opera in one act.

B66. *Hinrichsen's Year Book.* London: Hinrichsen, 1944.
Lists *Song of Faith* as a new work from America.

B67. *International Who's Who.* 11th ed. New York: Ziff Davis,
1947.
Lists name, degrees, reason for inclusion
("American musician"), birth year, and
education/teachers (Harvard, Ziehn, and Elgar).
Includes a partial list of works and current address for
Carpenter.

B68. Mize, J.T.H. *Who Is Who in Music.* 5th mid-century ed.
Chicago: Sterling, 1951.
Extensive secondary education information. Gives
all of his teachers. Lists works and first performances,
and honors. Describes his appearance and includes
organizations of which he was a member. Gives his
address and phone number.

B69. Moore, Elizabeth C. *An Almanac for Music-Lovers.* New
York: Henry Holt, 1940.
Mentions Carpenter's teacher at Harvard, John
Knowles Paine. Gives Carpenter's birth date and
dates of first performances for five of his works.

B70.   *Pierre Key's Music Year Book.* New York: Pierre Key, 1925-
1938.
Name included in the 1926-1927, the 1928, and the
1929-1930 volumes (includes his address in the last
two).

B71.   Rosenfeld, Paul. *Musical Chronicle (1917-1923).* New York:
Benjamin Bloom, 1972.
Meandering account of American composers
struggling to find identity.
"At moments, particularly in the second movement of the concertino, with its five-eight beat, its
extended swing, its traveling salesman sort of life,
Carpenter's music crosses the line that separates the
unborn from the born and is clothed in the colors of
existence."[p.169]
"Carpenter has succeeded in producing chiefly
some comfortable music."[p.170]
Krazy Kat "does not take jazz and transform it into
rhythm...Where Carpenter seeks to be dramatic and
passionate...he is helpless."[p.170-71]
Birthday of the Infanta "is music as decoration."
[p.172]
Quotes Carpenter's program notes for the *Piano
Concertino* and concludes with a discussion of his
"tone [?] by which Carpenter can be known among
the musicians."[p.172]

B72.   Saerchinger, César, ed. *International Who's Who in Music
and Musical Gazeteer.* 1st ed. New York: Current
Literature, 1918.
Biographical information listing his parents'
names, schools attended, and Carpenter's affiliations.
He was director of the Children's Home and Aid
Society and a member of the Saddle and Cycle Club
and the University Club in Chicago. Gives work and
home addresses.

B73.   *Who's Who in America.* Chicago: A.N. Marquis, 1946.
Gives birth date and place, parents, Harvard, Elgar
and Ziehn, wives, business, affiliations, compositions, French Legion of Honor award, and address.
[Tiny print!]

B74.   *Who Is Who in Music.* Chicago: Berghan, 1927.
"Born Chicago, 1876."[p.23] Mentions Harvard,
Paine and Ziehn, Carpenter as vice-president of his

company, the French Legion of Honor award, and lists well-known works including the three ballets.

B75.   *Who Is Who in Music.* Chicago: Lee Stern, 1940.
"Born in Park Ridge, Ill., 1876."[p. 26] Gives more teachers than earlier edition but still omits Seeboeck. Cites degrees, honors, more works, and gives address.

B76.   *Who Was Who in America.* Chicago: Marquis Who's Who, 1960.
Gives birth and death dates and places. Includes parents, Harvard, Ziehn and Elgar, and Carpenter's two wives. Lists his business, director of the Children's Home and Aid Society, Republican, Congregationalist and the clubs he joined. Cites seventeen works giving dates and, sometimes, performances. Mentions that he composed numerous published songs and the French Legion of Honor award. Gives home address.

CATALOGS

B77.   BBC Music Library. *Chamber Music Catalogue.* London: British Broadcasting Corporation, 1965.
Gives Carpenter's dates, lists the *String Quartet*, the *Violin Concerto*, and the *Violin Sonata.* Includes date and duration for the quartet, publishers for all, and a unique catalog number for each.

B78.   _____. *Piano and Organ Catalogue.* London: British Broadcasting Corporation, 1965.
Gives Carpenter's dates, lists four works for piano solo (including *Water Colors*) and the *Piano Concertino* arranged for 2 pianos. Gives publisher for all, date for *Danza,* and a unique catalog number for each.

B79.   _____. *Song Catalogue.* London: British Broadcasting Corporation, 1966.
Gives Carpenter's dates, lists seven individual songs and *Gitanjali, Negro Songs, Night Songs,* and *Water Colours* [sic] giving keys available for each, publisher or ms. form, a few dates and durations, and a unique number for each song or set.

B80.   Boston Public Library. *Catalogue of the Allen A. Brown Collection of Music in the Public Library of the City of*

Boston. Boston: Trustees, 1910-16.
Includes the 1897 Hasty Pudding play, *The Flying
Dutchmen,* and the 1913 *Violin Sonata.*

B81.   _____. *Dictionary Catalog of the Music Collection.* Boston:
G.K. Hall, 1972.
Twenty-four catalog card images for Carpenter.

B82.   California, University. *Institute of Library Research.*
Berkeley: University of California Press, 1963, 1972.
Union catalog of monographs cataloged by the
nine campuses of the University of California. One
reference only, to Carpenter's *Berceuse de guerre.*

B83.   California, University at Los Angeles. Music Library.
Dictionary Catalog. Los Angeles: University of Cali-
fornia Press, 1952.
Ten catalog card images for Carpenter.

B84.   Celentano, John and Reynolds, Creech, comp. *A Catalogue
of Contemporary American Chamber Music.* [n.p.]
American String Teachers Association, 1975.
Lists the *String Quartet* and the *Piano Quintet* giving
dates, instrumentation, publishers and comments
(e.g., the *Quartet* is an "impressionistic work").[p.8]

B85.   Shaw, John MacKay. *Childhood in Poetry.* Supplement.
Detroit: Gale Research, 1972.
A catalog with biographical and critical annota-
tions of the books of English and American poets in
this collection at the library of Florida State University. Both John and Rue Carpenter have entries here
for their children's songs. Cites words for three songs,
first lines for six other songs, and includes two more
song titles.

B86.   Eagon, Angelo. *Catalog of Published Concert Music by
American Composers.* 2nd ed. Metuchen, NJ: Scarecrow,
1969.
Arranged by composer, gives twenty-seven entries
with publisher, vocal ranges or instrumentation,
poet, and duration.

B87.   Eastman School of Music. *Catalog of Sound Recordings.*
Boston: G.K. Hall, 1977.
Of the thirteen catalog card images for Carpenter,
four are "see-references."

B88. *The Edwin A. Fleisher Collection of Orchestral Music in the Free Library of Philadelphia.* Boston: G.K. Hall, 1979.

Gives Carpenter's birth and death dates and places. Includes only *Adventures in a Perambulator* giving instrumentation, publisher, date of completion, first performance, copyright date, and length of score (117 pages).

B89. Famera, Karen McNerney, ed. *Catalog of the American Music Center Library, v.2: Chamber Music.* New York: American Music Center, 1978.

Information for Carpenter's *String Quartet* includes publisher, series, duration, and length of score (36 pages).

B90. New York Public Library. Music Division. *Dictionary Catalog of the Music Collection, New York Public Library.* Boston: G.K. Hall, 1965.

Carpenter is represented by eighty-seven catalog card images (seventy-one titles and sixteen "see-references") which include articles in journals and books.

B91. _____. *Dictionary Catalog of The Rodgers and Hammerstein Archives of Recorded Sound.* Boston: G.K. Hall, 1981.

Of the twenty-one catalog card images for Carpenter, some are continuations from previous cards. Radio transcriptions are included.

B92. Saltonstall, Cecilia D. and Saltonstall, Henry S. *A New Catalog of Music for Small Orchestra.* Clinton, NJ: European American, 1978.

Lists *Krazy Kat,* giving description: "jazz pantomime,"[p.51] publisher and date (1948), instrumentation, and duration.

B93. U.S. Library of Congress. *Library of Congress Catalog, Music and Phonorecords.* Washington, D.C.: The Library of Congress, 1954-.

Eighty-five Carpenter entries, some of which are repeated in a later edition.

DISSERTATIONS AND MASTERS' THESES

B94. Barnes, Carol A. "John Alden Carpenter and Ned Rorem: Two American Composers of Art Song Recital."

Master's thesis, Central Missouri State College, 1965.
Research document for her master's recital which included *Gitanjali* by Carpenter and seven songs by Rorem. Includes biographical information, song analysis consisting of technical matters, form, harmonic, and stylistic considerations, a bibliography, lists of the composers' published solo songs, and her recital program.

B95. Connor, Patricia Josephine. "A Critical Analysis of the Harmonic Idiom of Songs of Claude Debussy and Its Influence on Compositions of Charles Loeffler and John Alden Carpenter." Master's thesis, North Texas State, 1941.
Gives biography, stylistic traits, and bibliography. Discusses *Il pleure dans mon coeur, To a Young Gentleman* from *Watercolors*, and two songs from *Gitanjali: When I Bring to You Colored Toys* and *Light, My Light*. Includes musical examples.

B96. Crain, Martha. "John Alden Carpenter: American Art Music in the Early 20th Century with Emphasis on *Gitanjali*." Master's thesis, Bowling Green, 1981.
Gives the background for American art song, Carpenter's biography, and a descriptive discussion of the music and text for *Gitanjali*. Includes bibliography and musical examples.

B97. Dobbyn, Freddie Phyllis. "The Instrumental Music of John Alden Carpenter." Master's thesis, Indiana, 1952.
Gives biography, general style characteristics (meter, rhythm, melody, harmony, tonality, texture, and form), then discusses in more detail first the piano music, then the chamber and orchestral music, concluding with a bibliography, and two appendices: a letter from Mrs. Carpenter and a list of works.

B98. Hanke, Arline Maria. "A Study of the *Gitanjali* Songs by John Alden Carpenter." Master's thesis, Eastman School of Music, 1942.
Gives the life of John Alden Carpenter as it relates to his compositions, a brief discussion of the Tagore poems used in this cycle, and an analysis of *Gitanjali* including form, rhythmic and melodic development in relation to the words, and a tracing of counter melody in the accompaniment. Includes conclusion and bibliography.

B99. Kaczmarek, Regina A. "A Catalog of Selected Piano Rolls from the Library of Congress Collection." Master's thesis, Catholic University of America, 1960 .
Descriptive catalog of piano rolls at the Library of Congress with title and performer indexes, and a check list of piano roll manufacturers.

B100. Mendenhall, Miriam Lucille. "The Songs of John Alden Carpenter." Master's thesis, North Texas State, 1952.
Gives the history of art song and also art song in America, information about Carpenter and his songs. Includes bibliography and musical examples.

B101. Moran, Mary Anita. "A Survey of the Development of the Art Song in the United States." Master's thesis, Catholic University of America, 1949.
Chapter four discusses American art song.

B102. Pierson, Thomas C. "The Life and Music of John Alden Carpenter." Ph.D. dissertation, Eastman School of Music, 1952.
Written the year after Carpenter died, this dissertation contains information obtained from interviews with Carpenter's widow and other associates. Extensive theoretical analysis and list of works. Good bibliography. Available on microcard.

B103. Pike, Gregory Burnside. "The Three Versions of the Quintet for Piano and Strings, by John Alden Carpenter: An Examination of Their Contrasting Musical Elements Based upon a Formal Analysis of the Original 1934 Version." Ph.D. dissertation, University of Miami, 1981.
Gives biography, Carpenter's style, a structural and harmonic analysis of the 1934 version of the *Piano Quintet,* compares this with one complete and one incomplete revision, gives a conclusion. Includes bibliography and musical examples.

HISTORIES AND CHRONOLOGIES

B104. Austin, William. *Music in the 20th Century from Debussy through Stravinsky.* New York: W.W. Norton, 1966.
Lists teachers Paine, Elgar, and Ziehn, and influences. Gives birth and death years.

John Alden Carpenter learned something from Debussy and popular music, which he fitted into his essentially conservative habits...His sensitive songs [*Gitanjali* and *Watercolors*]... wear better than his later picturesque orchestral pieces, but these too are interesting, for in them John Alden Carpenter anticipates some of the traits of George Gershwin and Aaron Copland.[p.61-62]

B105. Bakeless, Katherine Little. *Story-Lives of American Composers.* Rev. ed. Philadelphia: J.B. Lippincott, 1953.

Carpenter's "early works were brought to the attention of the music-publishing house of G. Schirmer through Kurt Schindler, the violoncellist, who was also a music-editor."[p.273]

Quotes Carpenter: "American music is on its feet now, and there are signs that it will no longer be influenced by foreign or refugee composers."[p.275]

Written for children, this book gives biographical information and comments on several of his works placing them in an historical perspective. Includes port.

B106. Baldwin, Lillian. *A Listener's Anthology of Music, v.2.* New York: Silver Burdette, 1948.

"His music is distinguished by a delicacy and an exquisite coloring which shows the influence of the French Impressionists. This is particularly noticeable in the songs...[where] the mood of the poem seems to gleam through the music as through a translucent case which lends an added lovely tint."[p.484]

"His *Skyscrapers* may go higher, his *Sea Drift* farther, yet it is doubtful if he will ever come closer to the hearts of his listeners than in this naïve saga of infancy [*Adventures in a Perambulator*]."[p.485]

Discusses *Adventures in a Perambulator* including Carpenter's program notes and musical examples which contain *London Bridge Is Falling Down*, *Alexander's Ragtime Band*, a partial *Where, O Where Has My Little Dog Gone?* and *Ach, du lieber Augustin*.

B107. Baltzell, W.J. *Noted Names in Music.* Boston: Oliver Ditson, 1927.

Gives date and place of birth, where he studied: "Chicago and at Harvard Univ.," and his compositions: "(*Adventures in a Perambulator*), a 'jazz' ballet (1926), and songs."[p.17]

B108. Bauer, Marion. *Twentieth Century Music, How It Developed, How to Listen to It.* New York: G.P. Putnam's Sons, 1947.

Carpenter was "distinctly influenced by French impressionism. And yet he exhibited an individuality, a culture, a refinement of technic and maturity of style in these early works, as he has in later compositions."[p.159-60]

The *Piano Concertino* uses "made in America" melodies and syncopated rhythms. "Skillful workmanship...mark this work...[with] a waltz, and an impressionism more of America than of France." [p.160]

In *Skyscrapers* "is Carpenter at the acme of this new-found American realism, in which jazz and popular melodies rub shoulders with ultramodern dissonance."[p.160]

Patterns "shows that Carpenter, who has gone through interesting metamorphoses, has put his house in order for the neoromanticism which is rapidly becoming a reality. Other works in this later style include *Sea Drift, Danza,* a violin concerto; and a symphony."[p.161]

B109. Baumgartner, Alfred. *Musik des 20. Jahrhunderts.* Kiesel: Kiesel Verlag, 1985.

Gives birth and death dates and places. Student of Elgar and Ziehn. Lists Carpenter as an industrialist by profession and an amateur composer. Lists the types of works Carpenter composed (e.g., symphonies) and includes only one title *Crazy Cat* (Verrueckte Katze).

B110. Birge, Edward Bailey. *History of Public School Music in United States.* Boston: Oliver Ditson, 1938.

Mentions the 1918 address on "Music in the Camps," given by John Alden Carpenter at the music teachers' conference. Carpenter served on a joint committee to decide which version of a song should be included in the *Army Song Book.*

B111. Chase, Gilbert. *America's Music from the Pilgrims to the Present.* Rev. 2nd ed. New York: McGraw Hill, 1966.

Carpenter "was one of the first American composers to experiment with the use of jazz inflections. He employed ragtime rhythms in his *Concertino.*"[p.510]

The *Piano Concertino, Krazy Kat,* and *Skyscrapers*

"were symptomatic of the 'Jazz Age.' They now
appear to us as period pieces." Carpenter "will
perhaps be best remembered for his amusing
descriptive suite for orchestra, *Adventures in a
Perambulator* (1914)." [p.510]

B112. _____, ed. *The American Composer Speaks; A Historical
Anthology, 1770-1965.* Baton Rouge: Louisiana State
University Press, 1966.
See B113.

B113. _____. *The American Composer Speaks; A Historical
Anthology, 1770-1965.* 2nd printing. Baton Rouge:
Louisiana University Press, 1969.
Mentions Carpenter's teacher, Paine, and discusses
Adventures in a Perambulator.
"Debussy and Ravel are reflected in such contem-
porary American composers as Edward Burlingame
Hill and John Alden Carpenter, both of whom stud-
ied under Paine at Harvard in the nineties."[p.122]

B114. Copland, Aaron. *Copland on Music.* Garden City, NY:
Doubleday, 1960.
"Because of Stravinsky the period 1917-1927 was
the decade of the displaced accent and the polytonal
chord. Few escaped the impact of his personality. The
frenetic dynamism and harmonic daring of *Le Sacre*
were reflected in other ballets...[and] Carpenter's
Skyscrapers."[p.95]

B115. _____. *The New Music, 1900-1960.* Rev. & enl. ed. New
York: W.W. Norton, 1968.
Carpenter "used jazz with greater or lesser degrees
of politeness."[p.69]

B116. _____. *Our New Music: Leading Composers in Europe and
America.* New York: Whittlesey House, McGraw-Hill,
1941.
Carpenter "used jazz."[p.99] "The twenties saw the
older generation of 'young' composers come into
their own."[p.143]

B117. Craft, Robert, ed. *Dearest Bubushkin.* New York: Thames
and Hudson, 1985.
Correspondence of Vera and Igor Stravinsky.
Contains photograph of them with Mr. and Mrs.

John Alden Carpenter and Mr. and Mrs. Adolf Bolm. Caption: "1943-Los Angeles."[p.129]

B118. Downes, Olin. *Olin Downes on Music.* New York: Simon and Schuster, 1957.

Discusses premiere of *Skyscrapers*, "a free fantasy on certain phases of American life. These are symbolized by fantastical scenery and by choreography based upon American dances."[p.114] Downes describes the scenery, the action, and occasionally the music:

> Mr. Carpenter might reply to the criticism of a lack of substantial musical material in his score by saying that he had not tried to be ponderous or to attempt dramatic commentary, but to entertain and to amuse...What he has done is to invent some fairly fetching jazz tunes of his own and to include some scraps of familiar popular songs.[p.116]

B119. Duke, Vernon. *Listen Here! A Critical Essay on Music Depreciation.* New York: Ivan Obolensky, 1963.

> There existed a fourth genre, no longer held in great esteem by the musical cognoscenti; that was post-post-impressionism, made in U.S.A. The leading champions of the cult were John Alden Carpenter, Charles Griffes,...Louis Gruenberg, and Emerson Whithorne. All four, on occasion, permitted themselves a perilous excursion into the deep jungle of Americana—with French overtones, for safety's sake. Thus, Carpenter composed a *Krazy Kat* ballet, danced by Adolph Bolm and Ruth Page [only Bolm in this ballet], and the distinctly urbanistic *Skyscrapers* (indignantly turned down by the cruel Diaghilev, to whom the score was submitted in 1925).[p.43]

> Jazz—or what passed for it at the time—was hardly more than a vulgar musical joke to the 1924 diehards...There was no perceptible change in this attitude toward "jazz" intrusions in the concert hall for many years to come, in spite of Carpenter's vaguely syncopated *Krazy Kat* (1922) and Gruenberg's *Daniel Jazz* (1923) which never really caught on in this country...typically, both pieces produced a far greater effect abroad.[p.53]

B120. Edwards, Arthur C. and Marrocco, W. Thomas. *Music in the United States*. Dubuque: Wm. C. Brown, 1968.

Gives Carpenter's dates and teacher Paine at Harvard. "*Skyscrapers* (1926), a ballet of modern American life, and *Adventures in a Perambulator* (1941) are his most characteristic works. In a style that is harmonically European Romantic with considerable French Impressionism, jazz elements (mostly syncopated rhythmic patterns) are superposed on simple melodic lines."[p.104]

Quotes Oscar Thompson and Felix Borowski. Concludes: "Today the effects are dated and have lost their tang; the jazz elements seem synthetic and foreign against the refined, atmospheric harmonies and loosely constructed forms of the piece."[p.104-05]

Includes two record listings.

B121. Elson, Louis C. *The History of American Music*. New York: Macmillan, 1925.

Gives birth year, all teachers, business, early song titles, *Violin Sonata*, and descriptions of *Adventures in a Perambulator, Piano Concertino, Sermons in Stones, Birthday of the Infanta*, and *Krazy Kat*. Includes port.

B122. _____. *The National Music of America and Its Sources*. Boston: L.C. Page, 1924.

"Most representative of all, perhaps, are the works of John Alden Carpenter, whose *Adventures in a Perambulator* strikes an original and distinctively American note, to be found also in his ballet, *Krazy Kat*."[p.319]

"The best example [of jazz effects] is found in the ballet, *Krazy Kat*, by that striking and original genius, John Alden Carpenter."[p.332]

B123. Ewen, David. *The Complete Book of 20th Century Music*. New & rev. ed. Englewood Cliffs, NJ: Prentice-Hall, 1959.

Gives birth and death dates and places, Harvard and three teachers: Paine, Elgar, and Ziehn, his business and honors. Describes *Adventures in a Perambulator, Skyscrapers*, and *Sea Drift*.

Carpenter was essentially a conservative composer who was satisfied with traditional forms and techniques which, nevertheless, he endowed with the imprint of his own personality.

It is not easy to identify him with any one school or style, for he wrote in many different veins with equal success. His first important work was programmatic music spiced with wit and satire: the *Adventures in a Perambulator*, written in 1915. A change of style took place with the ballet *Krazy Kat* (1921), in which the influence of jazz is strongly felt; the jazz style found its culmination in the ballet *Skyscrapers*. In a work like *The Birthday of the Infanta* with its pronounced Spanish character, a new facet in Carpenter's creative idiom was uncovered. In the last decade and a half of his life, Carpenter turned to impressionistic writing. This manner identifies some of his finest works, notably *Sea-Drift* and parts of the *Second Symphony*.[p.54]

"*Skyscrapers* is Carpenter's most modern score, often resorting to dissonance...But its principal attraction is its spicy use of jazz."[p.56]

B124. _____. *Composers of Today*. New York: H.W. Wilson, 1934.
Gives birth date and place. Complete list of teachers and influences. Incorrectly states that *Skyscrapers* "had its première at Monte Carlo in 1925."[p.37]
Carpenter's *Violin Sonata* "was a work without very much character or originality...[However] *Gitanjali* [songs], impressed critics everywhere with their fresh approach and instinctive feeling for a tender loveliness."[p.37]
Quotes W.J. Henderson, Olin Downes, and Felix Borowski on Carpenter's music. Concludes, after stating that Carpenter was a businessman, with a list of principal works, bibliographic references, titles if pieces were recorded (no labels or performers). Includes port.

B125. _____. *David Ewen Introduces Modern Music: A History and Appreciation—from Wagner to the Avant-garde*. Rev., enl. ed. Philadelphia: Chilton Book Co., 1969.
"Among other American composers to enter the symphonic-jazz world were...John Alden Carpenter (1876-1951) with *Krazy Kat* and a remarkable jazz ballet, *Skyscrapers*."[p.220]

B126. _____. *Music Comes to America.* New York: Allen, Towne
& Heath, 1947.
Mentions that Carpenter is now being recorded.

> Thereafter [Gershwin's *Concerto in F*] jazz ceased
> to be an ugly stepchild of music. Serious
> composers borrowed the vitality and
> voluptuousness of its idiom for the expression of
> American rhythm...Jazz not only entered the
> symphony hall but the opera house as well:
> *Skyscrapers*, a ballet, came to the Metropolitan
> Opera House.[p.426]

B127. _____. *The World of Twentieth-Century Music.* Englewood
Cliffs, NJ: Prentice-Hall, 1968.
Begins by tracing Carpenter's style (verbatim) from
Ewen's *Complete Book of 20th Century Music*,
continues with three teachers, business background
and then specific treatment for five works: *Adventures
in a Perambulator, Birthday of the Infanta, Skyscrapers,
Sea Drift*, and the *Symphony no. 2*, giving action,
citing performances in original or altered versions,
and first performances.

B128. Farwell, Arthur and Darby, W. Dermont, ed. *Music in
America.* The Art of Music, v.4, by Daniel Gregory
Mason. New York: National Society of Music, 1915.
Notes his "work of singularly well-defined
individuality and notable maturity of style...his
modernity meaning complexity...is attained generally
by means of a veritable startling simplicity." [p.427]
Discusses *Eight Songs, Four Verlaine Songs,* and *Four
Songs.* "*Le Ciel* and *Il pleure dans mon coeur* attain the
most modern scheme of musical thought with
astonishingly simple means; the *Chanson d'Automne*
is sympathetically set, and *Dansons la Gigue* is
sufficiently sardonic."[p.428]

> [In *Gitanjali*] Carpenter wrestles with the problem
> of setting prose poetry to music, often with
> felicitous effect and yet not always convincingly,
> despite the intrinsic beauty of his musical ideas.
> The violin sonata in its themes, its strikingly
> individual harmonic intuitions, and its structure
> generally, is of great beauty and interest.[p.428]

Concludes with details of birth, education, work.

B129. Finney, Theodore M. *A History of Music.* New York: Harcourt, Brace, 1935.

> "Although the influences to which he [Carpenter] was subjected as a student were romantic and impressionistic, he refuses to be dominated by any style or aesthetic. His *Adventures in a Perambulator* and *Skyscrapers* are distinctly American products." [p.602]

B130. Foulds, John. *Music To-Day.* London: Ivor Nicholson, 1934.

> John Alden Carpenter chose to found American national music "upon the supernational classic-romantic schools."[p.274]

B131. Goldman, Richard Franko. "American Music: 1918-1960." *The Modern Age, 1890-1960.* Edited by Martin Cooper. New Oxford History of Music, v.10. London: Oxford University Press, 1974.

> Carpenter used "ragtime jazz" in his *Piano Concertino* and *Krazy Kat* and *Skyscrapers.*[p.584]
>
> "Carpenter's music enjoyed a vogue for a time, for it was basically conservative enough to appeal even to the conductors of major orchestras and their audiences."[p.585]

B132. Goss, Madeleine. *Modern Music Makers: Contemporary American Composers.* New York: Dutton, 1952.

> Extensive discussion of early training and family background. Lists some of his "best-loved" songs. Cites Carpenter's preface to *Adventures in a Perambulator.* Describes action of *Birthday of the Infanta,* "the first important ballet by an American composer to be produced in the United States."[p.38]
>
> "*Krazy Kat* brought John Alden Carpenter fame both at home and abroad."[p.39]
>
> Describes *Krazy Kat* performances.
>
> Gives history of *Skyscrapers:*
>
> > [Diaghileff] asked him if he would write a ballet for his company. At that time the Russian was trying to organize a second tour of the United States and he was anxious to include an American piece in the company's repertory. "Something typically American," he specified, "something that will describe the industrial atmosphere of your country." Diaghileff's idea of industrial America had mainly to do with strikes. "Grèves"—the

French word for strikes—would, he felt, make a fitting title. (Eventually the ballet was called "*Skyscrapers*").[p 39]

A year later Carpenter came to Venice...with the music and the impressario said it was just what he wanted. Carpenter discussed the ballet's choreography with Nijinska...and all apparently was set for a production in Monte Carlo the following March. But, the projected second American tour having failed to materialize, that was the last Carpenter heard from the Russian. "I do not write letters—not even telegrams," Diaghileff had warned him. When all means of reaching the ballet director had been exhausted, Carpenter finally agreed to let Gatti-Casazza produce *Skyscrapers* at the Metropolitan in New York.[p.39]

Quotes Robert Edmond Jones, Carpenter, Paine, Borowski, Whitman, and Lawrence Gilman. Discusses his next few works, especially *Seven Ages*. Lists honors.

Concludes with general descriptions about his music, a "chronological chart of main events and works," a chronological list of his music by genre (under Songs: "and others"), a facsimile of *Practicing* from *Improving Songs for Anxious Children*. Includes port.

B133. Hamm, Charles. *Music in the New World.* New York: W.W. Norton, 1983.

Discusses *Krazy Kat:*

But hearing it today, it is difficult to understand what the excitement was all about. Its most important musical reference is to French and Russian ballet music of the late nineteenth and early twentieth centuries; its most prominent "exotic" rhythms are those of Spanish dance, emphasized by use of castanets; and it is only in Krazy Kat's final "Katnip Blues" that occasional suggestions of jazz instrumentation and rhythm come through, in trombone and clarinet glissandos, the brief use of a muted "wa-wa" trumpet, and some hints of syncopated rhythms.[p.423]

Carpenter "is best remembered for his attempts to forge an American symphonic style out of elements of ragtime and jazz."[p.456]

B134. Hansl, Eva vB and Kaufmann, Helen L. *Minute Sketches of Great Composers*. New York: Grosset & Dunlap, 1932.
Gives birth date and place. Carpenter "has been called by one critic the logical successor to MacDowell."[p.153] Describes certain works briefly. "Warm, sensitive, full of color, elegance and refinement, they [*Gitanjali* and *Water Colors*] are wholly successful in their genre."[p.153]
Includes port.

B135. Hitchcock, H. Wiley. *Music in the United States: A Historical Introduction*. 2nd ed. Englewood Cliffs, NJ: Prentice-Hall, 1974.
"John Alden Carpenter's ballet scores *Krazy Kat* (1921) and *Skyscrapers* (1926) were indebted to some rhythmic aspects of American dance music."[p.175]

B136. Howard, John Tasker and Bellows, George Kent. *A Short History of Music in America*. New York: Thomas Y. Crowell, 1957.

> Even though Carpenter was to employ many phases of the American vernacular, his style of writing was still predominantly European. He had been a student of Paine's at Harvard, but went to England [i.e. Rome] to work with Elgar and while in Europe came under the influence of Debussy. But he had been quick to see the musical importance of ragtime (and later jazz)...Today many musicians feel that Carpenter's works are superficial and merely reflect an earlier era, but in his time he was an important musical figure. [p.229]

B137. Howard, John Tasker. *Our American Music; Three Hundred Years of It*. 3rd ed. New York: Thomas Y. Crowell, 1946.
Ranks the American tendencies in his compositions:
"Yet there are others who deny Carpenter his Americanism because of the French derivation of his style, or because he seems to feel so keenly, and so subjectively, the moods of nature."[p.368]
Discusses his early training, and describes some of

his works with dates and places of performances.

Carpenter's *String Quartet* "proved to be an interesting mixture of charm and whimsicality with moments of uncompromising severity."[p.370]

Carpenter's *Piano Quintet* "was natural and sincere music, and the use of the piano for percussive effects was altogether contemporary in feeling. The refinement of its idiom lent distinction to the work's rich chromaticism."[p.370]

Includes reviews by Francis Perkins and Virgil Thomson of the *New York Herald Tribune*. Concludes by mentioning some of his songs.

B138. _____. *Our Contemporary Composers: American Music in the Twentieth Century*. New York: Thomas Y. Crowell, 1941.

Includes photograph by Greystone. Begins by placing him in an educational and business background. "Carpenter's progress...shows an interesting evolution. Regardless of how truly creative he may be, it denotes an artist who attempts his own thinking." Gives an example of "whole-tone progressions" in *The Green River*, of "Franckian...spirit" in the *Violin Sonata*, and of "whimsy" in *Adventures in a Perambulator*.[p.35-36]

In the *Piano Concertino* he shows a "firmer grip on his tools, a more certain touch in his handling of them." Some innovations include "shifting accents that point to the jazz rhythms of later works, quadruple figures imposed on a triple pattern, and vice versa. There is also present a Spanish flavor." [p.36]

Discusses the three ballets and other major orchestral works.

B139. Howe, Mark Anthony DeWolfe. *The Boston Symphony Orchestra, 1881-1931*. Boston: Houghton Mifflin, 1931.

Pierre Monteux "abetted the growth of Carpenter, Loeffler, Hill, Converse, Gilbert."[p.149]

B140. _____. *The Boston Symphony Orchestra, 1881-1931*. New York: DaCapo, 1978.

Reprint of l931 ed.

B141. Hughes, Rupert. *American Composers*. Boston: Page, 1914.

Gives birth date and place and Carpenter's educational background including all of his teachers. "Carpenter is in business, but finds time to toss off

compositions that win remarkable eulogies." [p.541]
Briefly describes the *Violin Sonata* and some of the
songs. "Carpenter's work, on the whole, is modern
and modulatory, but distinctly and decidely original."
[p.543]

B142. _____. *American Composers.* Boston: Page, 1900.
Includes Harvard honors and the *Piano Sonata*
which do not appear in the 1914 ed.

B143. Johnson, H. Earle. *Symphony Hall, Boston.* Boston: Little,
Brown, 1950.
Lists works performed by the Boston Symphony
Orchestra, 1881-1949; gives date and year of first
performance, and years of other performances. Makes
several references to *Adventures in a Perambulator*: 1)
"pleased mightily" in 1915-1916; 2) included in Pierre
Monteux's farewell concert; and 3) Koussevitzky
wished to perform "that work featuring a vehicle"
which the orchestra librarian understood to be
Frederick Converse's *Flivver Ten Million.* [p.111]

B144. Kingman, Daniel. *American Music: A Panorama.* New York:
Schirmer, 1979.
Mentions *Krazy Kat* which "employed jazz idioms"
and *Skyscrapers* was "commissioned by the Russian
impressario Sergei Pavlovich Diaghilev." [p.386]
Mentions "Diaghilev's production of *Skyscrapers*
...in 1926."[p.396]
Refers to "the use of 'noise-like' sounds...from
John Alden Carpenter's typewriter...to [1960's
noise]."[p.512]

B145. Kolodin, Irving. *The Metropolitan Opera, 1883-1966: A
Candid History.* New York: Alfred A. Knopf, 1968.
Ballet new to New York: "*Birthday of the Infanta* on
Feb. 23 [1920]. Carpenter's score and the dancing of
Ruth Page (Infanta) and [Adolf] Bolm (Pedro) were all
liked; but there was time for only a single repetition
before the season ended."[p.289]

B146. Leichentritt, Hugo. *Music of the Western Nations.*
Cambridge: Harvard University Press, 1956.
"One of the most successful American scores in
the realistic vein was the ballet *Skyscrapers* by John
Alden Carpenter...The materialistic aspects of the

American scene prevail in this score, with its description of the noisy hubbub of New York life."[p.286-87]

B147. _____. *Serge Koussevitzky*. Cambridge: Harvard University
Press, 1946.
Carpenter's first time on a Koussevitzky program
was Dec. 9, 1927, but he had been performed by the
Boston Symphony Orchestra six times before.

> *Perambulator* has apparently come to the close of
> its career in Boston. The reason may be found in
> the gradual change of aesthetic maxims. A
> complicated score in six movements, for a
> tremendous orchestra, devoted to the adventures
> of an American baby...really does not make much
> sense at the present time, though the music is
> itself not—and undoubtedly has not been—
> without charms.[p.65]

Skyscrapers was performed four times between 1927
and 1939. Other works performed include: *Song of
Faith* (Feb. 23, 1932), *Patterns* (Oct. 21, 1932), *Danza* (Jan
17, 1937), and the *Violin Concerto* (Mar. 3, 1939).
"The elaborate literary, descriptive programs, the
exotic themes, landscape impressions, sociological
and technological topics, treated for instance in...Car-
penter's *Perambulator* were not relished anymore."
[p.75]

B148. Machlis, Joseph. *Introduction to Contemporary Music*. New
York: W.W. Norton, 1961.
"The new tendency [to portray machine sounds
musically] produced such works as...John Alden
Carpenter's *Skyscrapers* (1926)."[p.156]
"Carpenter achieved a vogue in the Twenties with
two ballets that sought to incorporate the rhythm and
tempo of American life: *Krazy Kat* (1922) and *Skyscrapers* (1926)."[p.454]

B149. Mason, Daniel Gregory. *The Dilemma of American Music
and Other Essays*. New York: Macmillan, 1928.
"Many of Carpenter's clever and refined—almost
too refined—songs and piano pieces might have been
written by Debussy, while his suite for orchestra,
Adventures in a Perambulator, is essentially Gallic in its
economy of means, its distinctiveness of color, and
its ironic wit."[p.6]

Adventures in a Perambulator and the *Piano Concertino* are on a list of most frequently played American works 1919-1920 to 1925-1926.

B150. _____. *Tune in, America*. New York: Alfred A. Knopf, 1931.
Lists performances of ten major orchestras giving seasons and repertoire; also lists American chamber music including Carpenter's *String Quartet* and his *Violin Sonata*. Orchestral works include *Adventures in a Perambulator*, the *Piano Concertino*, *Skyscrapers*, *Birthday of the Infanta*, and *Pilgrim Vision*.

B151. Mellers, Wilfrid. *Music and Society*. New York: Roy, 1950.
Discusses American music with its own provincialities and its own academicians, such as John Alden Carpenter and Deems Taylor who so completely failed "to achieve a vernacular adequately expressive of their environment that they accept[ed] ready-made a late nineteenth-century European convention which for them is [was] moribund." [p.204]

B152. Mueller, John H. *The American Symphony Orchestra: A Social History of Musical Taste*. Bloomington: Indiana University Press, 1951.
Lists how frequently ten orchestras performed certain works from 1925 to 1950. During the years 1925-1930 Carpenter works were performed 6.5% of the total; two of his compositions were performed by these orchestras between 1945 and 1950.

B153. _____. *The American Symphony Orchestra: A Social History of Musical Taste*. Bloomington: Indiana University Press, 1927.
Lists composers and dates, titles of orchestral works, durations and which orchestras performed them in which years. There is a separate listing by orchestra of their conductors with dates of tenure.

B154. Mueller, Kate. *The Music Makers*. New York: Harry N. Abrams, 1979.
Gives birth and death years, nationality, place of birth, Harvard, Elgar in Rome. "His music is colourful and witty...*Krazy Kat*...combine[s] jazz with the 'serious' orchestra...*Skyscrapers*...marked a development in his style. His lighthearted *Concertino*...has frequent performances." [p.166]

B155. Northouse, Cameron. *Twentieth Century Opera in England and the United States*. Boston: G.K. Hall, 1976.
Krazy Cat [sic] is listed as an additional opera lacking complete information.

B156. O'Connell, Charles. *The Victor Book of the Symphony*. Rev. ed. New York: Simon and Schuster, 1941.

> His music is of its own genre, original and unique, yet he can turn with facility from the often austere and grave patriotic affirmations of *A Song of Faith* to the problemmatical reflections of an infant in *Adventures in a Perambulator*, or from the vague and subjective musings of the Indian mystic Rabindranath Tagore, to the febrile flush and spasmodic rhythms of a Coney Island panorama.[p.175]

> Discusses stories and music of *Adventures in a Perambulator* and *Skyscrapers*. Gives orchestras and conductors for one recording each, but no label information.

B157. Osgood, Henry O. *So This Is Jazz*. Boston: Little, Brown, 1926.

> The learned gentlemen...lack the gift of writing good jazz tunes. Their thoughts are not rowdy enough. John Alden Carpenter is a striking example of this. We have in this country no better musician, no better composer of serious music, no better orchestrator. But when he tries to write jazz—and he unfortunately persists in the idea that he can do so—he is much too polished. The result is the lukewarm tunes that one hears in his two ballets, *Skyscrapers* and *Crazy Cat*; whereas his other ballet *The Birthday of an Infanta*, written in his natural idiom, is the most distinguished and best-sustained work for the stage an American has yet produced.[p.153]

> *A Little Bit of Jazz* suffers from that "musical politeness...that affects all Carpenter's jazz." [p.156]
> Quotes Carpenter on contemporary music.

B158. Otis, Philo Adams. *The Chicago Symphony Orchestra, 1891-1924*. Freeport, NY: Books for Libraries, 1924.

Programs for *Adventures in a Perambulator*, the *Piano Concertino*, *Home Road*, *Pilgrim Vision*, and *Symphony no. 1* include very brief commentary (usually the occasion of the first performance), and reviews from the *Evening Post*.

B159. Pannain, Guido. *Modern Composers*. New York: E.P. Dutton, 1933.

The composer's attempt [to reflect in *Skyscrapers* the primeval rhythmic movement of American life] is a valiant one, but it is no more than an attempt, and it is finally shipwrecked upon the reef of realism. He can do no better than to pass the creations of his imagination (rhythmic images of American life...) through the sieve of a Russian and French technique of the ballet; with the result that his idea does not get an adequate interpretation, but is covered by a mixture of two different styles. *Skyscrapers* is an ingenuous work, lively and full of rhythmic energy, but it has a duplicate background, fitted roughly into the conventional rhetorical framework of the French-Russian ballet of to-day with its symbolical gestures and varied choreography. It has music which sparkles, but the genuine American element is modelled by a European-acquired technique smacking of Ravel and Stravinsky.[p.244-45]

B160. Reis, Claire R. *Composers, Conductors and Critics*. Detroit: Detroit Reprints in Music, 1974.
Carpenter "experimented with jazz."[p.47] Gives the program notes for *Anxious Bugler* by Carpenter.

B161. Salazar, Adolfo. *Music in Our Time*. New York: W.W. Norton, 1946.
Carpenter "absorbed contemporary French manners of writing during study in Europe... Carpenter has exploited most successfully his dramatic and pictorial sense in his compositions for ballet."[p.312-13]

B162. Silverman, Faye-Ellen. "The Twentieth Century." *Schirmer History of Music*. New York: Schirmer, 1982.
Carpenter "aimed for a synthesis of jazz and traditional Western music."[p.775]

B163. Scholes, Percy A. *The Oxford Companion to Music*. London: Oxford University Press, 1970.

Carpenter is a "composer of exceptional sincerity and technical brilliancy, and though possessed of eclecticism, nevertheless expressed in ways suggestive of the American tempo and environment certain phases of the life of his place and time."[p.1057]

B164. Seldes, Gilbert. *The Seven Lively Arts*. 1st ed. New York: Harper & Brothers, 1924.

Discusses *Krazy Kat* and gives Carpenter's program notes for it. In the author's opinion "the theme is greater than the plot."[p.236]

It was in this show that the Herriman-Carpenter ballet of Krazy Kat was tried and dismissed, and the fault here is the fault of Mr. Anderson throughout...Everyone who has intelligence of Krazy knows that it should be done by an American stunt dancer until the time when Mr. Chaplin finds time to do it. Krazy Kat is exquisite and funny...[and] Mr. Anderson wanted him to be artistic at all cost.[p.144]

B165. _____. *The Seven Lively Arts*. New York: Sagamore Press, 1957.

Discusses *Krazy Kat*:

To put such a character into music was a fine thought, but Mr. Carpenter must have known that he was foredoomed to failure...Mr. Carpenter almost missed one essential thing: the ecstasy of Krazy when the brick arrives at the end; certainly, as Mr. Bolm danced it one felt only the triumph of Ignatz...The irony was missing.[p.214]

B166. Slonimsky, Nicolas. *Music since 1900*. 4th ed. New York: Charles Scribner's Sons, 1971.

Arranged by year; gives dates and performers of orchestral premieres. Includes thirteen performances of Carpenter's works.

B167. Spaeth, Sigmund. *Great Symphonies, How to Recognize and Remember Them*. Garden City, NY: Garden City Publ. Co., 1936.

Gives birth year and place. "Highly successful American composer, consistently maintaining the

true amateur attitude toward his work."[p.327]
Mentions *Adventures in a Perambulator, Birthday of the Infanta,* and *Skyscrapers.*

B168. Spalding, Walter Raymond. *Music at Harvard; A Historical Review of Men and Events.* New York: Da Capo Press, 1977.
Lists honorary (1922) and Harvard (1897) degrees. Includes port. Mentions an original minuet for orchestra performed Dec. 18, 1894 and Carpenter's membership in the Committee on Army and Navy Camp Music.

B169. Stevens, Denis. *A History of Song.* New York: Norton, 1960.
Discusses his musical style in general, then the songs:

[His songs,] except for a brief excursion into Mahler's folk-song style and the sparse part-writing of his accompaniment, fall entirely under the influence of Debussy's concepts, around 1910, and adhere to them for more than ten years. Their delicate sonorities and evocative poetic atmosphere reveal a musician of taste and craftsmanship but only within the limits of a style that was not sufficiently his own...He utilized the racy idiom of jazz [in *Four Negro Songs.*] He tried to paraphrase it...but actually surrendered to it.[p.426]

B170. Stringham, Edwin John. *Listening to Music Creatively.* New York: Prentice-Hall, 1943.
Carpenter's "music, delightful, intelligent, and witty, has attained wide popularity with the general public."[p.126]
"Fevered, restlessly pulsating rhythms of the work episodes alternate with the gay fox-trot and 'Blues' rhythms of the play episodes [in *Skyscrapers*]." A wealth of melodic ideas, of striking harmonies "abound in pungent dissonances united with never-flagging rhythms in a composition of great excitement and forward drive."[p.126-27]

B171. Thomson, Virgil. *American Music since 1910.* New York: Holt, Rinehart and Winston, 1972.
Mentions birth, degrees, teachers Ziehn and Elgar, two wives, profession and affiliations, honors, and

partial list of musical works.

"Carpenter was an impressionistic composer of superficial but perfectly real charm. His works embodying whimsy, gentle sentiments, and the picturesque are more striking than his monumental ones."[p.130]

B172. _____. *Music Reviewed, 1940-1954*. New York: Vintage Books, Random House, 1967.

Refers to Carpenter's "neoclassicized impressionism" [p.231]

B173. _____. *A Virgil Thomson Reader*. Boston: Houghton Mifflin, 1981.

Gives characteristics of the composer "whose chief revenue comes from invested capital...He tends to write playful music, to seek charm at the expense of emphasis. He abounds in witty ingenuities. He is not much given nowadays to writing introspective music."[p.124]

"The stylistic orientation of the rich composer is toward the French salon school. He goes in for imagistic evocation, witty juxtapositions, imprecise melodic contours, delicacy of harmonic texture and of instrumentation, meditative sensuality, tenderness about children, evanescence, the light touch, discontinuity."[p.124]

Carpenter is Thomson's American example.

B174. Upton, William Treat. *Art-Song in America*. Boston: Ditson, 1930.

Discusses Carpenter's songs. See B446.

B175. Weissman, Adolf. *The Problems of Modern Music*. London: J.M. Dent; New York: E.P. Dutton, 1925.

"Among the more prominent American musicians...[is] the refined, if somewhat superficial, John Alden Carpenter."[p.222]

B176. Yates, Peter. *Twentieth Century Music*. New York: Pantheon, Random House, 1967.

Carpenter "cultivated music as a skilled amateur."[p.284]

B177. Young, Percy M. *The Choral Tradition*. New York: W.W. Norton, 1962.

Twentieth century choral music has a "ruggedness

and a sense of purpose. We may recall, for instance, the fine swinging tunes of John Alden Carpenter's *Song of Faith* (a sort of aggregation of melodies which might be folksongs but aren't)."[p.314-15]

B178. Young, Stark. *The Flower in Drama, & Glamour*. Rev. ed. New York: Charles Scribner's Sons, 1955.
Colorful, descriptive account of the performance of *Birthday of the Infanta*: "All this innocent and grotesque, sombre, ornate gaiety Mr. Carpenter expressed, so austere is his music at times, so macabre, so hauntingly elaborated, so wistful, and so finely withdrawn."[p.202]
Praises Robert Edmond Jones' settings and the costumes in terms of theatrical presence.

B179. _____. *Immortal Shadows*. New York: C. Scribner's Sons, 1948.
Slightly abridged version of previous citation. Performance discussed took place at the Manhattan Opera House, Feb. 2, 1922.

DICTIONARIES AND ENCYCLOPEDIAS

B180. Altmann, Wilhelm. *Kurzgefasstes Tonkünstler-Lexikon*. 15th ed. Wilhelmshaven: Heinrichhofen's Verlag, 1971.
Lists date and place of birth, student of Elgar and Ziehn, and types of compositions: ballets, orchestral suites, piano concertino, chamber music and songs.

B181. Anderson, E. Ruth, comp. *Contemporary American Composers; A Biographical Dictionary*. 2nd ed. Boston: G.K. Hall, 1982.
Gives birth and death dates and places, teachers Paine, Ziehn, and Elgar, some honorary degrees and awards, twenty-five titles including "*The Player Queen*, piano."[sic][p.83]

B182. *ASCAP Biographical Dictionary*. New York: Crowell, 1929.
Includes Carpenter's birth, teachers, honors, address, and major compositions.

B183. _____. 2nd ed. Edited by Daniel I. McNamara. New York: Crowell, 1952.
Gives birth date and place. "Advanced studies, Amy Fay, piano."[p.57] Gives honors, works, and home address.

B184. _____. 3rd ed. Compiled and edited by The Lynn Farnol
  Group. New York: The American Society of
  Composers, Authors, and Publishers, 1966.
    Includes birth and death dates and places; gives all
  teachers except Seeboeck; lists honors and works.

B185. _____. 4th ed. New York: Jaques Cattell Press, R.R.
  Bowker, 1980.
    Gives dates, all teachers except Seeboeck, honors
  and a list of his works.

B186. *Baker's Biographical Dictionary of Musicians*. 3rd ed. New
  York: G. Schirmer, 1919.
    Includes birth date and place and three of his
  teachers: Paine, Elgar, and Ziehn. Lists some of his
  works. "In his compositions he follows the modern
  impressionistic tendencies."[p.142]

B187. _____. 4th ed. New York: G. Schirmer, 1940.
    Adds information about his career as a business-
  man, his awards, and his honorary degrees. More
  extensive list of works. Includes bibliography.

B188. _____. Supplement by Nicholas Slonimsky. New York: G.
  Schirmer, 1949.
    Mentions the 1947 gold medal. Adds to worklist.

B189. _____. 5th ed. Completely revised by Nicholas Slonimsky.
  New York: G. Schirmer, 1958.
    Adds death date and place. More extensive work-
  list. "From his musical contacts abroad he absorbed
  mildly modernistic and impressionistic techniques
  and applied them to his music based on American
  urban subjects, adding the resources of jazz
  rhythms."[p.254]

B190. _____. 6th ed. Completely revised by Nicholas Slonimsky.
  New York: Schirmer, 1978.
    Adds two titles to the bibliography.

B191. _____. 7th ed. Revised by Nicholas Slonimsky. New York:
  Schirmer, 1984.
    Almost identical to 6th ed. Omits Elgar.

B192. Barlow, Harold and Morgenstern, Sam. *A Dictionary of
  Musical Themes*. New York: Crown, 1948.

Gives incipits for *Adventures in a Perambulator* and the *String Quartet*.

B193. _____. *A Dictionary of Vocal Themes*. New York: Crown, 1950.
Gives incipits for *Gitanjali* (nos. 1 and 3), *Home Road*, and *Serenade*.

B194. Blom, Eric. *Everyman's Dictionary of Music*. New York: New American Library, 1971.
Incorrectly states that Carpenter studied with Elgar in 1895. Mentions *Sea Drift* (after Whitman) and *Birthday of the Infanta* (after Wilde).

B195. Butterworth, Neil. *A Dictionary of American Composers*. New York: Garland, 1984.
Gives dates and places of Carpenter's birth and death, two of his teachers: Paine and Elgar, his works and the circumstances of their first performances. "With choreography by Heinrich Kroeller, *Skyscrapers* was first produced in 1925 in Monte Carlo by the Ballet Russe."[sic][p.72]
"His early orchestral compositions are important as they represent most clearly the first American works to portray the American way of life. It is this rather than the intrinsic value of his music which established him as a composer of some significance." [p.73]

B196. Carlton, Joseph R. *Carlton's Complete Reference Book on Music*. Studio City, CA: Carlton, 1980.
Lists dates and country of origin, his principal works and dates of composition.

B197. Chase, Gilbert. "Carpenter, John Alden." *Dictionary of American Biography*, suppl. 5 (1951-1955). Edited by John A. Garraty. New York: Charles Scribner's Sons, 1977.
Discusses Carpenter's background and education, his first successes and their impact: "Carpenter's involvement with jazz culminated in the *Jazz Orchestra Pieces* (1925-26)."[p.103]
Lists other major works. Mentions his second marriage in 1933. "By this time he was the most famous American art-music composer of his generation, his works frequently performed by major symphony orchestras and choral groups."[p.103-04]

Impressionism left its mark on him, particularly
in his songs. What distinguished him from such
academic composers as Hill and Powell was his
flair for the American musical vernacular (as
distinct from folk music), evinced in such novel
works as *Krazy Kat* and *Skyscrapers*. Although
these have come to be regarded as period pieces,
their innovative contribution in the 1920's
remains important.[p.104]

Includes bibliography.

B198. _____. "Carpenter, John Alden." *Encyclopedia Americana*.
     Danbury, CT: Grolier, 1986.
          Includes birth and death years, teachers and
     business. Mentions briefly some of his orchestral
     works. "*Krazy Kat* and *Skyscrapers,* as well as the
     Concertino for Piano and Orchestra (1915), drew on the
     idioms of American popular music."[p.701]

B199. _____. "Carpenter, John Alden." *The New Grove Dictionary
     of American Music*. London: Macmillan; New York:
     Grove's Dictionaries of Music, 1986.
          Gives birth and death dates and places. Includes all
     his teachers, Harvard, business, awards and honors.
     "His numerous songs for voice and piano greatly
     enhanced his reputation and brought him
     recognition as an outstanding song composer of his
     generation." His "most successful [symphonic work]
     is *Sea Drift*...Apart from the merit of his songs, his
     place in American music is assured by the historical
     significance of his ballet *Skyscrapers* as an early
     attempt to depict 'modern American life'."[p.359]
          Includes a complete list of works and a short
     bibliography.

B200. _____. "Carpenter, John Alden." *The New Grove Dictionary
     of Music and Musicians*. London: Macmillan; New York:
     Grove's Dictionaries of Music, 1980.
          Includes birth and death dates and places. Lists all
     his teachers. "With the *Piano Concertino,* Carpenter
     began his mild but persistent flirtation with Ameri-
     can popular music, including ragtime and slight
     touches of jazz."[p.818]
          Discusses briefly some of his works. Gives selective
     list of works and bibliography.

B201. Claghorn, Charles Eugene. *Biographical Dictionary of American Music.* West Nyack, NY: Parker, 1973.
   Mentions performance of *Sea Drift* by the Chicago Symphony Orchestra under Frederick Stock in 1933.

B202. DeBekker, L.J. *DeBekker's Music and Musicians.* New York: Nicholas L. Brown, 1925.
   Lists works, teachers Ziehn and Elgar, birth and graduation dates—Chicago and Harvard.

B203. Einstein, Alfred, ed. *Hugo Riemanns Musik Lexikon.* 11th ed. Berlin: Max Hesses Verlag, 1929.
   Lists birth date and place, all teachers except Paine, and Harvard. Selective worklist.

B204. *Enciclopedia della musica.* Milano: Ricordi, 1963.
   Gives birth and death dates and places; all teachers except Seeboeck; lists three symphonies (1917, 1940, 1942), *Danza* (orchestra, 1935), *Anxious Bugler, Seven Ages,* and *Patterns.*
   "Grande industriale, si dedicò alla musica da dilettante, affermandosi tuttavia tra i migliori autori nordamericani."[p.417]

B205. *Encyclopedie de la musique.* Paris: Fasquelle, 1958.
   Seven lines list his works, birth and death dates and places, teachers Elgar and Ziehn. "Il collabora avec Diaghilev (*Skyscrapers,* ballet, 1926)."[p.492]

B206. Ewen, David. *American Composers: A Biographical Dictionary.* New York: G.P. Putnam's, 1982.
   Includes birth and death dates and places. Extensive account of his schooling and teachers. *Four Negro Songs* is incorrectly dated 1903. Traces Carpenter's development through his works and their influences, including premieres.
   "Carpenter would pursue most successfully: the use of popular American idioms—jazz particularly—within the context of serious composition."[p.108]

   With the *Jazz Orchestra Pieces* (1925-26) Carpenter's symphonic-jazz period was over. In his *Quartet for Strings* (1927)...he was the conformist and the romanticist faithful to conventional patterns and concerned mainly with expressivity of emotion. After 1930 he became increasingly impressionistic, seeking moods, atmosphere, subtle rather than outright suggestions, poetic insight, and tender rather than effusive sentiments.[p.109]

Concludes with the names of his wives, list of awards and honors, and the statement that performances on his seventy-fifth birthday were promoted by the National Arts Foundation. Includes a Carpenter quotation, list of principal works, and a bibliography.

B207. _____. *American Composers Today; A Biographical and Critical Guide.* New York: H.W. Wilson, 1949.

Includes birth date and place. Lists all his teachers, mentions his business, discusses his works, especially *Adventures in a Perambulator,* the three ballets, and *Song of Faith* and their influences (some in passing: "Carpenter has also written excellent chamber music together with a long list of songs.") [p.48] Quotes Felix Borowski and W.J. Henderson, lists principal works and recordings, includes honors and awards, gives two bibliographic citations. Includes port.

B208. _____, ed. *Composers since 1900; A Biographical and Critical Guide.* New York: H.W. Wilson, 1969.

Ewen's consistent beginning with teachers, continues with the family business and *When Little Boys Sing,* "his first publication appeared as early as 1904."[p.114] Here *Skyscrapers* "received its première performance at the Metropolitan Opera in New York on February 19, 1926." [This was incorrectly stated in Ewen's *Composers of Today* (B124).]

"Although Carpenter had favored a Romantic style developed along traditional lines, in 1921 he became interested in jazz as a significant tool with which to build an American musical art."[p.115]

Quotes Oscar Thompson and W.J. Henderson. Lists honors and wives, major works, and three bibliographic references. Includes port.

B209. _____. *Encyclopedia of Concert Music.* New York: Hill and Wang, 1959.

Gives birth and death dates and places. Lists background, major teachers: Paine, Elgar, and Ziehn, family business, major works and honors, and separate references to *Adventures in a Perambulator, Birthday of the Infanta, Sea Drift, Seven Ages,* and *Skyscrapers.* Presents the stories, influences, and first performances.

B210. _____. *Ewen's Musical Masterpieces: The Encyclopedia of Musical Masterpieces.* 2nd ed. New York: Arco, 1958.

Includes birth place and date, "studied music first privately, then at Harvard University, finally with Bernhard Ziehn. He was also a pupil of Elgar." Carpenter was a businessman and composer who used the "jazz idiom seriously" and who "died in Chicago in 1951."[p.149]

Discusses *Skyscrapers* which "was given its première in Monte Carlo in 1925."[sic][p.149] Also discusses *Adventures in a Perambulator* (including Carpenter's program notes).

B211. Gilder, Eric and Port, June G. *The Dictionary of Composers and Their Music.* New York: Paddington, 1978.

Gives a chronological list of his works (twenty-four titles) and his age at the time they were composed.

B212. Greene, David Mason. *Greene's Biographical Encyclopedia of Composers.* Garden City, NY: Doubleday, 1985.

Extensive discussion of teacher's backgrounds (e.g., "Liszt pupil Amy Fay"). Cites early works and their premieres. "Up to 1920 most of Carpenter's works had been of the international-genteel-eclectic school. Now he felt impelled to make them more 'American'—in theme, in inspiration, and even in music."[p.958]

Gives some titles, dates, and some short descriptions.

Carpenter continued to produce until a few years before his death, but his day was by then over...If his music is not very original or great (it speaks German with a French accent), it is not stuffy or self-conscious, and Carpenter must be regarded at the very least as a fine art-song composer."[p.958]

Gives titles (but no labels) and only one performer for recordings.

B213. *Grove's Dictionary of Music and Musicians.* American Supplement. Edited by Waldo Selden Pratt. New York: Macmillan, 1930.

Gives birth date and place. Lists all teachers except Paine, but does include Harvard. Mentions family business and early works. Carpenter has a "fortunate, straightforward and untrammeled faculty of musical expression, prompted by technical fluency and skill and marked by unusual charm and refinement." [p.154]

Appendix lists his ballet *Semiramis* [*Skyscrapers?*] which was produced at the Metropolitan Opera in New York in 1926.

B214. Hadley, Benjamin, ed. *Britannica Book of Music.* Garden City, NY: Doubleday, Britannica Books, 1980.

Includes dates, business, Harvard, and teachers Elgar and Ziehn. *Adventures in a Perambulator* shows a "gift for musical humor and effective orchestration." [p.155] *Krazy Kat* uses jazz. *Skyscrapers* is powerful. Lists titles for three recordings.

B215. Hart, James D. *The Oxford Companion to American Literature.* 4th ed. New York: Oxford University Press, 1965.

Gives composer's birth and death years. "Best known for his witty symphonic suite, *Adventures in a Perambulator.*"[p.136] Lists the *Piano Concertino* and the titles of his three ballets.

B216. Henderson, W.J. "Carpenter, John Alden." *Grove's Dictionary of Music and Musicians.* 3rd ed. Edited by H.C. Colles. New York: Macmillan, 1944.

Includes birth date and place, all five teachers and Harvard.

Carpenter has "a whimsical fancy, a delicate, even poetic humour, and tender sentiment. His melodic invention is facile and his themes have fluency and grace. He writes with an easy mastery of form, and his orchestral works are filled with colour, but never garish."[p.569]

B217. _____. "Carpenter, John Alden." *Grove's Dictionary of Music and Musicians.* 5th ed. Edited by Eric Blom. New York: St. Martin's Press, 1955.

Gives birth date and place. Lists teachers, incorrectly puts his study with Elgar in 1895 and "on returning to America [Carpenter] continued further work with Bernhard Ziehn." [While he was at Harvard!] "He was a composer who produced music with manifest enjoyment and whose quick impulses were governed by good taste."[p.91]

Includes list of works.

B218. Hermil, Helénè. *Musique, 10,000 compositeurs du XIIe ay XXe siècle*. Paris: G.R.E.M. (Groupe de recherches et d'études musicales), 1983.
    Gives his birth and death dates and places, and mentions *Krazy cat* [sic] recording.

B219. Hindley, Geoffrey, ed. *Larousse Encyclopedia of Music*. London, New York: Hamlyn, 1974.
    Refers to Carpenter as a student of Paine.

B220. Hughes, Rupert. *The Biographical Dictionary of Musicians*. New York: Blue Ribbon, 1940.
    Cites birth date and place. Mentions Harvard, Ziehn and Seeboeck. "His musical idiom is modern and his output fairly large."[p.92] Gives partial list of works.

B221. _____. *Music Lovers' Encyclopedia*. New York: Garden City, 1939.
    Same article as B220.

B222. Jablonski, Edward. *The Encyclopedia of American Music*. Garden City, NY: Doubleday, 1981.
    Gives dates and places of birth and death, and Carpenter's business and musical training. Traces his early published works. "Elegance and wit plus mastery of the orchestra were characteristic of Carpenter's music."[p.117]
    Quotes Carpenter on American music. Lists other major works and dates. No mention of honors or medals, but "he was also active as director of the Illinois Children's Home and Aid Society. He died in Chicago, April 26, 1951."[p.118]
    Separate entries for *Krazy Kat* and *Skyscrapers* (which was "presented for the first time in Monte Carlo in 1925 [sic].")[p.289] *Skyscrapers* is "a work of much charm and a worthy period piece."[p.289]
    Includes two record listings.

B223. Jacobs, Arthur. *A New Dictionary of Music*. Chicago: Aldine, 1961.
    Brief entry includes birth and death years, titles to two works, refers to two symphonies.

B224. _____. *The New Penguin Dictionary of Music*. 4th ed. New York: Penguin, 1977.

Same information as previous entry. Concludes: "combined music with a business career."[p.70]

B225. Karp, Theodore. *Dictionary of Music*. Evanston: Northwestern University Press, 1973.

Includes birth and death dates and places, teachers: Paine, Elgar, and Ziehn. "His style was influenced by French impressionism and by jazz. Among his better known orchestral works are *Krazy Kat*, *Skyscrapers*, and *Adventures in a Perambulator*. He wrote also chamber and keyboard music and songs." [p.84]

B226. Kennedy, Michael. *The Concise Oxford Dictionary of Music*. 3rd ed. London, New York: Oxford University Press, 1980.

Gives birth and death dates and places. "Like Ives ...business career."[p.118] Mentions Harvard. Lists major works and some songs.

B227. _____. *The Oxford Dictionary of Music*. Oxford, NewYork: Oxford University Press, 1985.

Same entry as B226.

B228. Kinkeldey, Otto. "Carpenter, John Alden." *A Dictionary of Modern Music and Musicians*. London: J.M. Dent; New York: E.P. Dutton, 1924.

Includes birth date and place, all his teachers, honors received, and his published works of any significance with premiere information.

"As a compr. he follows modern tendencies entirely, although he has not yet joined the extreme ultra-modernists. His work exhibits great variety and skill in the handling of the orchestra."[p.79]

B229. Mariz, Vasco. *Dicionário bio-bibliográfico musical*. Rio de Janeiro: Livraria Kosmos Editora Erich Eichner, 1948.

Born in "Park Bridge" [sic], Illinois, studied at Harvard, lists major works, describes Carpenter: "Autor de música delicada, cheia de poesia, graca, colorido, jamais extravagante. 1921, Legião de Honra."[p.47]

B230. _____. *Dicionário bio-bibliográfico musical*. 2nd ed. Rio de Janeiro: Livraria Kosmos Editora Erich Eichner, 1985.

Description changes: "Influência impressionista e de jazz. Gravaçôes nos EUA."[p.74]

B231. Moser, Hans Joachim. *Musik Lexikon*. 4th ed. Hamburg: Hans Sikorski, 1955.
> Gives birth and death dates and places. Lists three teachers, "1897 Bacc. art."[p.183] but Harvard is not mentioned, businessman, honorary degree from Wisconsin University, titles of major works and a bibliography.

B232. *Der Musik Brockhaus*. Wiesbaden: F.A. Brockhaus; 1982.
> Includes phonetic spelling of his last name, birth and death dates and places, and teachers Paine and Elgar. "Anregungen aus der amerikan. Unterhalt-ungsmusik, des Ragtime und des Jazz finden sich bereits in seinem Klavierkonzert (1915)."[p.96]
> Work list gives *Krazy Kat* and *Skyscrapers* by title and other works by genre.

B233. *Musikkens Hvem Hvad Hvor*. Kobenhavn: Politikens Forlag, 1950.
> Gives birth date and place, Harvard, businessman, Elgar and Ziehn, honors and list of major works. Includes port.

B234. _____. Kobenhavn: Politikens Forlag, 1961.
> Adds his death date and place, *Symphony (1940)*, *Gitanjali*, and *Water Colours*. Includes port.

B235. *The National Cyclopaedia of American Biography*. New York: James T. White, 1955.
> Gives birth date and place, all of his teachers, Harvard and business. Lists major works with dates and circumstances (e.g., for the Washington Bi-Centennial).
> "His style is distinguished for its simplicity, rich and varied harmonies, and apt phrasing; by a break with traditional theories and form and through his independence and originality he became one of the first completely American composers."[p.168]
> Includes affiliations, honors, and a port. Carpenter was director of the Illinois Children's Home and Aid Society and incorporator of the Illinois Composers' Guild. A Congregationalist and a Republican, he enjoyed reading, modern art, and travel.

B236. *The New College Encyclopedia of Music*. Edited by J.A. Westrup and F.Ll. Harrison. New York: W.W. Norton, 1976.

"Nothing amateurish about his music."[p.114]
Gives seven lines on the ballets.

B237. Pavlakis, Christopher. *The American Music Handbook.* New
York: The Free Press, Macmillan, 1974.
Lists holographs and manuscripts by Carpenter
held at Carnegie Library of Pittsburgh.

B238. Pratt, Waldo Selden, ed. *The New Encyclopedia of Music and
Musicians.* New York: Macmillan, 1924.
Includes birth date and place, profession, teachers:
"Amy Fay, Seeboeck and Ziehn and at Harvard
University." Gives titles of major works. He is "vice
president of a business."[p.270]

B239. _____. *The New Encyclopedia of Music and Musicians.* New
and rev. ed. New York: Macmillan, 1929.
Adds "and many striking songs" [p.270] to
previous entry.

B240. Prieberg, Fred K. *Lexikon der neuen Musik.* München: Karl
Alber Freiburg, 1958.
Gives birth and death year and state, Paine and
Harvard, business, major works and their premieres.

B241. Reis, Claire. *American Composers of Today.* 1st ed. New
York: International Society for Contemporary Musik,
1930.
Includes titles by genre with durations, publishers,
and dates of completion. Then a "record of performances" follows listing title, orchestras, opera
company, or festival, e.g.

CONCERTINO   Major American orchestras; Paris
[p.9]

B242. _____. *Composers in America.* New York: Macmillan,1938.
Gives birth year and place, Harvard, Paine, business, Elgar and Ziehn. Misleading: "In 1922 he took
his degree of Master of Arts at Harvard Univ...in 1933
the University of Wisconsin made him a Doctor of
Music."[p.55][These were honorary degrees.]
Includes titles for his major works with some
premiere dates. Lists by genre titles, durations, publishers and dates of completion.

B243. _____. *Composers in America*. Rev. and enl. ed. New York: Macmillan, 1947.

Eliminates "mother was a singer"[p.55, 1938] at the beginning of the article and adds *Seven Ages*, "his most recent work"[p.59] at the end. More extensive work list.

B244. _____. *Composers in America*. New York: Da Capo Press, 1977.

Reprint of the 1947 ed.

B245. Rock, Christa Maria and Brückner, Hans. *Judentum und Musik mit dem ABC jüdischer und nichtarischer Musikbeflissener*. 3. Aufl. München: Hans Brückner Verlag, 1938.

Gives birth date and place, business, Ziehn, and titles to two works: *Improving Songs for Anxious Children* (1907) and the *Violin Sonata* (1912).

B246. Sandved, Kjell Bloch, ed. *World of Music: An Illustrated Encyclopedia*. New York: Abradale, 1963.

Includes birth and death years and this description: "American composer." His "early works occasionally embodied jazz rhythms...but he also employed the impressionistic idiom he learned in Europe." [p.251] Gives titles of well-known works as well as several symphonies, some chamber music, and attractive song cycles. Includes port.

B247. Schmidl, Carlo. *Dizionario universale dei musicisti*. Milano: Casa Editrice Sonzogno, 1926.

"Buon compositore dilettante e grande industriale nord-americano."[p.299] Gives birth place and date. Studied with Elgar and Ziehn. Lists best-known works.

B248. Scholes, Percy A. *The Concise Oxford Dictionary of Music*. 2nd ed. London, New York: Oxford University Press, 1964.

Mentions birth and death years and places; Harvard. "Wealthy business man who attained popularity as composer of orch. works, piano pieces, songs, etc."[p.95] Separate entries for: *Adventures in a Perambulator, Birthday of the Infanta, Krazy Kat, Sea Drift*, and *Skyscrapers* giving premiere information. (e.g., "*Skyscrapers* prod. Monte Carlo, 1925.") [sic][p.535]

B249. Siegmeister, Elie, ed. *The New Music Lover's Handbook.*
Irvington-on-Hudson, NY: Harvey House, 1973.
"The Creole, Cuban, Mexican, and native American dance melodies appeared in our home-grown
composers."[p.328] Carpenter "absorbed Impressionist
influences."[p.506]

B250. *Sohlmans Musiklexikon.* Stockholm: Sohlmans Forlag AB,
1975.
Includes Carpenter's dates, Harvard, Elgar and
Ziehn. Mentions *Krazy Kat* and *Skyscrapers.* Lists
major works. Includes honorary degree from
University of Wisconsin (1933), a bibliography, and a
port.

B251. Stieger, Franz. *Opernlexikon.* Tutzing: Hans Schneider,
1977.
Gives genre, librettist, and place and date of
premiere for: *Flying Dutchman, Birthday of the Infanta,
Krazy Kat,* and *Skyscrapers.*

B252. Thompson, Oscar, ed. *The International Cyclopedia of Music
and Musicians.* 10th ed. Edited by Bruce Bohle. New
York: Dodd, Mead, 1975.
Includes birth year and place, all his teachers, a list
of major works with premieres, and honors.
"Carpenter is best remembered as a song writer,
and his songs reveal his leanings toward the French
school of impressionism. His style, however, is his
own, and is marked by refinement and aristocratic
elegance."[p.363]

B253. Wier, Albert E., ed. *The Macmillan Encyclopedia of Music and
Musicians in One Volume.* New York: Macmillan, 1938.
Gives dates, degrees, and institutions, e.g.

| 1922 | BA | Harvard |
| 1933 | PhD | U. of Wisc. |

Mentions *Skyscrapers, Birthday of the Infanta,* and
Krazy Kat.

B254. Woerner, Karl H. "Carpenter, John Alden." *Die Musik in
Geschichte und Gegenwart.* Kassel: Bärenreiter, 1952.
Gives birth and death dates and places. Lists teachers Paine, Elgar, and Ziehn. Includes stylistic characteristics, a partial list of works, and a bibliography.

B255. Young, Percy M. *A Critical Dictionary of Composers and Their Music.* London: Dennis Dobson, 1954.

 Lists poets whose works Carpenter set to music. In *Song of Faith*: Whitman and Lincoln; uses trumpet calls and drumrolls, narrator and chorus.

MUSIC THEORY

B256. Persichetti, Vincent. *Twentieth Century Harmony: Creative Aspects and Practice.* New York: Norton, 1961.

 Carpenter used "altered parallel writing" in *Skyscrapers* (p.39 of the reduction).[p.210]

B257. Ziehn, Bernhard. *Canonical Studies, A Very New Technic in Composition.* Milwaukee: Wm. A. Kaun, 1912.

 Contains an eight-part canon in the fourth, written by Carpenter.

DANCE

B258. Arvey, Verna. *Choreographic Music.* New York: Dutton, 1941.

 [William Grant] Still and Carpenter are among those few composers to stride definitely away from the regular-rhythmed dance music to which the public is accustomed. Their music is at once valuable as music, racially fascinating, not imitative, and choreographic. Both of them first wrote ballets with foreign backgrounds; both of them later came to write ballets expressing the American scene in good-humored, satirical music.[p.286]

 [*Birthday of the Infanta* and *Krazy Kat*] were created simultaneously with the choreography, when Carpenter himself was in the closest collaboration with Adolph Bolm. *Birthday of the Infanta* was based on the Oscar Wilde story...though the actual working scenario was planned by Carpenter...Bolm declares, however, that during the creation of the ballet, he left Carpenter entirely alone, until the composer began to send him completed parts of the score from time to time. [p.286-87]

Carpenter himself admits that as between the two methods of composing a ballet, the one he used in *Skyscrapers* (writing the music first, to follow the basic idea inherent in the subject; leaving the choreographic details to be imposed on the finished score) is to him far more congenial and logical. Diaghileff commissioned *Skyscrapers* in 1924...[and] suggested writing the music in general terms of contemporary American life without regard to story or action...Diaghileff <u>did</u> make some suggestions...which Carpenter adopted... Diaghileff's production of the ballet never took place.[p.289]

The title was to be *Song of the Skyscrapers*...[After] Carpenter completed his score...then, were the detailed actions and dances imposed on the music, having been worked out in a collaboration of Carpenter, Robert Edmond Jones, and Sammy Lee. Working according to this method, Carpenter believes that any composer has greater freedom and a better chance of achieving a general unity of form with a resulting work which should be available for concert purposes without rearranging.[p.289-90]

[Bolm] considered Carpenter's subject weak: lacking a logical sequence of events, or even an organized plot...His premise is that a ballet is essentially of the theater and, being so, should have all the attributes of the successful theatrical drama, plus fine music and superlative dancing, in which case it would exceed in entertainment value any other form of theater art.[p.290]

Carpenter's fragmentary, incomplete thread of story led to the application of strange remedies in a later (1933) Hollywood Bowl production of the ballet. No one approves of dancers ruthlessly changing scores to suit their own ideas, nor dancing a totally different ballet and calling it *Skyscrapers*. But perhaps there is a little to be said for them, in view of the circumstances. It appears that one of the reasons for changes was that some imaginary authorities had obligingly opined that life had greatly changed since the ballet was composed. Whereas in 1926 people ate hot dogs for diversion, in 1933 a hot dog constituted a full meal. For that, and similar reasons, the ballet was changed. Robots worked on the Skyscraper and waited on table in the cabaret, while a bloated plutocrat known as The Boss had a dream in which angels sang, a seductive lady charmed him and demons pursued him. Into the mêlée was thrown a prizefight. The new scenarists openly admitted that their "reasons" permitted them to retain the title of the ballet and eliminate the subtitles. Lo, the poor composer! Has he no jurisdiction over his brain children?[p.290-91]

[*Skyscrapers*] placed Carpenter in the front rank of American composers, for many believed that his greatest strength lay in composing serious jazz (of this sort) with a view toward dynamic and forceful characterization. It brought him to the attention of musicians as an orchestrator, a producer of rich effects and varied tone colors.[p.291]

In the printed score, Carpenter gives yet another reason for the lack of plot:...American life reduces itself essentially to violent alternations of work and play, each with its own peculiar and distinctive rhythmic character. The action of the ballet is merely a series of moving decorations reflecting some of the obvious external features of life.[p.291-92]

There follows a blow-by-blow description of the meter, music, and action. Robert Edmond Jones describes his role:

Carpenter would play the music, giving me an idea of the changing orchestration...Countless patterns were made during six months of grueling, unremitting labor. From those we selected the final succession of designs, one growing from the other, parallel with the music.[p.293]

B259. Beaumont, Cyril W. *Complete Book of Ballets*. London: Putnam, 1956.
The Heinrich Kröller production of *Wolkenkratze*

(*Skyscrapers*) was performed at the Opernhaus in Munich, 1929, as a ballet in two acts.

Act I. The rising of the curtain reveals a skyscraper in course of construction. In the foreground a group of workmen are engaged in a series of mechanical movements; in the background the endless chain of an everyday crowd in the capital passes by in silhouette.

Presently the workers exit through an opening in the curtain surround, moving with a heavy dragging step. But almost immediately they return by another opening, stepping gaily, each with a girl on his arm. These simultaneous actions heighten the contrast.

Act II. Coney Island. Various amusements are in progress and groups of merry-makers appear and depart. Suddenly, lightning flashes and thunder rolls; all stop and remain motionless, while out of the darkness the groups of workers appear and perform their duties mechanically, as though the sudden thought of their work had flashed through the minds of the crowd.

Soon they disappear, the storm passes, and all is bright and joyous again. A very unusual mirror dance is executed in a rotatory movement. A dancer appears through a trap. First he dances alone, then he is joined by four girls. The dance ended, he exits by jumping over their bent backs. Some of the women begin to quarrel, their friends take sides, and a fight ensues. It ends with the police marching off the brawlers. Only a road-sweeper remains, a negro clad in white. His work finished, he lies down and sleeps.

The back-cloth rises and through gauze curtains his dream is revealed. Far down south where his own folk live, types long forgotten sing à chorus and perform their religious dances. These become more and more fanatical. The negro begins to stir in his sleep. He tosses from side to side, until, finally, he jumps up and joins in the mad dance. Suddenly the light fades and a procession of sandwichmen crosses the stage. As the scene lightens the action returns to Coney Island with merriment at its height.

The black surround re-appears and this time

the men and girls exit through one opening and the serious-faced workers enter by the other. A factory whistle screams shrilly, and the skyscraper is again seen, with men at work on the scaffolding. As another group moves to the front, the curtain slowly falls.[p.756-57]

B260. Buckle, Richard. *Diaghilev*. New York: Atheneum, 1979.
Carpenter "wanted Diaghilev to put on a ballet he had written. He came over from America, bringing his score, for two days only. In a letter to Boris on 19 July, Diaghilev described the 'unbelievable circumstances' in which he found himself." [p.436]

Kahn and Gest find him [Carpenter] a serious and important person...Happily, his ballet is not as bad as I expected...it is American de Falla, with appropriate folk-lore. Also, the famous "policemen's strike" no longer takes place on the Strand but in an American factory, with alarm whistles and workers and such. Carpenter asks whether the décor couldn't be assigned to a Russian <u>Bolshevik</u> painter because, in his ballet, he is "not far away from Bolshevism." I find this notion amusing.[p.437]

"Diaghilev never did put on Carpenter's ballet *The Policeman's Holiday*."[p.437]

B261. Chujoy, Anatole and Manchester, P.W. *The Dance Encyclopedia*. Rev. and enl. ed. New York: Simon and Schuster, 1967.
Gives Carpenter's birth and death dates, titles of his three ballets with the choreographers and dates of production.

B262. Cohen-Stratyner, Barbara Naomi. *Biographical Dictionary of Dance*. New York: Schirmer, 1982.
Entries for Adolf Bolm (who choreographed *Birthday of the Infanta* and *Krazy Kat*), Sammy Lee (*Skyscrapers*), Ruth Page (who danced the leading role in *Birthday of the Infanta*), and two others associated with a 1922 production of *Birthday of the Infanta*: Andreas Pavley, performer and director, and Serge Oukrainsky, ballet master.

B263. Gadan, Francis and Maillard, Robert, gen. eds. *Dictionary of Modern Ballet*. New York: Tudor, 1959.
Entry for Robert Edmond Jones, American artist, who worked on *Birthday of the Infanta* (1919) with Adolph Bolm and on *Skyscrapers* (1920)[sic] with John Alden Carpenter and Sammy Lee.

B264. Junk, Victor. *Handbuch des Tanzes*. Stuttgart: Ernst Klett, 1930.
Includes birth year. Lists three ballets with dates and places of performance. Each ballet has its own entry.

B265. Kochno, Boris. *Diaghilev and the Ballets Russe*. New York: Harper & Row, 1970.

Diaghilev only once considered having an American composer collaborate on a ballet. That was during his preliminary talks in Venice with Otto Kahn and Morris Gest about a possible tour of the Ballets Russes in the United States...Kahn stipulated that Diaghilev stage an American ballet, and Diaghilev agreed to present a work by J. Alden Carpenter in New York. [p.222]

B266. Kriegsman, Sali Ann. *Modern Dance in America—The Bennington Years*. Boston. G.K. Hall, 1981.
Carpenter's *That Soothin' Song* (1926) was performed by Ethel Luening, soprano, and Lionel Nowak, piano, at a concert of contemporary music on Aug. 10 and 17, 1941.

B267. Magriel, Paul David, comp. *A Bibliography of Dancing*. New York: H.W. Wilson, 1936.
Describes *Krazy Kat* and *Skyscrapers* and lists published scores and information about premieres. Incorrectly dates *Skyscrapers* Feb. 14, 1926.

JOURNALS

B268. "Adventures in a Perambulator." *Notes* 15 (Mar. 1958): 333.
List of record reviews for Mercury MG 50136.

B269. "American Encores from a Russian Tour." *The New Records* 31 (Sept. 1963): 13.

Review of Golden Crest CR 4065 record which includes Carpenter's *Impromptu*.

B270. "American Sampler." *The New Records* 44 (July 1976): 14-15.
Review of OLY-104. "With the help of a grant from the Washington State American Revolution Bicentennial Commission, this recording was consummated."

B271. Ardoin, John. "American Giant." *Musical America* 84 (May 1964): 53.
Review of CRI 180. Carpenter's *Piano Concertino* is "a blend of piano and singing strings."

B272. Austin, Fred. "Skyscrapers." *The Dance* 5 (Apr. 1926): 24-25, 58-59.
Review of premiere performance Feb. 19, 1926 at the Metropolitan Opera House. Includes six illustrations: two of the ballet and four of the composer, the choreographer, the scenarist, and the dancers.

> It tells no story, it has no pantomime. It is a picture, a moving, living picture, revealing to the ear, in music, and to the eye, in dancing, the emotions that sway, in the conception of composer and choreographer, the lives of teeming millions of men and women in the mood and environment of the present.

Narrates Carpenter's meeting with Diaghileff in Venice. Carpenter played *Skyscrapers* and it "swept the Russian entrepreneur off his feet." Carpenter then met with Nijinska, the wife [i.e. sister] of Nijinski. An explanation follows of how the Metropolitan Opera Company obtained the premiere.
Here is a detailed account of the action:

> In front of a drop suggesting iron work are two traffic lights, incessantly blinking their red eyes, symbolic of the rush of both work and play. The drop rises disclosing the partly completed tower of a skyscraper, surrounded with steel skeletons and scaffolding. In its lattice work, on the scaffolding and clinging to girders are the iron workers. Steam comes from a fissure where metal glows. The workers bend and sway, wield

hammer, toss rivets and catch them, throw ropes, lift and heave with the rhythmic movements of the skilled worker, to the rhythm of the music which depicts the clang of steel on steel, the whistle of the hoisting engine and the clash of metal—a symphony of industry.

The whistle blows. A drop descends, having at one side of the stage a time clock and entrances. The workers "punch out" on the clock and are met at the other entrance by their "steadies." The drop rises showing an amusement park with booths for side shows and part of a ferris wheel. The workers and their "steadies" romp in for play. Every step is a dance, a dance to jazz rhythm. The workers on the ground dance as hard as they worked. On one of the side show platforms a "couchee" dancer wriggles and the crowd dances over to her. They swerve in a rollicking mass, strutting and jazzing across to the booth on the other side. They are attracted to the rear and the music suddenly changes from jazz to classic tempo to allow two side show performers to do a toe dance. As suddenly the orchestra changes back to jazz and they are strutting.

There is a fight, the crowd in a melee and then they disappear, leaving the ground strewn with litter. "White Wings" (Roger Dodge of the Metropolitan Ballet Corps), a negro street cleaner, strolls in and spears waste paper for his trundled can. He lies down to rest and falls asleep. Depicting his dream, a band of negroes sing spirituals behind a gauze curtain, breaking suddenly into a Charleston. "White Wings," still in his sleep, joins them, thus awakening.

The workers and their "steadies" reappear. While they are jazzing their hardest darkness comes and the moon. The work of the morrow lies like an unseen shadow beneath their gaiety. To symbolize this shadow the movie "cut back" is employed. A group of workers, still in their steel blue work suits, gather in the centre of the stage, and, assuming the postures, go through the motions of toil. As suddenly as they had stopped their gambols they resume them with renewed ardor.

"The Strutter", (Albert Troy of the Metropolitan Ballet Corps), shoots up from beneath the stage in white trousers, tall silk hat and sleeveless jersey. He is joined by "Herself" (Rita de Leporte of the Metropolitan Ballet Corps). She symbolizes her kind and the extremes that meet and clash in them. She wears a ballet dress, draped by a flag, and toe slippers. The tempo changes and she dances on her toes, in ballet technique. Another change and she struts. With "The Strutter" she does a Charleston, a moment later a fouetté pirouette.

Darkness falls and the drop showing the time clock descends. A whistle blows. The "steadies" come with their men to the entrance and leave them with much lingering of arms round jumpered necks. The workers punch the time clock. The drop rises and the clang of steel is heard again, the hissing of rivets and the rat-tat-tat of the steam hammer is in the music to whose rhythm the workers bend and dip, heave and tug. They work as hard as they played, for "steadies" and the night of play are just beyond the five o'clock whistle.

B273. Bauer, Marion. "Impressionists in America." *Modern Music* 4 (Jan.-Feb. 1927): 17-18.
    Details the Impressionistic characteristics in Carpenter's music. "His unusual gift for translating each word of a poem into its exact musical counterpart is pure impressionism."

B274. Bellamann, Henry. "Charles Ives: The Man and His Music." *Musical Quarterly* 19 (Jan. 1933): 47.
    Compares Carpenter to Ives; both men were businessmen and composers.

B275. Berger, Arthur. "Spotlight on the Moderns." *Saturday Review* 35 (31 May 1952): 43.
    Review of CHS 1140, *Adventures in a Perambulator*. Mentions the "French orchestration" and an "American ingredient...[which] has found its niveau in the scores for the smart, fluffy films."

B276. Borowski, Felix. "John Alden Carpenter." *Musical Quarterly* 16 (Oct. 1930): 449-68.
    Discusses the nineteenth century ideas distinguishing the amateur and the professional. Gives the history of the George B. Carpenter & Sons business,

and of Carpenter's education and teachers. *Gitanjali* reached a larger public than Carpenter had reached before.

> In this form [with orchestra] the lyrics were somewhat less convincing than they had been in the form in which originally they had been conceived—a circumstance due, it is probable, to the fact that the composer at that time was less familiar with the orchestra than he became later.

Gives dates of premieres.
About *Skyscrapers*:

> [Diaghileff] asked the composer to send to him in Paris the score of that work [*Krazy Kat*] and some photographs of the action. Having assimilated that material, he proposed that Carpenter should write for him a ballet which should embody the bustle and racket of American life...Diaghileff suggested that Carpenter should write the music of his ballet as an expression...of contemporary American life, without regard to details of story or action.
>
> The composition was finished in 1924 and Carpenter went into further conferences with the Russian producer, who not only evinced great interest in the work, but made numerous suggestions which were acted upon by the composer. The première was arranged to take place in 1925, at Monte Carlo, but negotiations fell through, and...the sagacious Mr. Gatti Casazza...made a bid for it.

Skyscrapers was performed Feb. 19, 1926 at the Metropolitan Opera House, and Feb. 10, 1928 at the National Theatre in Munich.

Carpenter had a "fondness—in the earlier songs at least—of making use of the lowest range of the piano in writing the accompaniments."

The second movement of the *Violin Sonata* "is spoilt by the middle section, whose style suddenly plunges into the sort of tuneful obviousness that tickled the ears of music-lovers in mid-Victorian days." There is "sheer beauty and imaginativeness" in the third movement.

The Spanish strain [of the *Piano Concertino*]...peeps out in the opening movement, with not a little of Carpenter's characteristic whimsicality as well. There is real and nostalgic beauty in the slow movement, and while the 5-8 section which follows it does not quite convince one that this particular quintuple setting of the music was the only one that could express its creator's inspiration, it is undeniably clever.

The composer's smaller piano pieces are worthy of respect as musique de salon contributions that have more than mere elegance to recommend them. The *Polonaise Américaine* has...gusto and a certain breezy spiritedness which make it attractive. The *Impromptu*...is rather less appealing ...*Little Indian* and *Little Dancer*, (1916) are short, pleasant and not difficult...*Tango Américain*...is full of interesting rhythm, even if its melody is less immediately striking than that of the *Polonaise* ...The first of these [*Diversions*] is really imaginative and charming. There is quaintness in the *chinoiserie* of the second and piquancy in the character—again Spanish—of the third and fourth.

The symphonic works have "brilliancy as colorists." Carpenter established "a mood with often light and simple touches."
    Adventures in a Perambulator "has humor, fantasy and that romantic whimsicality that figures in so much of the composer's work...The *Miserere* from *Il Trovatore* is ground out ludicrously by a xylophone, a celesta and a piano" in *The Hurdy-Gurdy*.
    The only connection *Sermons in Stones* has to Shakespeare's *As You Like It* is optimism. It is a "remarkably fine work, but scarcely of the type whose beauty is apparent at one hearing." It remains unpublished.
    "Taken as a whole, *A Pilgrim Vision* is not one of the works of which their creator has most reason to be proud."

[*Birthday of the Infanta*] abounds in vivid touches...Skillful handling of the orchestra in the ballet, [and] the fine manipulation of color were demonstrated with unerring skill. Only in the closing scene—the death of Pedro—did one feel that Carpenter had somehow missed the mark at which he aimed. High emotions and tragedy are planes of expression on which his gifts rest somewhat uneasily.

In *Krazy Kat* Carpenter "manipulate[s] the bizarre tints on the orchestral palette." He displays a "clever handling of equally bizarre harmonies...transforming ordinary dance-rhythms into novel and exciting lilts of tune."
Carpenter uses Afro-American music in the Coney Island scene of *Skyscrapers*. Harmonic complexity is observed. "He always has definite subject-matter upon which to hang his chord-progressions." Although one finds "maturity of his orchestral scoring in the work, there is no groping for 'effects'."

[The *String Quartet* is] in the modern rather than in the classic vein. The opening of the piece, with its syncopated complexity of rhythm, is more curious than beautiful, but, having had his fling with cross-accents, the composer carries his four instruments into a region of truly alluring charm.

Concludes with a work list giving dates composed and published.

B277. Brandt, Leonard J. "Songs by Carpenter, Griffes, and MacDowell." *Fanfare* 1 (May-June 1978): 114-15.
Review of Orion ORS 77272. *Gitanjali* "shows the influence of the French impressionists, an influence that unfortunately led toward songs, however competent and well-written, more inflated than inspired."

B278. "Carmel." *Opera and Concert* (Dec. 1949): 38.
"In New York, on November 20...Stokowski and the New York Philharmonic Symphony broadcast John Alden Carpenter's *Carmel Concerto*...At times, even, it was strongly suggestive of both Indian and Chinese music."
Adventures in a Perambulator "caused considerable comment last season when it was played by the Portland Symphony."

B279. "Carmel Concerto." *Pan Pipes* 43 (Dec. 1950): 114.
Carmel Concerto was broadcast on the radio in late

1949 with the New York Philharmonic Orchestra,
Leopold Stokowski conducting.

B280. Carpenter, John Alden. "Music as Recreation." *Recreation*
40 (Oct. 1946): 352-53, 392-93.
"Music is as important as recreation as it is to
recreation." Gives the history of the formation and
success of Chicago's Choral and Instrumental Music
Association.

B281. "Carpenter among Notables Lost by Music." *Musical
Courier* 143 (15 May 1951): 7.
Lists all of Carpenter's teachers except Seeboeck.
Gives his works and some honors: "He held Master's
degrees from Harvard and Wisconsin Universities."
Includes names of survivors.

B282. "Carpenter Concerto Played in Chicago." *Musical America*
57 (25 Nov. 1937): 26.
The *Violin Concerto* was first performed Nov. 18-19.
Carpenter described it as "moderately modern" in
one movement. It is "timid about asserting itself. The
thematic material is not as original as it has been
customary to expect from Mr. Carpenter."

B283. "Carpenter, John Alden." *Current Biography* (1951): 99.
Obituary. "Composer noted for the American
character of his work and for using the jazz idiom in
orchestral suites and ballets." Cites the *New York
Times* obituary.

B284. "Carpenter Returns from Sweden." *Musical America* 57 (10
Oct. 1937): 32.
John Alden Carpenter returned "on the Manhattan [ship] after a summer in Sweden." Announces
performance of the *Violin Concerto*.

B285. "Carpenter Violin Concerto Played by Balokovic." *Musical
America* 59 (25 Mar. 1939): 10.
"Breezy rather than profound...its one-movement
form and its lightweight material considered, the
concerto is too long to rivet attention."

B286. Casey, Robert P. "Some Facts about John Alden Carpenter,
'97." *Harvard Musical Review* 4 (Jan. 1916): 3-5.
Mentions his mother's musical influence, Harvard where Carpenter conducted the Glee Club, and

Ziehn whom Carpenter met in 1908 through Frederick Stock. As a composer Carpenter has originality, sincerity, fertility, and undisputed mastery of technique. Describes the song, *Dansons la Gigue!* as a "merry rollicking bergerette." Finds the *Piano Concertino* "rather free in form" using American rhythms. Cites performances for *Gitanjali* and the *Violin Sonata*. Finds Carpenter's chief charm to be his "frank individuality and Americanism." He is the "logical successor of MacDowell."

B287. Cincinnatus. "Cincinnati Orchestra Plays Carpenter Score." *Musical Courier* 108 (23 Nov. 1916): [n.p.]
Review of the first Cincinnati performance of *Adventures in a Perambulator*. "All the harmonic and contrapuntal originality with which Ziehn and, consequently his élèves overflow, is to be marked in this work. The interest never flags and new effects ever bring fascinating surprises."

B288. Coggi, Anthony D. "Conchita Supervia, vol.2." *Fanfare* 5 (Nov.-Dec. 1982): 264-66.
Rubini GV 583 recording includes *When I Bring to You Colored Toys* from *Gitanjali* with Conchita Supervia and unidentified orchestras, conductors, and pianists. Review about the singer, not the songs.

B289. Cohn, Arthur. "Americans at Rochester." *Modern Music* 17 (May-June 1940): 255-56.
Tenth annual Festival of American Music at Eastman School of Music included *Skyscrapers* "with all its bombastic trivialities and 'super-corny' orchestration."

B290. _____. "Concertino." *American Record Guide* 30 (May 1964): 765.
Review of CRI 180:

[Carpenter's *Piano Concertino*] is enjoyable fare concocted of many eclectic ingredients. These show the well-bred writing of a composer who at one time was forward-looking, but who then fell rather behind the times in which he worked. Eclectic though it is, there is little academic dust on the score.

B291. _____. "Skyscrapers." *American Record Guide* 31 (May 1965): 838.
    Review of Desto D-407, stereo DST-6407.

> Carpenter's piece [*Skyscrapers*] is a ballet score "in six scenes" written for a proposed tour by the famed Diaghilev ballet. The tour fell by the wayside and Diaghilev forgot about the work—it was first produced by the Metropolitan Opera Ballet. Since then it has fallen into oblivion. Properly? Yes, because listening now to Carpenter's feeble jazz-infected score we realize how interest in a particular idiom (or fondness for it) does not mean absorbed knowledge...It is terribly square, obvious, and sometimes rather embarrassing. *Skyscrapers* makes some noise, but even in this case (representing the symbol of restlessness) it is merely diluted <u>Les Six</u> machine music. The ragtime is ragged in its fast movements, and sourly square in its slower moments.

B292. _____. "America's Musical Bounty: A Compendious New Survey from Grove." *Symphony* 37 (Dec. 1986): 41-43.
    Review of the *New Grove Dictionary of American Music*. Gives examples of coverage (space ratios): "Compared to Carter, John Alden Carpenter is given a mere two and one-half columns. It is sufficient in terms of the relative importance of these composers. Further, within the succinctness of the Carpenter article, complete information is presented."

B293. Conly, John M. "Record Reviews." *Atlantic Monthly* 200 (July 1957): 94.
    Review of Mercury MG-50136 (*Adventures in a Perambulator*). "Charming old friends in new hi-fi guise. Carpenter's canine ballet and Philips' midnight ride with Paul Revere may not sound daringly modern any more, but they still can enchant."

B294. Cook, J. Douglas. "The Composer Tells How." *Saturday Review* 37 (26 June 1954): 41-42.
    Quotes Carpenter: "I'm a complete believer."

> Ideas or inspiration come from God, or from a Divine Origin. All good comes from this source. In my own case, 75 per cent of my compositions

have been based upon literary compositions.

[The two requisites necessary to produce music:] (1) Cut yourself off from all tradition. Get loose. I'm from New England and I know what a Puritanical influence can do. (2) A regular work schedule.

I'd like to make a prediction. The next big move to come in music will come from this country or from Russia; both are the least shackled by tradition.

B295. Copp, Laura Remick. "Why Modern Music is Modern— and What, Please, is 'Atonal' Music? An Interview with Nicholas Slonimsky." *Etude* 49 (June 1931): 395.
    Discussion of harmony. Includes port. of Carpenter and others.

B296. Cowell, Henry. "Summer Festivals in the U.S.A." *Modern Music* 19 (Nov.-Dec. 1941): 42-44.
    That Soothin' Song was performed at the Bennington Festival. The song is a "commonplace attempt to incorporate Negro feeling into a white man's song and its Negro folk-like tune dwindles off into a curious, French impressionistic, vague close."

B297. Curtis, William D. "Guide to Records." *American Record Guide* 41 (Nov. 1977): 38-39.
    Review of Mercury Golden Imports SRI 75095. Individually banded reissue from old Mercury Olympian series. Compares this to ERA 1009 which "was cut at a higher volume level with a greater degree of background hiss." *Adventures in a Perambulator* is "lightweight in character, but there is certainly nothing trivial about any of it." There is an "absence of pretension."

B298. D., J. "Orchestral." *Fanfare* 11 (Jan.-Feb. 1988): 274.
    Entry for CD version of NW 321-2. Refers to the record review by P.S. [B425].

B299. D., O. "Muck Again Plays Carpenter's Suite." *Musical Courier* 108 (1 Jan. 1916): [n.p.]
    Review of the Dec. 27th performance of *Adventures in a Perambulator*. "It is not music of surpassing originality, but it has been written with taste and wit, and is free of affectation and bombast. Its composer writes modestly but exceedingly well, so far as

instrumentation and the manipulation of themes is heard."

B300. Daehn, Larry. "Australia's Grainger Museum." *The Instrumentalist* 42 (Sept. 1987): 33-40.
"Grainger preferred to collect music by lesser-known writers; his collection includes works by John Alden Carpenter [and others.]"

B301. "Dancers from Four Corners of the Globe." *Vanity Fair* 14 (May 1920): 47.
Includes illus. of Ruth Page as the Infanta.

B302. Daniel, Oliver. "Americans from Vienna." *Saturday Review* 48 (26 June 1965): 51-53.
Review of Desto D-407, stereo DST-6407. "Carpenter's ballet *Skyscrapers*, which goes back to 1926, has some of the self-conscious overjoy of the roaring Twenties. Roar it does not, but it dances along merrily with snatches of old tunes remembered and bits of jazz discreetly interwoven."

B303. _____. "Take Me to Your Lieder." *Saturday Review* 48 (30 Oct. 1965): 84.
Review of Desto 411-12. *Looking Glass River* is a "song of such tender lyric loveliness."

B304. "The Descent of Jazz upon Opera." *Literary Digest* 88 (13 Mar. 1926): 24-25, 27.
Skyscrapers "carried the syncopated form [jazz] into the heart of America's most conservative music world and seems to have emerged with a meed of critical approval."
"It is not parodistic, it is not cruel, this music of his; it is closer to tragic irony, to a richly compassionate understanding, than we had fancied it would be."
Quotes Lawrence Gilman, *Herald Tribune,* and Olga Samaroff, *New York Evening Post.* Includes illustrations of "Work," "Coney Island," and "Dancers Exploiting the Rhythms of Modern American Life."

B305. "Design by Robert Edmond Jones for the *Birthday of the Infanta*." *Theatre Arts Magazine* 4 (1920): 133-35, 147-50, 189-90.
Contains eight illustrations of scenes, designs, and costume sketches for the Chicago Opera Association's production of *Birthday of the Infanta.*

B306. Deutsch, Babette. "America in the Arts." *Musical Quarterly* 7 (July 1921): 305.

> As examples of distinctively American music, he [Leo Sowerby] brings forward the first movement of John Alden Carpenter's *Symphony*, parts of his Concertino, and the last movement of DeLamarter's *Sonata* for the violin. These things Sowerby describes as our own by virtue of their big sweep, their vigor, their lack of sentimentality, affectation and diffuseness...The composers' idiom, as distinguished from the poets', is more a purely personal than a national one.

B307. Devries, René. "America Comes of Age as a World Power in Music." *Musical Courier* 151 (1 Feb. 1955): 37.
Carpenter was "America's first native impressionist." Includes port.

B308. D[evries], R[ené]. "A Chat with John Alden Carpenter." *Musical Courier* 110 (4 July 1918): 14.
Gives Carpenter's thoughts on the war, music, and life in general. "Everyone should be interested in two things, as only when one is interested in more than a single thing can he hope to progress in life in general." The war brought out a national feeling which will "stimulate the development of our national music."

B309. Devries, René. "Chicago Opera Association Revives *Don Pasquale* Starring Galli-Curci." *Musical Courier* 112 (8 Jan. 1920): 14.
Describes the "gorgeous spectacle" of the *Birthday of the Infanta* which was "presented at the Auditorium in a most sumptuous manner."

> Although the score is sincere, beautiful—ofttimes brilliant—colorful, striking the keynote of individuality...there is a feeling of restraint in the music which seems to miss the excitement of childish moments.
>
> It is a pantomime for children, since the occasion is the birthday of the Royal Infanta of Spain, for whom a surprise party has been arranged. The time is that of Velasquez, when huge hoopskirt costumes and hairdress to match were worn. There are two scenes, the first outside

the palace and the second the entrance hall of the palace. Altogether it makes an array of rich, exquisite color, charming to the eye.

Praises the dancers and describes all the many characters: "banderilleros, picadors, matadors, bull-fighters and a Major Domo taking part, besides gardeners, playmate girls and boys, foreign ambassadors, ministers, cook, palace servants, grooms, guards, etc."

B310. "Died." *Time* 57 (7 May 1951): 86.
Obituary. Notes his use of jazz, lists some of his works, and quotes Carpenter on peaceful music.

B311. Ditsky, John. "Skyscrapers and Other Music of the American East Coast School." *Fanfare* 11 (Jan-Feb. 1988): 276-77.
Review of EMI Angel CDC-7 49263-2. The "jazzy 1926 ballet score *Skyscrapers*" achieved "something identifiably national." The Desto recording of *Skyscrapers* is "ancient, and now best forgotten."

B312. Dommett, Kenneth. "Déjà vu: American Anthology." *Hi-Fi News & Record Review* (Aug. 1982): 74.
Review of SRI 75095 which "shares in varying degrees American extraversion and French sophistication. Carpenter's attractive suite [*Adventures in a Perambulator*] has always been popular and has tended to eclipse his more consciously American expressions such as *Skyscrapers* and *Sea Drift*."

B313. Downes, Olin. "J.A. Carpenter, American Craftsman." *Musical Quarterly* 16 (Oct. 1930): 443-48.
Carpenter is "probably the most sensitive, sincere and accomplished American-born composer that we have today among us...his heart is bigger than his head, which is essential for a composer."

Carpenter's work...is to him the most salient and brilliant that is being done to-day in American music. It appears to gain steadily in substance and decisiveness because...he is getting constantly nearer to life as well as constantly more mature and unhesitating in the moulding of his musical material.

> *Birthday of the Infanta* has "something of the professedly unemotional brilliancy and laconicism...of the earlier Stravinsky." *Skyscrapers* "has some of that aroma of life and dream which no real music is without." Carpenter "has created, and he has contributed indispensably to the erection of the great future edifice of a national music." Includes port.

B314. Dunton, James G. "The Ballet Record." *The Dance* 12 (Oct. 1929): 48.

> Describes *Krazy Kat* "set to syncopated music by John Alden Carpenter" and tells the plot.

B315. Engel, Carl. "Views and Reviews." *Musical Quarterly* 8 (Aug. 1922): 612.

> "What distinguished the first songs of Mr. John Alden Carpenter was the admirable handling of the prosody."

B316. _____. "Views and Reviews." *Musical Quarterly* 9 (Jan. 1923): 148-49.

> Mr. Carpenter has overlaid it [the plot of *Krazy Kat*] with appropriate music that is always clean cut and crisp, though not conspicuous for that indefinable "cleverness" which was needed to make the most of that grand and final Fox-trot. They do order this matter better in Broadway. And even Debussy...delved deeper into the secrets of animal nature, than did Mr. Carpenter in the case of his Indomitable Kat, whose cousinage with the Sphinx he entirely suppresses in the pedigree. Nevertheless, a charming score...to be remembered...for the history of incipient "American" music.

> Suggests that Fred Stone replace Adolf Bolm dancing the role of Krazy Kat.

B317. _____. "Views and Reviews." *Musical Quarterly* 19 (July 1933): 356-57.

> [In *Skyscrapers* Carpenter] can do no better than to pass the creations of his imagination (rhythmic images of American life, as they might be called) through the sieve of a Russian and French technique of the ballet; with the result that his

idea does not get an adequate interpretation but is covered by a mixture of two different styles.

B318. F., J. "American Art Songs." *The Gramophone* 44 (July 1966): 83.
  Review of DWR 6417-8. Does not mention Carpenter's song *When I Bring to You Coloured Toys* which is included in the album.

B319. Field, Hamilton Easter. "Adolph Bolm and *The Birthday of the Infanta*." *Arts and Decoration* 12 (Feb. 1920): 250-51.
  Describes the action of *Birthday of the Infanta* and "Grotesque Pedro" the "misshapen young man, who, having been brought up far from men in the forest, has no idea of his ugliness or deformity." When Pedro sees an image before him in the hall of mirrors he makes a face at it, walks towards it, strikes at it and discovers that the grotesque figure is himself. "Little by little the truth comes over him. He dances before the mirror, a dance in which he expresses his pent-up emotion and drops dying."
  When the Infanta comes in with her playmates "they wonder. The Infanta goes up to Pedro lying on the floor; she finds her handkerchief clasped in his hands; she divines the truth and tiptoes off the stage."
  Adolph Bolm, who danced the role of Pedro, found in Pedro "such innate dignity and such purity of soul that there is in the final scene a pathos for which I can find no parallel in the entire repertoire of the ballet."

B320. "The Final Curtain." *Billboard* 63 (5 May 1951): 48.
  Obituary. Carpenter "began composing about 1900, and his compositions caught on in 1912. An American strain in all his works was a distinguishing mark, and he...transposed the jazz idiom for concert recital."

B321. Fine, Irving. "Reviews of Records." *Musical Quarterly* 38 (July 1952): 482-83.
  Review of Concert Hall CHS 1140.

  [Carpenter] was not an innovator by temperament; yet he seems to have been impelled to keep abreast of the latest musical trends. The resultant paradox—his own music was born out of date. Carpenter was formed as a young composer in the German Romantic tradition; his earlier works are strongly influenced by Strauss and Elgar. In spite of his subsequent identification with Impressionism and with the jazzy wrong-note school of the twenties, in spite of his sincere interest in some of the newer musical trends in the music of our time, in his own music he never got beyond the externals, the gadgets that later became the stock in trade of the Hollywood arranger.

Adventures in a Perambulator "leans heavily on Strauss for its style and subject matter...It is neither light nor funny. Nor is it even cute. But it is skillfully made orchestral music, and pleasant, if somewhat soporific, listening."

B322. ["Finston's 'Skyscrapers'."] *American Dancer* 6 (Sept. 1933): 19.
     The July 30, 1933 Hollywood Bowl performance of *Skyscrapers* was devised by Harold Hecht and conducted by Nathaniel Finston.

B323. Flanagan, William. "The Art Song in America." *Hi Fi/Stereo Review* 18 (Jan. 1967): 99-100.
     Review of DWR 6417-18 which contains *When I Bring to You Coloured Toys* but the review makes no reference to this song. "The bulk of the material [in this album] represents the Age of Innocence of the American art song."

B324. _____. "Classical." *Hi Fi/Stereo Review* 13 (July 1964): 71, 73.
     Review of CRI 180.

John Alden Carpenter's *Concertino* which fills out the second side of the disc, seems to me to be of even less interest than is indicated by the modest claims made for it in the jacket notes. I would be the last man in the world to hold its lightness or even its innocence against it, but its nineteen-fifteenish view of Impressionism is so strongly naïve that it seems almost to be mocking.

B325. _____. "Skyscrapers." *Hi Fi/Stereo Review* 14 (June 1965) 66-68.
Review of Desto DST 6407. The Carpenter and Converse pieces "show their respective ages pretty badly. *Skyscrapers*...stands at a high enough level of craftsmanship, but the interpolated jazz and the innocent programmatic indulgences that parallel the ballet's action all seem a little beyond being taken seriously today."

B326. Foote, Arthur. "A Bostonian Remembers." *Musical Quarterly* 23 (Jan. 1937): 41.
Mentions *Adventures in a Perambulator*.

B327. Frankenstein, Alfred. "Records in Review." *Hi Fi* 4 (Apr. 1954): 44-45.
Review of ARS 37.

Skyscrapers was for many years the only sizable piece of American music one could get on records. It is a machine-age ballet produced at the Metropolitan in the 1920's. It's a coarse and careless affair, but there is still some vitality and amusement in it, and it is of considerable interest as an historic landmark.

B328. _____. "Records in Review." *High Fidelity* 7 (Aug. 1957): 52.
Review of Mercury MG 50136. *Adventures in a Perambulator* "has the most delightful program ever written. The composer's notes on the music are worthy of E.B. White, but the music itself is on the insubstantial side."

B329. _____. "Records in Review." *High Fidelity* 14 (June 1964): 75.
Review of CRI 180.

John Alden Carpenter's *Concertino* is no concertino at all but a full-blown concerto lasting twenty-five minutes. Like most of Carpenter's music, it begins well, in a witty dialogue of piano and orchestra which sounds like a bit of jazz by MacDowell, but before long the work bogs down in Carpenter's kind of banality.

B330. _____. "Records in Review." *High Fidelity* 16 (June 1966): 91.

Review of DWR 6417B. "There is simply no excuse, in an anthology published by a great university, for such obvious and much recorded trash as ...and John Alden Carpenter's *When I Bring You Colored Toys*."

B331. Freed, Richard. "The Bicentennial Corner: A Sampler of American Music." *Stereo Review* 36 (June 1976): 101.

Review of OLY-104 which "is based on a concert given at the University of Washington in 1973." Carpenter's *The Player Queen* and the Griffes songs "are especially worthwhile."

B332. Freeman, John W. "Collections of American Songs." *Opera News* 41 (June 1976): 52.

Review of DWR 6417, *The Art Song in America*, and NW 247, *When I Have Sung My Songs*. DWR 6417 "is a fair look at writing from Edward MacDowell's day up through Barber and Rorem." NW 247 "consists of twenty songs by Americans from MacDowell to Ives." Does not mention the Carpenter songs.

B333. French, Florence. "Here and There." *The Musical Leader* 32 (26 Oct. 1916): 419.

Upon hearing violinist Albert Spalding and Mr. Benoist at the piano perform Carpenter's *Violin Sonata* John McCormack proclaimed it "immense in its bigness of thought and working out."

B334. Gann, Kyle. "CARPENTER: Collected Piano Works." *Fanfare* 9 (July-Aug. 1986): 115-16.

Review of NW 328-29. Carpenter is "still considerably underrated today." This recording provides a "fuller picture" of him but contains no major works.

The early pieces, written in the 1890s, tend to be stodgy and unimaginative. The 1898 *Nocturne*...imitate[s] Chopin (badly), and the earlier *Minuet* is far too muddy and thickly written to qualify for its title. The sonata...contains a lot of pretty writing marked by an earnest, mildly sensuous, fin-de-siècle sensibility. Its harmony, though, tends toward predictability...and the amount of repetition deals a fatal blow to its undeniable melodic charm...Given more fluidity of tone color, some of Carpenter's overbusy fingerwork could disappear beneath a more singing melody, and a greater sense of melodic sweep might render the repetitions less tedious.

Some of the latter are absolutely delightful. *Impromptu* (1913), with its unpredictable harmonies and a little melody that suddenly springs into jazz from time to time, is a little classic of American impressionism. Spanish influences...[in] *Diversions*, five spicy little vignettes...and the 1935 *Danza* (in its orchestrated form, one of Carpenter's better-known works) exhibits a rhythmic vivacity that is often very subtly understated. The *Polonaise Américaine* [has] harmonic brashness, while the tame jazz of the *Tango Américain* [sic] still retains a dash of the daring...*Little Indian*, [with] its pentatonic melody and droning bass... [is] one of the most charming and noncondescending examples...of the American Indian.

B335. _____. "CARPENTER: Collected Piano Works." *Fanfare* 11: (Jan.-Feb. 1988): 106.

Review of the CD version of NW 328-29. Still finds the "sonata's redundancy maddening" and Oldham's playing "just short of poetic." The reviewer prefers the piano sound on the "vinyl: its upper harmonics are a little muted on the CD."

B336. Garvelmann, Donald. "A Good Survey—But Flawed." *American Record Guide* 40 (May 1977): 11.

Review of Vox Box SVBX 5303. Carpenter's "*Impromptu* from 1913 is especially affecting, a deeply contemplative interpretation."

B337. Gilder, Rosamond. "The American Theatre, 1916-1941." *Theatre Arts Magazine* 25 (Feb. 1941): 158.

"1927—Met Opera House, recognizing Am. talent, follows the previous season's ballet by John Alden Carpenter, *Skyscrapers*, with *The King's Henchman* by Deems Taylor and Edna St. Vincent Millay."

B338. Gilman, Lawrence. "Drama and Music: Significant Happenings of the Month." *The North American Review* 202 (Dec. 1915): 912-14.

Adventures in a Perambulator was performed by the New York Symphony with Walter Damrosch last month. "Mr. Carpenter's symphonic perambulator [was] (delightfully limned for us, in the orchestral narration, by strings and celesta)." Includes Carpenter's program notes.

Gives an example of the orchestral effects: the Policeman "has stopped the music—that irresistible waltz, dazzingly [sic] adorned with glockenspiel, harp, celesta, xylophone, is silenced."

B339. _____. "Music of the Month: Monsieur Satie and Mr. Carpenter." *The North American Review* 215 (May 1922): 695-97.

[Carpenter] has a wholly un-American flexibility. Mr. Carpenter's responsive and versatile genius enables him to turn at will, for the subject-matter of his music, to the Spain of Velasquez, or the Comic Section of the daily paper, or the poetry of Tagore, or the hedonistic life of a perambulating baby in a city park, or his own untabulated reveries as a poet in tones; and not long ago he paid his respects to the memorable year 1620.

Carpenter "paints the picture, suggests the vision, on his orchestral canvas; he elucidates and enforces it, with admirable conciseness and felicity, in his argument." Quotes Carpenter. Analyzes the thematic structure of *A Pilgrim Vision*.

Carpenter "has sought merely to extract the emotional essence of that great adventure of 1620 and state it in terms of musical speech; and he has done this admirably—with gravity, pith, and tenderness; with a rich sense of the nobility and drama of his theme."

B340. Goldberg, Albert. "Novelties Are Featured by Stock." *Musical America* 52 (10 Nov. 1932): 6.

In *Patterns* the "melodic and rhythmic aspects are somewhat episodic." There are "Puccinian" melodies, and rhythms that flirt with waltz, habanera, and American jazz. "Though combined in no cumulative scheme of coherence, the skillful scoring...and the constant rhythmic life, hold interest throughout."

About the performance: "A more muscular artist [than Carpenter at the piano] might have given the piano a more rightfully prominent place in the ensemble."

B341. Goodfriend, James. "Going on Record: Second Comings."
Stereo Review 37 (Oct. 1976): 60.
Review of ERA 1009.

> Carpenter was once considered one of the big guns
> of American music (the other was MacDowell),
> but today he would be more correctly placed as a
> sort of American Roger Quilter (no disrespect
> intended). *Adventures in a Perambulator* is a piece of
> American impressionism, pleasant, mildly
> whimsical, eminently listenable—light music.

B342. Gunn, Glenn Dillard. "The Present Status of American
Music." *M.T.N.A. Proceedings* 13 (1918): 36-37.
Carpenter "first adventured into symphonic environment" with songs, e.g., *Gitanjali*. His orchestral
works "have found a place in the repertory of one
European orchestra, whence they will return to a
permanent place in our American symphonic repertory."

B343. Hager, Mina. "Speak for Yourself, John Alden Carpenter."
Music Journal 28 (Mar. 1970): 66-67.
Mina Hager first sang for Carpenter at The Great
Lakes Training Base. She recalls how he composed.
"He used to hum, however, while he was
composing—an octave below the melody line! I have
often wondered if that might not be the reason that
practically none of his songs go below B flat or higher
than G."
Although the melody in *The Green River* is not
Sprechstimme, it "sings almost as one would speak
it." In *Water Colors* "the vocal line follows almost
exactly the speech line."
Includes comments of some critics. From Berlin:
"John Alden Carpenter has learned his idiom in the
French school, but he has incorporated this influence
in a style of his own capable of eloquence, pathos,
folk humor and sprightly and pastoral calm."
John A. Carpenter had "an exceptional gift of
comprehension and of expressing his opinions with
clarity, honesty and humor." Includes port.

Review of Carol Brice song album, Columbia ML
2108. Nothing about Carpenter.

B345. Hanson, Howard. "A Forward Look in American
Composition." *M.T.N.A. Proceedings* 20 (1925): 121.
Survey of American orchestral literature perform-
ed 1919-20 to 1925-26. Carpenter's *Adventures in a
Perambulator* and his *Piano Concertino* are included.

B346. _____. "John Alden Carpenter." *Saturday Review* 34 (24
Feb. 1951): 50-51.
Adventures in a Perambulator "has been played by
virtually every major orchestra in the United States."
His "creative personality is so many-sided, complex,
and subtle."

> He was one of the first composers...to break
> successfully with the German tradition...to bring
> to American music a subtlety and delicacy of
> expression which had been up to that time
> generally lacking...He continued the excursion
> into the expression of humor in music...Finally,
> though primarily a melodist and colorist, he has
> remained an interested experimenter in rhythmic
> techniques.
>   My favorite of all Carpenter's scores,
> however, is his symphonic poem *Sea Drift* on the
> poems of Walt Whitman. Here Carpenter reveals
> not only his descriptive powers, of which we are
> well-aware, but an emotional depth of which we
> had not always been conscious...What sensitive
> listener who heard it will ever forget that
> translucent sound at the end where muted horns,
> low strings, and vibraphone combine the
> sonorities of four keys with such delicate beauty
> that one strains one's powers of hearing to
> prolong the sheer ecstasy of the sound.

Sea Drift is "more profound, more tragic, and more
mysterious" than Debussy's *La mer.*

B347. Harvey, Trevor. "Adventures in a Perambulator." *The
Gramophone* 35 (Oct. 1957): 177.
Review of Mercury MRL 2542.

It all seems emphatically to be children's music for grown-ups to listen to, not children. I quite enjoyed it but I felt that each piece was too long and ambitious for its slender idea, especially the final one, which takes a long time to come to an end.

B348. Howard, John Tasker. "American Composers. VI: John Alden Carpenter." *Modern Music* 9 (Nov.-Dec. 1931): 8-16.

Discusses his major works and American characteristics, his conservative and modernist tendencies (he is a romanticist in the *Violin Sonata*), his use of cacophony (in *Skyscrapers*) "merely to depict the din of rivets." Carpenter did not reach for lofty heights. Although there are Gallic tendencies in his songs, Carpenter "intensified the fundamental Americanism of exaggeration in symbolism." Includes port.

B349. Howe, Mark Anthony DeWolfe. "John Knowles Paine." *Musical Quarterly* 25 (July 1939): 266.

Carpenter recalls Paine:

I find that it is difficult to recapture anything of my contacts with "J.K." beyond rather vague impressions of a cheerful but reluctant teacher, full of pessimism as to his pupils, and filled with a fine defiance of the necessities which prevented him from getting on with his own creative work. I was fortunate to be under his guidance when he was in the throes of <u>delivering</u> the last pages of his opera, and there were magnificent moments watching those stubby fingers and marvelling at that "composer's voice" struggling with *Azara* and her companions from [high C (2 octaves above middle C)] to [low C (2 octaves below middle C)].

And these moments were sometimes followed by tea during which J.K. produced some of his favorite puns and pretended to be unaware of the sweet and peaceful presence of Mrs. J.K. whom we all, and he, adored.

And when I saw him for the last time in June of '97 he walked out with me to his gate, and as I turned to go, he threw at me over his shoulders as a parting admonition: "Better change your mind about going into <u>that business!</u>"

B350. "Illinois: John Alden Carpenter." *Violins and Violinists* 12 (Mar-Apr. 1951): 62.

> The Chicago Symphony Orchestra paid tribute to Carpenter on his seventy-fifth birthday. Rafael Kubelik conducted the *Birthday of the Infanta* on Feb. 27 and *Skyscrapers* on Feb. 27 and Mar. 1-2.

B351. Jacobi, Frederick. "American Music Conference: I, Milestones in the Development of Musical Composition in America." *M.T.N.A. Proceedings* 21 (1926): 219.

> Quotes Rupert Hughes: Carpenter "is gently supplying it [the Yankee wit] to us—in the light strokes of his amusing children's songs and in the broader lines of *Krazy Kat* and *Skyscrapers*."

B352. "A Jazz Ballet." *Literary Digest* 73 (15 Apr. 1922): 33.

> Includes a Deems Taylor quotation on *Krazy Kat*, a mention of Carpenter's business and three of his teachers: Paine, Elgar, and Ziehn, and a partial list of works. Carpenter's program notes "display an English style of limpid clarity, a keen sense of words, and a delicacy and charm of humor that makes them good reading anywhere."

B353. Jellinek, George. "Kirsten Flagstad: Recital." *Hi Fi/Stereo Review* 16 (Apr. 1966): 86.

> Review of RCA Victor LM 2825. "The Kramer and Carpenter selections, all three worth many rehearings, are also done with near-perfect artistry."

B354. "John Alden Carpenter." *Pan Pipes* 43 (Dec. 1950): 114.

> *Carmel Concerto* "has an oriental flavor and at times suggests both Chinese and Indian music."

B355. "John Alden Carpenter: A Musical Humanist." *Musical America* 71 (May 1951): 12.

> Obituary. "American music has lost one of its most lucid and humanistic spirits." Quotes Carpenter. Traces his development through *Gitanjali* which "reveals his sensitive imagination, keen color sense, and romantic aspirations." Discusses *Birthday of the Infanta*, *Krazy Kat*, *Skyscrapers*, and *Sea Drift*.

B356. "John Carpenter Dies." *Symphony* 5 (May 1951): 3.

> "Member of one of the [Chicago] city's pioneer families...His best known orchestral work was *Skyscrapers*."

B357. Keats, Sheila. "Reference Articles on American Composers: An Index." *Juilliard Review* 1 (Fall 1954): 24.
Contains an annotated bibliography of the Borowski and Downes articles in *Musical Quarterly* (Oct. 1930) and the Howard article in *Modern Music* (Nov.-Dec. 1931).

B358. Kolodin, Irving. "Recordings Reports: Classical LP's and Albums." *Saturday Review* 33 (24 June 1950): 54.
Review of Columbia LP 2108 which includes Carpenter's song *The Day Is No More.*

B359. _____. "Recordings Reports I: Orchestral LP's." *Saturday Review* 40 (27 July 1957): 38.
Review of MG 50136 with *Adventures in a Perambulator.* "Carpenter whimsy has to do with Gallic influences circa 1914."

B360. _____. "Recordings Reports I: Orchestral LP's." *Saturday Review* 47 (25 Apr. 1964): 60.
Review of CRI 180. The *Piano Concertino* "doubtless had an aura of freshness and charm in 1916."

B361. Kresh, Paul. "Classicals Discs and Tapes." *Stereo Review* 39 (Dec. 1977): 140.
Review of Mercury SRI 75095 which "features American symphonic music at its most winning and agreeable."

> [Carpenter] composed some of the most inventive scores ever produced in this country. It is a pity that his songs, his orchestral suite *Krazy Kat*, and his elaborate, high-voltage ballet score *Skyscrapers* (represented only by a thin, abridged performance on Desto) are not more readily available on records today.

B362. _____. "Classical Discs and Tapes." *Stereo Review* 41 (July 1978): 86.
Review of NW 228, "a slightly abridged performance" of *Krazy Kat.* Narrates story.

B363. Kyle, Marguerite Kelly. "AmerAllegro: Premières, Recent Performances, New Releases." *Pan Pipes* 44 (Jan. 1952): 23.
Lists the works performed for Carpenter's seventy-fifth birthday. "Works included in the ISCM

[International Society for Contemporary Music]
program were his *Sonata for Violin and Piano* and his
*Quintet for Flute, Oboe, Clarinet, Bassoon, and French
Horn.*" [sic]

B364. Lancaster, J.B. "Record Reviews." *American Record Guide*
23 (June 1957): 138.
Review of Mercury MG 50136. *Adventures in a
Perambulator* has "American charm and spontaneity."

B365. Laubenstein, Paul Fritz. "Jazz—Debit and Credit." *Musical
Quarterly* 15 (Oct. 1929): 621.

[Carpenter said:] "It would be impossible to give
jazz through the medium of a symphony
orchestra." Hence, to get something of the
sonorous jazz effect in his *Skyscrapers*, he added
saxophones and a banjo. Even so he regards this
composition as "jazz once removed" and filtered
through a symphony orchestra.

B366. Lawrence, Robert. "Kirsten Flagstad: Song Recital." *High
Fidelity* 16 (Feb. 1966): 103-04.
Review of RCA Victor LM 2825. "The American
songs are delivered with style and definite charm."

B367. Ledermann, Minna. "Skyscrapers: An Experiment in
Design." *Modern Music* 3 (Jan.-Feb. 1926): 21-26.
Interview with Robert Edmond Jones. *Skyscrapers*
began with only the music, no libretto, no plot, no
dance designs, not even a locale, only moods of work
and play. Discusses the musical structure, the scenery
background, and the form. Jones and Carpenter
worked for six months in a farmhouse in Vermont
planning the scenario. Samuel Lee worked on the
choreography. Includes an illus. of the transitions in
the exits and entrances.

B368. Leigh, E.S.V. "American Songs." *The New Records* 46 (June
1978) : 11.
Review of Orion ORS 77272. *Gitanjali* is "without
oriental allusions."

B369. Leonard, William. "Carpenter Birthday Observed in
Chicago Symphony Season." *Musical America* 71 (1 Apr.
1951): 21.

Skyscrapers "today sounds like a pallid imitation of 25-year-old jazz." *Birthday of the Infanta* proved more "colourful."

B370. Lowens, Irving. "American Music on One Hundred Records." *High Fidelity* 26 (Sept. 1976): 80-82.
    Describes the "giant undertaking" of the Recorded Anthology of American Music series and lists the records produced, including NW 247.

B371. _____. "Piano Music in America: vol. 2, 1900-45." *High Fidelity* 27 (Sept. 1977): 115.
    Review of Vox Box SVBX 5303. Mentions "the accomplished academicism" of John Alden Carpenter. "Among the rarities I found especially interesting were Carpenter's 1913 E flat minor *Impromptu*."

B372. _____. "Sonata for Violin." *High Fidelity* 27 (June 1977): 88.
    Review of Orion ORS 76243. The *Violin Sonata* is "one of the Chicago musician/businessman's earliest works in an extended form. It strongly reflects French influences (César Franck comes immediately to mind), as did most of his later music, but it lacks the virility that makes the Foote sonata memorable."

B373. Mason, Daniel Gregory. "Making American Music Accessible." *Arts and Decoration* 12 (Jan. 1920): 188, 222.
    States that Carpenter was president of the Society for the Publication of American Music (SPAM). Includes port.

B374. _____. "Music as Decoration: Mr. Carpenter Uses It Skilfully [sic] in his New Pantomime." *Arts and Decoration* 12 (Mar. 1920): 322, 362.
    American music "must be not only home-made but well-made." Carpenter is a "capable craftsman." *Birthday of the Infanta* has a Russian tinge. Includes illus. of "The Death of Pedro."
        [*Birthday of the Infanta*] is vivid, solid, vibrant, picturesque, not too preoccupied with harmonic confectionery, and unashamed of frank contagious rhythm...[Its limitation] is that it seldom gets below the surface, it rarely penetrates below the decorative of the deeper function of music, in which alone music is most itself, that of emotional interpretation and mood-creation.

B375. Maxwell, Leon R. "America's Contribution to Song
Literature." *M.T.N.A. Proceedings* 14 (1919): 156.

> Whatever the source of Carpenter's style, it
> has long since become extremely individual and it
> has always been very beautiful. If a love of refined
> detail, of closely united and very expressive
> melodic phrases, of color, of atmosphere, is
> French and only French, then of course
> Carpenter's work is French; but I think I hear a
> beautiful American work when I listen to a
> Carpenter song which has these qualities.
>   But the humorous songs, the negro and
> Dorsetshire dialect songs, the songs inspired by
> the war, some of the Chinese *Watercolors* and
> certain of the *Gitanjali* songs are purely American
> because they are Carpenter's most individual
> expression.

B376. Mell, Albert. "A Bicentennial Celebration: Music for and
by Americans." *Journal of the Violin Society of America* 2
(Summer 1976): 11-13.
Recital of Carpenter's *Violin Sonata* at Music
Mountain, Inc., Falls Village, CT, on Sept. 18, 1976.

> This year marks the one hundredth anniversary
> of John Alden Carpenter's birth (1876-1976).
> Carpenter was one of the first American
> composers to celebrate the American experience
> in such works as *Skyscrapers, Adventures in a
> Perambulator,* and the ballet *Krazy Kat,* based on the
> comic strip of the same name. His violin sonata,
> written in 1912, is a large scale work in four
> movements which shows various influences
> including French impressionism and early 20th
> century jazz.

B377. Milano. "The Journal Reviews." *Music Journal* 23 (Mar.
1965): 26.
Review of CRI 180. Carpenter's *Piano Concertino* is
"a relaxed and atmospheric work; form is clear and
simple and the texture is lightly colorful."

B378. Miller, Philip L. "American Vocal Music of Today and
Yesterday." *American Record Guide* 31 (May 1965): 808-
09, 812.
Review of Desto D-411-12. "John Alden Carpenter

looked mostly to France for his models, but his
smoothly flowing *Looking Glass River*...seems very
thoroughly American...Carpenter was one of the first
serious composers to interest himself in jazz.
Somehow this miniature [*Jazz Boys*] has special
poignancy today."

B379. _____. "An Anthology of American Art Song." *American
Record Guide* 32 (May 1966): 784-85.
    Review of Duke University album. *When I Bring to
You Color'd Toys* is an American classic which recalls
"the one-time popularity of Tagore's poetry."

B380. _____. "Audio-Visual Materials." *Library Journal* 75 (1 Oct.
1950): 1682.
    Review of Columbia ML 2108 which includes *The
Day Is No More*. Recommends those songs which are
sung in English.

B381. _____. "Guide to Records." *American Record Guide* 42
(Nov. 1978): 48-49.
    Review of Orion ORS 77272. Quotes Upton who
admired *On the Seashore of Endless Worlds* as
"transmitting the fragility and transparent beauty of
the child-spirit into tones."

B382. _____. "Recorded Music." *Library Journal* 77 (Aug. 1952):
1297.
    Review of CHS 1140. "Carpenter's fantasy (1915)
[*Adventures in a Perambulator*] has long been a favorite
because of the composer's imagination and his
mastery of the Straussian orchestra."

B383. _____. "Recorded Music." *Library Journal* 90 (1 June 1965):
2538.
    Review of Desto DST 6411-12 which includes
Looking Glass River. This is "the most important
collection of American songs yet issued."

B384. _____. "Two Sopranos—Both Wagnerians, Both
Scandinavians." *American Record Guide* 32 (Feb. 1966):
516-17.
    Review of RCA Victor LM 2825. "Mr. McArthur
tells us that the rest of the songs included were all
favorites with the singer [Kirsten Flagstad]."

B385. _____. "Voice." *American Record Guide* 16 (June 1950): 337.
Review of Columbia 2108. "The Carpenter [song *The Day Is No More*], too, is effective."

B386. Mitchell, William J. "Reviews of Books." *Musical Quarterly* 37 (July 1951): 439, 441.
Book review of *Bernard Ziehn, Der Deutsch-Amerikanische Musik-Theoretiker*, by Hans Joachim Moser. Carpenter contributed some canons to Ziehn's *Canonic Studies*. Includes a letter from Carpenter to Julius Gold dated 10 January 1924.

B387. Morris, Harold. "Contemporary American Music." *The Rice Institute* 21 (Apr. 1934): 120, 126-27.
Discusses the "rhythmic explorations" in Carpenter's *Piano Concertino*. Includes musical examples.

B388. N. "Adventures in a Perambulator." *The New Records* 25 (July 1957): 3.
Review of Mercury ME-MG-50136. "Carpenter's thoroughly enjoyable *Adventures* receives its second and better LP recording."

B389. Nairn, Norman. "21st American Festival at Eastman School." *Musical Courier* 143 (June 1951): 16-17.
Announces a performance of *Sea Drift*.

B390. "Nazi Index." *Time* 31 (27 June 1938): 36-37.
Carpenter was included in the "Nazi *Who's Who* of Jewish musicians," *Judentum und Musik mit dem ABC jüdischer und nichtarischer Musik-beflissener*. Includes port.

B391. "The New Etude Gallery of Musical Celebrities." *Etude* 48 (Feb. 1930): 101-02.
Gives Carpenter's birth place and year. Lists four of his teachers: Elgar, Seeboeck, Paine, and Ziehn. Mentions that Carpenter combined "the careers of a businessman and an art creator." Lists titles of some of his works. "Few of Carpenter's piano pieces have been published." Includes port.

B392. "A New Spirit in American Musical Composition." *Current Opinion* 54 (Jan. 1913): 32-33.
Carpenter has "an originality so compelling that

his admirers have been driven to the use of daring comparisons." Alma Gluck says that he has the "force and originality of Strauss, and the refinement and charm of Chausson." Kurt Schindler and Arthur Farwell "are in a sense the 'discoverers' of Carpenter." Quotes P.G.C. from the *Boston Transcript*:

> Mr. Carpenter has something to say, and says it very expressively, apparently without any apologetic feeling of shame for not being completely Europeanized...[He is] a master both of expression and of style...His melodies are as obvious and inevitable as a folksong, and yet as free from platitude; in his harmonies he is audaciously chromatic or unblushingly diatonic, as he sees fit.

Arthur Farwell, in *Musical America*, discusses *The Green River*. His children's songs "reveal a subtle insight into child psychology and an intangible something we may call the comic spirit in music." Kurt Schindler, in Schirmer's *Bulletin*, states: "Mr. Carpenter is still young, but he knows his own way... He has his individual message to bring, and it is going to be a thoroly [sic] Americanized message."
Carpenter brings "personality, originality, culture, a sense of comedy, and above all, a truly American spirit into musical composition." Includes port.

B393. Newlin, Dika. "Discs." *Pan Pipes* 57 (Jan. 1963): 33.
    Review of Desto (formerly St/And) 411-12, *Songs by American Composers*. Carpenter's songs are sung by the baritone Ronald Gramm.

B394. [Obituary] *The American Organist* 34 (Apr. 1951): 130.
    Carpenter "studied music seriously but [was] an active businessman till his retirement in 1936; [he] composed chiefly for orchestra, nothing for organ."

B395. "Obituary." *Musical America* 71 (May 1951): 24.
    Obituaries of Carpenter and Adolf Bolm. Lists all Carpenter's teachers except Elgar. Includes major works.

B396. "Obituary." *Musical Times* 92 (June 1951): 280.
    Obituary. "In 1915 he made his debut as a composer at Chicago with *Adventures in a Perambulator*

...Other successes...[were] *Concertino...Skyscrapers*
...[and] *Sea Drift*." Lists a few of his "other works."

B397. "Obituary." *Newsweek* 37 (7 May 1951): 58.
Obituary. "In the '20s [Carpenter] integrated the
jazz idiom and the nervous rhythms of city life into
symphonic forms."

B398. ["Obituary."] *Opera News* 16 (17 Dec. 1951): 31.
Obituary. *Skyscrapers* "achieved five performances
at the Metropolitan Opera House in the season 1926-
1927. Other stage works, *The Birthday of the Infanta*
and *Krazy Kat,*, were presented soon after World War
I by the Chicago Opera."

B399. ["Obituary."] *Variety* 182 (2 May 1951): 75.
Carpenter was called the "most American of composers" by Walter Damrosch. He is known chiefly
"for bringing wit into serious music."

B400. ["Obituary."] *Violins and Violinists* 12 (June-July 1951): 180.
Carpenter was "a member of one of Chicago's pio-
neer families and internationally known composer."

B401. "100th Anniversary of John Alden Carpenter." *Pan Pipes*
68 (Jan. 1976): 26.
Lists all of his teachers. "While in Europe he came
under the influence of Debussy." Includes honorary
degrees and titles of three of his works: *Gitanjali*,
Adventures in a Perambulator, and *Skyscrapers*.

B402. "Peaceful Music." *Time* 36 (4 Nov. 1940): 58.
Carpenter's *Symphony 1940* was commissioned by
the Chicago Symphony Orchestra and premiered at
Orchestra Hall. "Critics, praising its tuneful themes,
its crystal clear orchestration, were polite too, found it
one of the most gentlemanly of symphonies."
Edward Barry commented in the *Tribune*: "The end
of the piece contains something as near to an
apotheosis as a man of Mr. Carpenter's discretion
would ever go. The music becomes broad and majestic and affirmative, only to drop off at the end in a
charmingly deprecatory manner."
Claudia Cassidy, in the *Journal of Commerce*, said it
was "attractive with no apparent intent to be profound, call it a graceful compliment to the jubilee
season." The composer called it "peaceful music."

B403. Pierce, Edwin Hall. "In Behalf of the 'Popular' Elements in Musical Art." *Musical Quarterly* 9 (Oct. 1923): 474.

"It is not impossible that certain elements coming from popular music may have unexpected and important influence on art-music of the not too distant future. (Witness, for instance, Carpenter, in his *Krazy Kat*)."

B404. Potamkin, Harry Alan. "Music and the Movies." *Musical Quarterly* 15 (Apr. 1929): 292.

"Jazz converters like Copland and Antheil, or John Alden Carpenter, might find a profitable field in the cinema."

B405. "Premieres." *Symphony News* 31 (Apr. 1980): 46.

Watercolors was performed by the Brooklyn Philharmonia with Lukas Foss conducting on 1 Nov. 1979.

B406. R., B. "J.A. Carpenter as Musical Humorist." *Musical America* 23 (13 Nov. 1915): 34.

Several reviews of the New York premiere of *Adventures in a Perambulator* by the New York Symphony Orchestra with Walter Damrosch conducting. The music is "decidedly diverting and colorful...a queer hybrid of Debussy, Charpentier, Strauss, Ravel, even Puccini." Includes quotes by Richard Aldrich from the *New York Times*, Mr. Halperson of the *Staats-Zeitung*, William James Henderson with *The Sun*, Henry Krehbiel from *The Tribune*, and Mr. Ziegler with *The Herald*.

B407. "Records in Brief." *Musical America* 77 (July 1957): 28.

Review of Mercury MG 50136 with *Adventures in a Perambulator*. Rated: ****. "Although his music is European influenced, he was one of the earliest composers to seek out American themes for his subject matter."

B408. Reed, Peter Hugh. "Record Notes and Reviews." *American Record Guide* 18 (May 1952): 267.

Review of Concert Hall CHS-1140.

When first presented in 1914, this score [of *Adventures in a Perambulator*] soon found success, but through the years it has not endured in the orchestral repertory. Like all Carpenter's music, there is charm and refinement in the workmanship though enjoyment would seem contingent on acceptance of the program which is a bit implausible.

B409. Rich, Alan. "Programs of American Music." *High Fidelity* 15 (June 1965): 84.

Review of Desto DST 6407. "The American Recording Society's subscription series, supported in part by the Alice M. Ditson Fund of Columbia University, was a noble effort of the Fifties. Most of its recordings were made in Vienna (with the...ARS Symphony)."

B410. _____. "Records in Review." *High Fidelity* 15 (Apr. 1965): 103-04.

Review of Desto SLP 411-12 and DST 6411-12. "There is a bit of ragtime, naïvely comprehended, in Carpenter's *Jazz Boys*; the treatment...resembles most strongly the skittish, polytonal folksettings of Benjamin Britten."

B411. Rockwell, John. "Essay-Review: Recorded Anthology of American Music. New World Records." *Musical Quarterly* 65 (Apr. 1979): 296-304.

Gives the history of the Recorded Anthology of American Music series including a list of titles and performers.

B412. Rogers, M. Robert. "Jazz Influence on French Music." *Musical Quarterly* 22 (Jan. 1935): 53.

Others "used rag-time and jazz" before an American, Carpenter, wrote *Krazy Kat*, a jazz ballet, in 1922.

B413. Rosenfeld, Paul. "Taylor, Carpenter and Loeffler." *The New Republic* 66 (Mar. 1931): 128-29.

Possibly it is a mistake to take any issue with a composition as debonair of spirit, as unpretentious and disarming, as the recent lightly rhythmical work [Carpenter's *String Quartet*] of the Chicago amateur. His wit and playfulness and cleverness have gone into it more happily than into any of the *Concertino's* successors, the somewhat Debussyish adagio and the part jazzy, part Spanish moderato are very diverting.

However "the quartet is insufficiently engaging and substantial."

B414. S. "A Carol Brice Recital." *The New Records* 18 (July 1950): 9.
Review of Mercury C-ML-2108 which includes *The Day Is No More.*

B415. S. "Adventures in a Perambulator." *The New Records* 20 (July 1952): 2.
Review of Concert Hall CH-CHS-1140. "Swoboda gives an idiomatic reading which could stand a bit more unbending and point to the humor in the score."

B416. Salter, Sumner. "Early Encouragements to American Composers." *Musical Quarterly* 18 (Jan. 1932): 100.
Carpenter is an active member of the Manuscript Society of Chicago (organized July 6, 1896).

B417. Salzman, Eric. "Modern Music in Retrospect (for the Fortieth Anniversary of Its Founding)." *Perspectives of New Music* 2 (1964): 17.
Review of the journal *Modern Music.* "Important, established, and more conservative figures—Whithorne, Carpenter, Jacobi—do, of course, receive respectful attention."

B418. Sanborn, Pitts. "Making the Grand Tour." *Modern Music* 6 (Mar.-Apr. 1929): 35.
"MacDowell,...Carpenter, Hadley, Cadman, Griffes, Taylor, and Whithorne belong in the Anglo-Celtic current."

B419. Sargeant, Winthrop. "Bernhard Ziehn, Precursor." *Musical Quarterly* 19 (Apr. 1933): 169-77.
As Ziehn's pupil, Carpenter contributed to Ziehn's *Canonical Studies.*

B420. Sears, William P., Jr. "'Buying 'American' in Music." *Literary Digest* 118 (29 Dec. 1934): 24.
"The poles of the modern conflict, and the struggle for a unified expression of the American spirit, are represented by George Gershwin, on the side of jazz, and Carpenter, on the side of austere classicism." Includes port.

B421. Shupp, Enos E., Jr. "New LP Samplers: Orchestra." *The New Records* 32 (May 1964): 2-3.
Review of CRI-180. "Orchestra and conductor produce the Piston and Carpenter concertinos with no little dash and style."

B422. "Skyscrapers." *Outlook* 142 (3 Mar. 1926): 314-15.
Too much emphasis has been laid upon the element of jazz in it...What Mr. Carpenter does in this score of his is to take jazz as he takes the other sounds and movements of American city life and blend it with the rest of the ingredients to make up his musical interpretation.

Although *Skyscrapers* is distinctively American, Carpenter has used Russian ballet and musical techniques such as those Stravinsky used. Includes illus. of the final scene: Modern City Life.

B423. Smith, Cecil. "Carpenter's Carmel Concerto Given Premiere by Stokowski." *Musical America* 69 (15 Dec. 1949): 8.

[*Carmel Concerto*] is a loosely constructed one-movement work, about twelve minutes in duration employing a conventionally syncopated main theme...Oriental and Spanish-American [tinged subsidiary materials.]...The piece is urbane, forthright, and friendly in spirit, but its episodic construction and its tendency to overwork the rather thin subject-matter of the principal theme contribute to a generally labored effect. It is not one of the composer's most successful works.

B424. Snook, Paul. "The Kat's Meow." *Fanfare* 1 (May-June 1978): 27-29.
Review of NW 228.

There's no escaping the fact that Powell and Gilbert at least—if not Carpenter—wrote basically 19th century program music tricked out with "ethnic" embellishments. Thus, three of these scores...have a slightly faded and genteel aura about them.
[Carpenter] is now best remembered for four works which combine an affable impressionist-picturesque esthetic with a very personal

adaptation of what is more accurately described as ragtime rather than real jazz: [the *Piano Concertino*, *Adventures in a Perambulator*, *Skyscrapers*, and *Krazy Kat*.]

[*Krazy Kat*] offers a tuneful medley of Carpenter's most prominent characteristics: saucy sweetness, antic whimsy, and a touching naïveté which more often suggests the nursery rather than the cabaret. On its own undemanding terms, this is a lilting and irresistible confection.

B425. _____. "Orchestral." *Fanfare* 8 (Mar.-Apr. 1985): 360-62.
Review of NW 321. Mentions the "jazz-tinged" ballets *Krazy Kat* and *Skyscrapers* which "demonstrate a wondrous flair for the graphically theatrical and the humorously mechanistic." *Sea Drift* is serious and introspective, showing a "quasi-Anglican, post-impressionistic evocation of a multi-hued, ever-changing seascape." The two "shattering climaxes ...carry a more personal weight of intensity and possibly even despair." This recording has more "pulse and power" than "Karl Krüger's loving but somewhat limp perusal."

B426. "Song Recital." *The Gramophone* 28 (Sept. 1950): 9.
Review of Columbia ML 2108. No mention of the Carpenter songs.

B427. Sonneck, O.G. "The American Composer and the American Music Publisher." *Musical Quarterly* 9 (Jan. 1923): 123, 125.
Carpenter is in "the forefront of American composers." His *Birthday of the Infanta* moves "on terms of artistic equality, even superiority, with some of the best European works."

B428. Soria, Dorle J. "Treasures and Trifles." *Opera News* 52 (Sept. 1987): 24-28.
Article about the Metropolitan Opera Archives.

In a letter of December 24, 1925, the Metropolitan writes a certain F.H. Wilson, engaging him "to furnish Twelve Colored Singers to sing the music allotted to them in John Alden Carpenter's Ballet *Skyscrapers*...For their services and for yours we will pay you One Hundred and Twenty Dollars for each performance, this price to be inclusive of all fees for performances, rehearsals and preliminary work."

B429. Stevenson, Joseph. "New Reviews." *Stevenson Compact Disc Review Guide* 4 (Apr.-May 1988): 2.
Review of EMI Angel CDC-7 49263-2.

> The wild card in the set is...[*Skyscrapers*], a raucous, post-War (I) romp which is stylistically miles away from the more pastorale and classically inspired quartet of older composers...The piece is even wild in its orchestration, which includes banjo, saxophone and an air whistle. From a pounding opening designed to suggest building construction, Carpenter whirls kaleidoscopically through a succession of dance-rhythm set-pieces which is delightfully off-base.

B430. Stiller, Andrew. "Music Reviews." *Opus* 3 (Feb. 1987): 35.
Review of NW 328-29.

> As recently as 1950, John Alden Carpenter (1876-1951) was still considered by most critics the most important American composer of his generation...Carpenter's reputation suffered a considerable battering in the two decades following his death. *Adventures in a Perambulator*, his most popular work, was subjected to so much ridicule that it was driven right out of the repertoire.
>
> There is no question that Carpenter's music was significantly overvalued during his lifetime; but his admirers were not fools, and his current almost complete effacement is scarcely merited.
>
> Unfortunately, piano music was not one of Carpenter's central concerns; he's best known for his songs and orchestral music...Half the total [of his piano music] is student work.

Includes port.

B431. Stutsman, Grace May. "Boston Men Play Carpenter Music." *Musical America* 59 (25 Mar. 1939): 11.
Describes and criticizes the *Violin Concerto* which has "volubility in the central portion."

B432. _____."New Works Given by Boston Forces." *Musical America* 52 (10 Nov. 1932): 22.

Patterns is "free in form,...a fantasia in one long movement" of three more or less distinct sections. It is not a "strikingly original work, nor are there arresting themes for development, yet the music makes a pleasant excursion into the realm of composition and was received with extreme cordiality."

B433. Taylor, Deems. "America's First Dramatic Composer: Carpenter, Whose Pantomime Music May Presage an American School of Ballet." *Vanity Fair* 18 (Apr. 1922): 59, 106.

Reviews a performance of *Krazy Kat*.

> For when the curtains parted, displaying Adolph Bolm, simply and tastefully attired as a kat, peacefully asleep in the shade of an outrageous Herriman tree, and the small orchestra manfully girded up its loins to give an excellent imitation of a snore, everybody relaxed and grinned. Nothing arty about this exhibit. Here were funny noises that were meant to be funny.
> The *Krazy Kat* score, for all its broad burlesque—its vulgarity, if you like—is a logical, well-developed piece of dramatic composition. Its themes are low comedy, but what makes them effective is the immense technical skill with which they are handled. The orchestra is small, and the instrumentation is jazzy; but it is sophisticated jazz.

Lists other Carpenter works. *Birthday of the Infanta* "is probably the best ballet score anyone has done since *Petrushka*." Carpenter "gave the Metropolitan [Opera Company] the first chance at *Birthday* ...only to have it refused because it was 'too intimate'." Includes illus. from these two ballets.

B434. Teat, Sue Ellen. "American Art Song and the Beginning Voice Student." *NATS Bulletin* 41 (May-June 1985): 8-10.

Lists American art songs suitable for beginning voice students. Thirty seven teachers recommended *The Sleep That Flits on Baby's Eyes* and thirty recommended *When I Bring to You Colour'd Toys*. Includes range, level of difficulty for the vocalist and accompanist, and the pedagogical uses for the songs (e.g., phrasing, interpretation, breathing, legato, and sostenuto).

B435. Thompson, Oscar. "Koussevitzky's Bostonians Give Second American Program." *Musical America* 59 (10 Dec. 1939): 27.
Reviews a performance of *Skyscrapers*.

> "But its verve, its wit, its unabashed tunefulness and brilliant orchestration—bordering on the popular but still essentially symphonic—well justify any conductor in keeping it on the active list. It is music for the theatre but does not lose its zest in the concert hall."

The vocal soloists "were seated inconspicuously among the players." Includes port.

B436. Thompson, Randall. "The Contemporary Scene in American Music." *Musical Quarterly* 18 (Jan. 1932): 11.
Carpenter "used jazz mainly in the episodic manner and with considerable success."

B437. Thornton, H. Frank. "The Art Song in America." *The New Records* 34 (July 1966): 11.
Review of the Duke University album. "The aim has been to select songs according to a double criterion of the historical importance of the composer and the artistic value of the song itself."

B438. _____. "Songs by American Composers." *The New Records* 33 (Feb. 1965): 10-11.
Describes *Looking Glass River* as impressionistic and *Jazz Boys* as carefree.

B439. Thorpe, Harry Colin. "Interpretative Studies in American Song." *Musical Quarterly* 15 (Jan. 1929): 106-11 .

> At the very beginning [of *Serenade*] he prevents an almost inevitable misapprehension by plainly stating in the bold phrases of his introduction, that here stands no languishing lover, brushing pale fingers over tinkling strings.
> [The poem] is a silent serenade to the absent beloved, chanted in the crypt of remembrance and heard only by the listening psyche. It is love's eternal effort to regain and retain its ecstasy by the

imagined re-living of its transports.

The ability to combine the formal or aesthetic in music, with the expressive, is so rare that it is interesting to peer curiously into the workshop, just for a moment...Those four measures at the beginning, with one or two other ideas, compose the whole show! The repeated notes, tip-tapping interminably, the motive and its inversion are the warp and woof—the entire musical fabric.

Instead of repeating the first measure literally, the composer shifts the first chord of the right-hand part to the second beat... Certainly that ending, in which the opulent baritone resonance of the voice and massive sonorities of the orchestra-like accompaniment combine in an overwhelming torrent of tone, is one of the noblest and most stirring in the entire literature of American song.

B440. _____. "Sidney Lanier, A Poet for Musicians." *Musical Quarterly* 11 (July 1925): 376.
Both Carpenter and Edward C. Moore set Lanier's poem *May the Maiden* to music.

B441. Trudeau, Noah André. "Sea Drift." *High Fidelity/Musical America* 35 (Apr. 1985): MA44.
Review of NW 321.

Freed from the need to "make it" in the music world, Carpenter let his imagination take him where it would; in this sense, he proved quite a world traveler. French art song and impressionism, American jazz and Tin Pan Alley, Far Eastern timbres and scales—all were grist for his creative mill.

Although the title and rhapsodic mood of this work [*Sea Drift*] superficially suggest the influence of Debussy, it is shaped by deeper Wagnerian currents.

B442. Turok, Paul. "An American Tragedy." *Music Journal* 35 (Mar. 1977): 46.
Review of Orion ORS 76243. The *Violin Sonata* is here "revived and performed with great style and relish."

B443. _____. "Buried Treasure." *Music Journal* 34 (Nov. 1976): 44.

> Review of NW 247. No mention of Carpenter.

B444. _____. "Classical." *Music Journal* 36 (Sept. 1978): 35.

> Review of NW 228. "Carpenter's *Krazy Kat* is made up of a series of pleasant vignettes that are simply too fragmentary to hold together."

B445. Upton, William Treat. "Nature in Song." *The Chesterian* 7 (Apr.-May 1926): 185.

> "Debussy is more pictorial, but no more sincere or consistent" than Carpenter in his songs.

B446. _____. "Some Representative American Song-Composers. *Musical Quarterly* 11 (July 1925): 392-97.

> "Carpenter's songs which were published in 1912 "spoke a new voice, permeated with French influence."

> > [*Green River* has a] keen harmonic sense, exceedingly plastic and capable of being molded with the utmost freedom; charming bits of melody, fashioned with greatest refinement of line and content; invariable correspondence of text with its embodying music...The close is exquisite with its bit of whole-tone color...I have never been able to reconcile the cloying harmonies in the accompaniment.
> >   The voice part [in *Don't ceäre*] runs on in characteristically monotonous monologue fashion, while the piano score abounds in the most fascinating double rhythms and the merriest counterpoint imaginable, and the harmonization, although appropriately simple, is anything but commonplace.

> Carillon effects, clever manipulation of the subdominant harmony, filmy harmonies, simplicity and artistic restraint, broad expressive meditative song and atmospheric writing using antiphonal effects can be found in *Looking Glass River, Go, Lovely Rose, Little Fly, A Cradle Song, Chanson d'automne,* and *Le ciel* respectively.
>   Carpenter uses two different simultaneous rhythms, in 3/4 and 3/2 time, in *Dansons la gigue!*. The dull grey monotone of *Il pleure dans mon coeur*

contrast with the naturalness of *Where the Misty Shadows Glide*. The rhythmical germ in *Les silhouettes* continues to the very end. "One of Mr. Carpenter's most fluent and facile songs" is *Her Voice*.

> [*To One Unknown* has] rich sonority...[not] strikingly original either in its means or manner...Mr. Carpenter's admirable economy of means, the entire passage of six very full measures being built up upon only three major chords, but enriched by a wealth of chromatic octaves, wide-flung arpeggios and the like.

Carpenter treats the text of *Fog Wraiths* in an imaginative and suggestive way. Upton finds oriental mysticism in *The Day Is No More* and an imaginative setting in *Player Queen*. While *Slumber Song* lacks his usual sense of cohesion and unity, *Serenade* is closely knit and unified. "Full of perverse rhythms, its mood is rather distraught, but it [*Serenade*] is a powerful song, well put together."

The songs in *Gitanjali* vary such characteristics as rich texture in *When I Bring to You Color'd Toys*, solemnity in *When Death Comes Knocking at Your Door*, tenderness in *When Sleep Flits on Baby's Eyes*, poesy in *Autumn*, fragility and transparent beauty of the child-spirit in *By the Seashore*, and great bursts of golden tone in *Light, my Light*.

Upton finds in these songs "the meditative spirit. the love of expressing the genius of nature, the out-of-doors, in its quieter aspects and in its influence upon human experience."

B447. Veilleux, C. Thomas. "Guide to Records." *American Record Guide* 40 (Apr. 1977): 21.

Review of Orion ORS 76243. Found the *Violin Sonata* "refreshingly complex" with "some fine moments for violin." The work could have been written by "Debussy on a not particularly creative day."

B448. _____. "Piano Music in America (1900-1945)." *The New Records* 45 (Oct. 1977): 13.

Review of Vox Box SVBX-5303. "Some of my personal favorites include...Carpenter's *Impromptu*."

B449. _____. "Violin Sonata." *The New Records* 45 (Feb. 1977): 6.
Review of Orion ORS 76243. There are "some
excellent, sweeping moments for violin." Includes
notes by the violinist, Eugene Gratovich.

B450. Waldo, Fullerton. "High Spots in American Music." *Etude*
51 (Apr. 1933): 231, 279.
Carpenter "was 'chief' among America's musical
<u>amateurs</u> in the best sense of that word." Includes
port.

B451. "Walter Camryn Stages Krazy Kat." *Dance News* 14 (Feb.
1949): 10.
"To climax the Tavern Club's 20th anniversary
...*Krazy Kat* ballet was offered in revised form for the
Children's Party, Dec. 19." Bolm's pupil Walter
Camryn did the choreography which was danced by
members of the junior ballet group, stars of the
Children's Civic Theatre. Krazy Kat was danced by
John Sharpe, Jr. and Rudolph Ganz accompanied.
Camryn plans to present the ballet at PTA meetings
this spring.

B452. Ware, Alice Holdship. "Skyscrapers; Settings by Robert
Edmond Jones for a Ballet by John Alden Carpenter."
Survey 56 (1 Apr. 1926): 35-37.
Review of the 1 April 1926 *Skyscrapers* production
at the Metropolitan Opera House. "It is a serious
interpretation of America and modern life, and it is
devastating." Sets, costumes and light intensify the
expression of America at play and at work. "It all
spells despair, terrible and revealing...here are
challenging hungers fiercely clamorous." Includes
five illus: "Shadows," "Morning," "Night,"
"Subway," and "Coney Island."

B453. Waters, Edward N. "Annual Reports (on Acquisitions):
Music." *The Library of Congress Quarterly Journal of
Current Acquisitions* 18 (Nov. 1960): 17-18.
Lists new accessions of works by Carpenter.

B454. Wiborg, Mary Hoyt. "Notes on Modern Soloists and
Composers." *Arts and Decoration* 22 (Dec. 1924): 40-41,
90.
Discusses the use of jazz and the music of the
dance hall as the proper musical expression for
America.

"Jazz syncopations and drum beats, typifying as they do American musical satire and popular humor, would be bound to attract the sensibilities and rhythmic appreciation of a man like Carpenter, both in humorous as well as serious vein."

Announces that "Diaghilew [is] to give to John Alden Carpenter the writing of the first American ballet to be performed under his personal direction ...this coming spring...[about] the Boston police strike of 1920."

B455. Yestadt, Sister Marie, S.B.S. "Song Literature for the 70's: A Socio-Musical Approach." *NATS Bulletin* (May-June 1933): 25-26.

Four Negro Songs, popular "among singers for a couple of decades, has every jazz and blues element contained in the poetry...realized...in the music."

B456. Young, Percy M. "John Alden Carpenter." *Musical Opinion* 66 (Aug. 1943): 361-62.

Carpenter's music is ideal to introduce the British to American music. Besides the "simplicity of utterance and coherence...there are no obstacles in the way of our listening." Elgar's presence is observed in Carpenter's "use of the orchestra, spacious, brassy, and percussively eloquent, his blunt melodic diatonicism in moments of large effort, his elliptical modulations...and his almost pre-Raphaelite attention to details of illustration."

[Carpenter] has progressed harmonically not very far out of the nineteenth century...he has never allowed himself to stagnate. His poetic charm has been made to rub shoulders with the contrary quality of boisterous wit. *Skyscrapers* (1926) is rough-edged realism, ballet music which is hard to assimilate without its décor and choreography. The score gives a forced impression of uncongenial slang idioms and its obvious approximation to the general English idea of American life renders it less palatable than the more familiar and more funny *Adventures in a Perambulator* (1915)...[In] the *Violin Concerto* (1936) he has rebuked the introvert tendencies of much contemporary music, and has maintained the apparent thesis of his artistic creed that music, like literature, must proceed from tradition to novelty and not vice versa.

B457. Young, Stark. "Krazy Kat." *The New Republic* 32 (11 Oct. 1922): 175-76.

Carpenter "begins with the jazz and funny-paper world and forces something out of it, abstracts from it a purer pattern." The performance at the Greenwich Village Follies by Mr. Yakovleff, Fortunello, and Cirilinno "is not yet up to the level of Mr. Carpenter's music and Mr. Herriman's picture."

> About this picture, as you see it on the stage, there is something that seems in an odd way to let the eye through. The light is so managed that the cartoons at the back, turning on rollers and changing every two or three minutes against the action in front of them, the costumes in black and white, the walls, the grayish trees on either side, take on a strange pearl color, as if we were seeing in some crazy dream the fantastic action of these fabled creatures whose human traits are all turned now to flickering inclinations and fragile passions and the shadows of whims. And meanwhile the music has about it a kind of added light that shines on this laughing unreality; it is bright, dramatic; it has also, vaguely underneath its animation, something very grim and pathetic and comic and original.

Young compares *Krazy Kat* to an American commedia dell'arte; both have similar stories, vagaries, music, gestures, action and movement, stream of vitality, buoyancy, incessant rhythm, excitement of changing line, bland cruelty and abounding love of life and of oneself, the "character of being so intent upon one's own foolish and capricious and inexorable ends."

NEWSPAPERS

B458. "American Ballet *Skyscrapers* Feb. 19." NYT (8 Feb. 1926): 25.

"Carpenter's 'Syncopated Time' music to be a novelty at Metropolitan." Announces the forthcoming production of *Skyscrapers*. Carpenter can be

"recalled for the Chicago Opera Company's production of his romantic ballet, *The Birthday of the
Infanta.*"

B459. "Baby's Ideas of Park Trip Described in Novel Music."
NYHT (6 Nov. 1915): 12.
Review of *Adventures in a Perambulator* conducted
by Walter Damrosch at Aeolian Hall.

> With its suggestion of the Debussy whole tone
> scale, its modern orchestration and its unusual
> combinations of sound, [*Adventures in a
> Perambulator*] was not intended to amuse children.
> The effect on a child of a policeman who flirts
> with the nurse, the sound of a hurdy-gurdy, the
> sight of a lake, an encounter with a pack of dogs
> and finally the feeling of drowsiness are pictured
> most cleverly, with some unusual effects from the
> orchestra. Piano, bells, xylophone, celeste and
> harp are used in a striking manner. No American
> work has been found so amusing and at the same
> time so musical in a long time.

B460. Barry, Edward. "New Carpenter Piece Played by Balokovic." CDT (19 Nov. 1937): 24.

> Except for the second division of the work,
> where the broad Carpenter serenity is fully
> apparent, the concerto does not on first hearing
> reveal the charm of idea which it
> doubtless...possesses. There is a certain angularity
> in the themes and they do not seem to lie well for
> the violinist. Opportunities to exploit the
> instrument's best effects are few and far between.
> [Balokovic] played with a thin tone deficient
> in character. Its periods lacked sweep and vigor. A
> suspicion that these somewhat tepid remarks
> represent a personal rather than a universally
> valid truth is strengthened by the fact that last
> night's audience applauded the work cordially
> and called its composer and its interpreter to the
> stage.

B461. _____. "New Symphony by Carpenter Wins Acclaim."
CDT (25 Oct. 1940): 23.
Although the *Symphony in C* has "moderation,
urbanity, sensitiveness, a certain wistful delicacy of

address [it]...seems graver and more profound" than Carpenter's earlier music. Its structure has a greater solidity and its texture a greater richness.

> [The themes] possess a remarkable evocative power, notably the one in 5-4 time, which climbs into the stratosphere so delicately and becomes more luminous and serene the higher it goes. The end...contains something as near to an apotheosis as a man of Mr. Carpenter's discretion would ever go. The music becomes broad and majestic and affirmative, only to drop off at the end in a charmingly depreciatory manner.

The reviewer notes that "either the composer or the conductor miscalculated in his handling of the symphony's close. The chord which ends the maestoso was an invitation to applause—a fact which partially spoiled the odd beauty of the actual conclusion."

B462. Borowski, Felix. "Carpenter's *Second Symphony* Presented First Time Here." CST (19 Nov. 1943): 21.
Carpenter "began as an impressionist, developed into a quasi-radical, and now, in his late maturity, has retired into conservatism." In the closing movement of his *Symphony no. 2* the music "is flooded with pictorial suggestiveness." The conductor "made much of the vivid colors in the score, and only in larger intensification of tonal light and shade could the interpretation have been improved."

B463. Bowes, Julian. "A Dissenter." (Letters to the Editor) NYT (28 Feb. 1926): 6.
Response to the *Skyscrapers* review by Olin Downes. The writer feels that this American ballet "with its Russian realism and pure hokum" was given a "boresome and rather ridiculous performance." The dancing and pantomime were neglected. The "entire idea was simply a steal on the legitimate performances of Broadway musical comedies, burlesque, and moving picture prologues."

> [*Skyscrapers* does not] express our art consciousness...It does not "suggest the confused and prodigious architecture of a great city" ...[and] cannot lead to anything but absolute chaos and

insanity in our expression. Any acetylene welder would laugh outright at the sledge strokes in the pantomime used to depict rhythm in the work scenes when the light of the torch flares for realistic purposes.

B464. Brock, H.J. "Jazz Is To Do a Turn in Grand Opera." NYT (14 Feb. 1926): 5.
   Skyscrapers is "jazz incorporated into a symphonic composition and uplifted on the powerful swell of all the precious instruments of grand opera...More power to jazz...[and] this slogan of musical Bolshevism." Includes two illus.: "Steel Construction" and "Coney Island Abstracted."

B465. "Composer Carpenter 75." NYT (1 Mar. 1951): 32.
   Carpenter "received 200 congratulatory wires, flowers and hundreds of letters and cards" for his seventy-fifth birthday. Quotes Carpenter on the role of music and art today:

> Their task is to nourish and sustain people. The day of American leadership has dawned and it is necessary for us to become spiritual leaders. It is not enough to deal with things. In addition, we must express our ideas and ideals. It is the role of music and the arts to be the medium for this expression.
> I recommend prayer and a return to religion and art as solution to today's problems. They speak to the best that is in us. These troubled times are not a healthy period for the creator. Artists cannot be afraid of today and afraid for tomorrow and express themselves freely.

B466. "Composer To Be Honored by Arts-Letters Institute." NYT (14 Feb. 1947): 19.
   Douglas Moore, president of the institute, made the announcement that Carpenter will be presented the annual gold medal. Carpenter was "elected in 1918 to the institute...and in 1942 to the academy." Includes port.

B467. David, Peter G. "A Deluge of Musical Americana." NYT (4 July 1976): D1, D19.
   Review of New World Record series. Lists ERA 1009 which contains *Adventures in a Perambulator*.

B468. _____. "The Imported and Homespun Charms of Our
Musical Past." NYT (3 July 1977): D11, D14.
Review of Orion ORS 76243. Carpenter "draws on
the French school for his pungent *Violin Sonata*."

B469. DeLamarter, Eric. "Percy Grainger at Orchestra Hall." CDT
(11 Mar. 1916): 14.
Adventures in a Perambulator, "a freakish fantasy of
stunning harmonic and orchestral effect, is paralleled
in this 'concertino' by a racy, barbarian fantasy of
equally stunning rhythmic effects. It is involved,
enigmatic, mesmeric...no end clever." This idiom,
"agonizing to the mid-Victorian ear, and
yet...'seizing,' as the French phrase puts it, ambushes
the interpreter with novel terrors." Mr. Carpenter
and Mr. Grainger "owe each other profound
gratitude. The one created an ideal of rhythmic
pulchritude, and the other galvanized it into life."

B470. Downes, Olin. "*Anxious Bugler* by Philharmonic." NYT (18
Nov. 1943): 28.
Anxious Bugler was commissioned by the League of
Composers to express an aspect of the war. "The
music has psychological as well as heroic connota-
tions." Includes Carpenter comments.

[Downes heard] confused sounds and rhythms
and thoughts; the din of machines—the jog of
drill, a musical reference to *Ein Feste Burg* and to
the "V"-motive, as it is now called, from the *Fifth
Symphony;* the chorus of *Old Folks at Home,* the
tune broken into bits...and toward the last the
sounding of *Taps.* All these lines and colors merge
in Mr. Carpenter's tonal canvas, admirable in its
workmanship, unmistakable in its sincerity and
with humorous details which point up the
essential earnestness of his commentary.

B471. _____. "Composers and Their False Images—Fiction
Preferred by the Public." NYT (14 Feb. 1926): VIII: 7
Skyscrapers is the "first attempt in a ballet of serious
dimensions to bring into being a purely American
choreography as an art form."

B472. _____. "Operas of a Day." NYT (5 Mar. 1926): 25.
Skyscrapers was danced "for the fourth time in a
fortnight...to continuous rounds of applause."

B473. _____. "Philharmonic Led by Bruno Walter." NYT (23 Oct. 1942): 26.

> *Symphony no.* 2 "did not, on an initial hearing, appear to be one of Mr. Carpenter's most distinguished utterances." Although there are "touches of phrase and development" and the themes have "vigor or melodic lilt" the composer's intention seems to be "too impersonal."

B474. _____. "*Skyscrapers* Here with 'Jazz' Score." NYT (20 Feb. 1926): 15.

> *Skyscrapers* is a "free fantasy on certain phases of American life. These are symbolized by fantastical scenery and by choreography based upon American dances, as Mr. Carpenter's score is based upon 'jazz' rhythms."

> > [Downes has] some reservations on the purely musical grounds. They lie principally in the direction of a lack of very striking inventiveness in the score. The technic [sic] is superb, though the procedure as well as some of the rhythmical ideas themselves savor strongly of Stravinsky. The workmanship is so fine, and imbued with such a spirit, that it conceals itself.

B475. Durgin, Cyrus W. "Symphony Hall." BG (22 Oct. 1932): 6.

> Review of the premiere of *Patterns* by the Boston Symphony Orchestra. "It is 'absolute' music, purest of the pure, and its substance is a series of short motives. These themes are varied and include one of Spanish character, one in the manner of a waltz and one which resembles jazz." The piano obbligato "is treated very nearly as one of the orchestral voices, and it is heard in short, highly rhythmic interludes." More lyrical than *Skyscrapers*, the strings have "many passages of broad, sustained melody. His harmonic scheme is on the whole less rigorously modern" than *Skyscrapers*. *Patterns* is "ingratiating, but not profound ...evocative of thought but not of emotion." Its greatest weakness: its "themes are not developed; they are presented in all their refreshing variety, but are not worked upon and reiterated sufficiently to make them seem part of a balanced, ordered whole."

B476. "Events in the World of Music." NYT (25 Nov. 1945): 4.

> Announces the world premiere of *Seven Ages*.

B477. Gilman, Lawrence. "An American *Song of Faith*." NYHT
(1 May 1932): VII: 6.
Review of RCA Victor 1559-60. Mentions first
performances and radio broadcast of *Song of Faith*.
Reviewer finds fault with the singers' enunciation
and the nameless narrator "who speaks the words of
Washington...with...uncultivated voice and diction."
Quotes Carpenter on his inspiration from Washington's words:

> It is from that [selfless integrity of his] character
> that we inherit the Great American Dream—the
> dream which has sustained us through our
> storms and trials...the whole world is beset by a
> dangerous psychology of defeat. And it is for our
> country now to raise its eyes in the faith of its
> founders and lead the way out...if my *Song of Faith*
> can succeed in lighting one single candle of
> reaffirmation, I shall be content.

Includes text for chorus and narrator. Observes
that Carpenter does not use brass bands or bombs
bursting in the air.

> The most impressive moments are moments of
> an almost devotional quiet and absorption.
> Rhetoric is absent from its meditative and sober
> pages. For this is music of faith and love and
> elevation...One must look to the thought and
> feeling implied by the words if one would find the
> measure of the music's eloquence...[This is]
> patriotism that is deeply sensitive and aware,
> even a little humorous (as in the allusions to
> *Yankee Doodle*); finding its most searching
> expression in the thought of the beloved and
> cradling land.

B478. Hale Philip. "Symphony Concert." BH (22 Oct. 1932): 11.
Review of *Patterns*. There is a "highly sentimental
waltz bit." Carpenter's musical nature has a "decidedly sentimental rather than emotional streak." The
reviewer would have preferred "longer passages with
jazz prominent; not merely implied—and 'an absurd
bubbling up of my concealed Spanish blood;' for
some of us the Spanish blood was not concealed; it
was congealed."
Skyscrapers would have been more effective staged:

Perhaps the putting of the orchestra in overalls to remind the audience of riveters and other laborers would be an aid to appreciation, though the music itself is here adroitly imitative; but for the scenes in "any Coney Island" stage settings and characters are essential. Here music alone gives no allusion of the island life: the Negro sweeper going to sleep, comic policemen, or tingle-tangle booths and barkers. Even ultra-modern music has its limitations in suggesting, much-less expressing, scenes in everyday life. But as a suite *Skyscrapers* is amusing; it is a genuine contribution to American music.

B479. Hubbard, W.L. "John A. Carpenter's *Infanta* Ballet Wins High Approval." CDT (24 Dec. 1919): 11.

Birthday of the Infanta "had been postponed because of the death of Mr. Campanini." The premiere "left not a place vacant" in the Chicago Auditorium. Describes the ballet.

Carpenter's music is "original, individual, essentially of today and yet possessing many beauties that make immediate appeal. It is music that catches the unusual fanciful spirit of the play and its mood and time, and reflects it skillfully. There is much of the Spanish flavor."

B480. Hughes, Allen. "The Art of the Art Song." NYT (7 Aug. 1966): D16.

Review of Duke University album, DWR 6417-18. It was "reasonable" to include Carpenter's *When I Bring to You Colored Toys.* Concludes that there is "no consistency in this album's coverage of the art song in America from either a historical or an esthetic standpoint."

B481. James, Pence. "Dr. Stock's 'Rabbit' Writes Symphony Called 'Symphony'." CDN (24 Oct. 1940): 9.

Title refers to Carpenter's comment: "I'm just a rabbit that Dr. Stock pulled out of his hat!" Dr. Stock is known for encouraging American composers. This symphony, *Symphony (1940)*, was written for the fiftieth anniversary of the Chicago Symphony Orchestra. Carpenter feels that "short symphonies ...are in step with our times. As in everything else, people are in a hurry with their music. They can't wait for the old leisurely way of spinning out an idea." Carpenter acknowledges his dual career in business and music but "wouldn't advise anyone to do likewise." Carpenter went to Dr. Stock "for advice like you would go to your father."

B482. "John Alden Carpenter 75 Today." NYT (28 Feb. 1951): 31.
Carpenter spent his birthday in Sarasota after suffering from a stroke a few weeks before. The National Arts Foundation gave him its award of merit "for distinguished achievements in musical composition."

B483. "John A. Carpenter, Composer, to Marry." NYT (25 Jan. 1933): 12.
Carpenter will marry Mrs. Borden at the home of her aunt and uncle, Mr. and Mrs. Kingsley Porter, in Cambridge, MA. They will sail abroad Feb. 1.

B484. "John Carpenter, Noted Composer." NYT (27 Apr. 1951): 23.
Obituary. Damrosch called Carpenter the "most American of composers." His importance to American music "was at its highest point in the Nineteen Twenties, when the composer was an instrumental force in transferring the spirit and feeling of the jazz idiom to the concert room."

B485. "Markedly American." BET (18 Apr. 1918): 14.
Sermons in Stones was performed in Norfolk, CT once and twice in Chicago. The reviewer felt "awe that he [Carpenter] did what he did, and bewilderment as to why he did it in the manner he chose." The musical public finds "neither the form nor the spirit [of a symphony], and in the meantime more people are talking about John Alden Carpenter than ever before, which is a nourishing comfort to the composer. The more talk, the plumper the halo."

[Carpenter] gives no mere indication of his trend of direction than one of those little "hell-diver" ducks of our boyhood shooting. He burst into view first as a wizard of tone-painting in *Adventures in a Perambulator*, whimsical, expert, a psychologist; he reappeared as an incarnation of verve and frantic rhapsody in the concertino for piano...and this time, after a season of meditation, he has spoken in the symphonic medium, reverently, deliberately...his music is peculiarly of our own place and time, American, 1917.

[*Sermons in Stones* has] great depths in the musical idea of the first theme, variety and color and movement, power in the climaxes, wisdom in the staging, and of no subject may it be said that it is trite...Let us trace directly to such moments as the majestic opening of the slow movement, the sparkle and the vividness of the scherzo, and the last dozen bars of all, the delight we take in this new work...No one may question the skill of orchestration or the skill of the polyphonist. They are present in every bar...He has put into the most formidable pattern of all, the best in him, without studious imitation of a scheme he did not feel instinctively, and without fear of the tradition.

B486. Moore, Edward. "John A. Carpenter Provides Humor for Chicago Symphony." CDT (24 Dec. 1921): 15.
  Krazy Kat is the "best bit of musical humor I have heard in many a year." Carpenter has "elevated jazz music to a position in the great orchestra." Katnip Blues is a "corking good tune, and it can be danced to." Suggests that Fred Stone and Violet Zell dance the principal roles.

B487. _____. "Stock Closes Holiday with Happy Concert." CDT (1 Dec. 1933): 17.
  Sea Drift is a "tone poem of marine serenity." Carpenter's picture is a "pleasant one, based, it would seem, on his earlier technical manner, and developed with the same color and skill which for a long time has been his habit."

B488. "Mrs. Ellen Borden Engaged to Marry." NYT (11 Jan. 1933): 16.
  The wedding will take place after she finishes her work as chairman of the committee seeking money to complete a temple of music for the Century of Progress exhibition opening in June.

B489. "Mrs. J.A. Carpenter, Art Authority, Dies." NYT (8 Dec. 1931): 42.
  Rue W. Carpenter "died suddenly...in the waiting room of Dr. Walter H. Theobald's office." She had gone there with her daughter for treatment of a cold.

"She soon slumped in her chair and was dead within a few minutes. Death was attributed...to a cerebral hemorrhage."

B490. "Mrs. Waller Borden Wed." NYT (31 Jan. 1933): 21.
Only her aunt, uncle, and two daughters witnessed the ceremony performed by Rev. Samuel Eliot of the Arlington Street Church of Boston. Carpenter's daughter lives in Texas and did not attend.

B491. "Music Notes." NYHT (4 Nov. 1934): V: 9.
Carpenter will discuss his *Sea Drift* in Henry Cowell's composer symposium at the New School for Social Research. It will be performed by the Philharmonic-Symphony Orchestra under Werner Janssen's direction.

B492. "Music Stage Dedicated." NYT (28 July 1952): 12.
Mrs. John Alden Carpenter dedicated a concert stage in her husband's memory at the Castle Hill estate of the late Mrs. Richard T. Crane. At the ceremony Mina Hager sang some of his songs and the New Music Quartet performed his *String Quartet*. His widow lives in Beverly, MA.

B493. Perkins, Francis D. "Dr. Stock Leads Musicians in New Symphony." NYHT (23 Nov. 1940): 9.
Symphony (1940) contains "peaceful music." It "does not err...on the side of too consistent placidity ...[It] avoids sonorities which might be received with disaffectation by conservative-minded concert goers." Although the "basic theme was previously used in an earlier symphony composed in 1917...the new work gives no sense of heterogeneity of style. The idiom is consistent and individual." Perkins finds it "sincere and appealing music generous in melodic content, well knit and concise in form, ably wrought in its scoring and in the employment of its ideas."

B494. Rich, Alan. "American Encores." NYT (18 Aug. 1963): X10.
Review of Golden Crest 4065 which contains Carpenter's *Impromptu*. Grant Johannesen "played [these works] on his recent tour of Russia. Most of the music is old-fashioned in language."

B495. "Rodzinski Returns from Salzburg Fete." NYT (2 Oct. 1937): 18.

Carpenter returned on the ship Manhattan after a summer in Sweden. Announces premiere of his *Violin Concerto*, Oct. 19, in Chicago.

B496. Schonberg, Harold C. "Music: Fry's Challenge." NYT (30 July 1975): 15.

Krazy Kat was performed at the Newport Music Festival:

> The Ballet Repertory Company, dancing to unimaginative choreography by Richard Englund, is little more than an amateur group. In addition, the score was played in a reduction for two pianos. But enough of the music came through to suggest that *Krazy Kat* is a delightful period piece—fluffy, amusing, lightweight, and ever so much fun if it is approached for what it is.

B497. _____. "Records: Americans." NYT (13 Dec. 1953): X15.

Review of the American Recording Society's release of Carpenter's *Skyscrapers* and Elwell's *The Happy Hypocrite*. "Both are rather dated scores. The jazz features in the Carpenter recall the days of bathtub gin and the drawings of John Held Jr. but there is little in the musical content of *Skyscrapers* to enable it to hold its own today."

B498. "*Skyscrapers* at Matinee." NYT (28 Feb. 1926): 29.

Skyscrapers was danced for the third time as an afterpiece to the regular Metropolitan opera matinee.

B499. "*Skyscrapers* Given Again." NYT (23 Feb. 1926): 26.

Skyscrapers, "following its successful premiere the week preceding, was again very well received."

B500. "*Skyscrapers* Rehearsed." NYT (19 Feb. 1926): 18.

Skyscrapers "involves 60 dancers and an orchestra of 100." The afternoon rehearsal with "a chorus of special voices for negro melodies introduced Flora Sutton and Ralph Northern in brief solo episodes."

B501. Sloper, L.A. "Boston Hears *Skyscrapers*." CSM (10 Dec. 1927): 12.

The reviewer comments on the method which Carpenter and Robert Edmond Jones worked on the scenario for *Skyscrapers*. "But the average listener cannot spend six months listening while the composer plays over the same passage hour after hour. If he could, it is possible his chief idea of movement would be one to a great distance."

The reviewer had seen the ballet at the Metropolitan earlier. In the opera house, the "action so thoroughly [sic] engaged the eye that the ear failed to notice how long drawn out was the use of one of the popular tunes in the 'play' scenes; yesterday [in *Suite no. 1*] we thought it never would be done with."

He compares *Adventures in a Perambulator* which is "amiable, fanciful, charming music" with *Skyscrapers* which "employs certain American tunes in the endeavor to depict the American scene, but its rhythmic pulse and its dissonances are imported from Russia."

B502. Smith, Warren Storey. "Symphony Performs New Music." BP (22 Oct. 1932): 12.

> [*Patterns*] seemed better to deserve the title "Patchwork."...[It] evinces an exhilarating briskness offset by a lush but not particularly distinguished lyricism. Structurally, however, the piece is overmuch of a hodepodge and its melodic ideals are by no means memorable. Like many another composer, Carpenter needs a poetic idea to give wings to his musical fancy. As a composer of absolute music he has never been more than half successful.

B503. Strongin, Theodore. "U.S. Art Songs Reissued." NYT (14 Mar. 1965): X22.

Review of Desto DST 411-12, stereo 6411-12, which contains forty-three songs by twenty-six composers. This was a project of the Alice M. Ditson Fund. The label St/And is a contraction of the names Eleanor STeber and her husband Gordon ANDrews. One thousand copies were distributed free to NATS (National Association of Teachers of Singing) members. Carpenter is one of the "other composers represented" in this review.

B504. _____. "U.S. Music Reissued." NYT (25 Apr. 1965): X20.

Review of Desto DST 407; stereo 6407. The sound "is not by any means the slickest available today."

B505. Thompson, Oscar. "American Work Is Introduced." NYS (10 Mar. 1939): 26.

[Balokovic's performance of the *Violin Concerto*] was one of winning tone and technical brilliance, very much alive and brimful of enthusiasm...In the instrumentation the composer has expanded the usual percussion to include snare drum, oriental drum, wood block, gong, glockenspiel, bells and—for a dulcet close—a vibraphone. But the effect of the scoring is not that of thickness and ponderosity. All is neat and transparent, with momentary suggestion here and there of contemporary popular music in the use of the pulsatile instruments as well as in fleeting rhythmic suggestions of ragtime—one would hardly go so far as to term it jazz or swing. There is in the thematic substance more that is breezy than profound.

Certain sweet sections are reminiscent of Richard Strauss. "There are stretches that do not readily hold attention. Others make a very agreeable impression. The modernity of the work is not disturbing."

B506. Thomson, Virgil. "Mahler Revealed." NYHT (23 Oct. 1942): 15.

[*Symphony no. 2*] was spread out for us with equal confidence in its values. These are not extraordinary, but they are respectable. It is rich man's music, gentleman's composition. Mr. Carpenter has been to Harvard and Paris; he has traveled in Africa and attended the best musical comedies, remembering both pleasantly. His mind is cultivated and adult. He writes with force and some charm. This work is well woven and contrapuntally alive; it has no empty spots in it. Its orchestration is almost too full. I do not mean that it is thick. I mean that it seems to have plenty of instruments available at all times to meet any caprice of the author's musical day. The whole is opulent and comfortable, intelligent, well organised, cultured and firm without being either ostentatious or unduly modest. Beyond these virtues I found little in it to remember.

B507. Tircuit, Heuwell. "New Classical Albums—an American Collection Series." SFC (10 Apr. 1977): 30.

Review of Vox Box SVBX 5303. No mention of
Carpenter.

B508. _____. "Special Karajan Discs among the New Albums."
SFC (16 Oct. 1977): 47.
Review of Mercury SRI 75095: "This is a 'fun'
reissue of three light American works, two suites and
a busy little overture. All are on the Romantic side,
nostalgic even in their day. John Alden Carpenter,
for instance, studied with Elgar but leaned toward
Impressionism in his 1914 *Adventures*."

B509. "Tone Painter Sees Subjects Near at Hand." CSM (30 Oct.
1915): 19.
Discusses Carpenter's development and works
thus far and quotes Carpenter:

> Since you mention the musical possibilities right
> here at home...I do sincerely believe Chicago
> presents tremendous opportunities, but a kindly
> and discriminating ear for the works of the new
> composer. No one could be more helpful and
> thoughtful in this regard than Director Stock of
> the Symphony Orchestra ...Now as to your query
> concerning the American school of music, I do
> not see just how such distinction is to be
> attained...All of our art is bound to be more or less
> polyglot...This harking back to the elemental to
> define nationalism in music is a moot point as it
> concerns us. The American Indian is elemental,
> but as a musical inspiration on the basis of his
> own idea of music he is hard and inflexible. The
> moment you take him away from his natural and
> picturesque surroundings he becomes unnatural,
> unpicturesque—not an object to inspire the muse.

B510. W., V.W. "Boston String Quartet." BH (24 Jan. 1935): 28.
Carpenter's *Piano Quintet* "remains, in spite of its
surface charm in spots, a singularly commonplace
piece. Its imitation of a Spanish atmosphere in the
last movement and in part of the first reminds one of
some gim-crack Hollywood hacienda." The Boston
String Quartet and pianist Jesus Maria Sanroma
performed the work which seemed better suited to a
larger ensemble.

B511. Webster, Ronald. "Symphony Orchestra Concert." CDT (20 Mar. 1915): 13.

Review of the premiere of *Adventures in a Perambulator*. "I can think of no higher praise than to say that the music exactly reflected the spirit of the 'story.' It cannot be called a serious work." Describes some of the pictorial and musical allusions .

B512. Weil, Irving. "*Skyscrapers* Ballet Has Premiere." NYEJ (20 Feb. 1926): 5.

The premiere was a "tradition shattering affair" revealing "out and out expressionism." Reviewer feels that Carpenter and Jones sketched too roughly the humor in the recreation scenes. A "still more notable defect of omission is a careful elision of any robust reference to the kind of sex enjoyment men and women seek and find when they get free of their workday." The music is "self-conscious and fearfully timid...jazz idiom. Melodically it is trivial, harmonically it is Stravinsky through the back door, and instrumentally it is the muddily obvious. To sum it up, it is uninteresting parrot-music." The scenery and costumes were as "imitative as Mr. Carpenter's music."

B513. Wiborg, Mary Hoyt. "A Rare Spirit in Art." (Letters to the Editor) NYT (12 Dec. 1931): 18.

"The late Mrs. John Alden Carpenter gave much to this country." She was talented as a painter and decorator.

B514. "Writers, Artists Revive Honors for Achievements in Fête Here." NYT (23 May 1947): 18.

Carpenter received the gold medal at the two-hour program of the American Academy of Arts and Letters and the National Institute of Arts and Letters. Arnold Schoenberg was given the Institute Award for Distinguished Achievement and grants were given to Alexei Haieff, Ulysses Kay, and Norman Lockwood. Three men in music were inducted into the Institute: Louis Gruenberg, Bernard Rogers, and Paul Hindemith. Includes port.

Appendix

ADVENTURES IN A PERAMBULATOR

I.

En Voiture!

Every morning—after my second breakfast—if the wind and the sun are favorable, I go out. I should like to go alone, but my will is overborne. My Nurse is appointed to take me. She is older than I, and very powerful. While I wait for her, resigned, I hear her cheerful steps, always the same. I am wrapped in a vacuum of wool, where there are no drafts. A door opens and shuts. I am placed in my perambulator, a strap is buckled over my stomach, my Nurse stands firmly behind, —and we are off!

II.

The Policeman.

Out is wonderful! It is always different, though one seems to have been there before. I cannot fathom it all. Some sounds seem like smells. Some sights have echoes. It is confusing, but it is Life! For instance, the Policeman; —an Unprecedented Man! Round like a ball; taller than my Father. Blue—fearful—fascinating! I feel him before he comes. I see him after he goes. I try to analyze his appeal. It is not buttons alone, nor belt, nor baton. I suspect it is his eye and the way he walks. He walks like Doom. My Nurse feels it too. She becomes less firm, less powerful. My perambulator hurries, hestitates and stops. They converse. They ask each other questions,—some with answers, some without. I listen, with discretion. When I feel that they have gone far enough, I signal to my Nurse, a private signal, and the Policeman resumes his enormous Blue March. He is gone, but I feel him after he goes.

III.

The Hurdy-Gurdy.

Then suddenly there is something else. I think it is a sound. We approach it. My ear is tickled to excess. I find that the absorbing noise comes from a box—something like my music box, only much larger, and on wheels. A dark man is turning the music out of the box with a handle, just as I do with mine. A dark lady, richly dressed, turns when the man gets tired. They both smile. I smile too, with restraint, for music is the most insidious form of noise. And such music! So gay! I tug at the strap over my stomach. I have a wild thought of dancing with my Nurse and my perambulator—all three of us together. Suddenly, at the climax of our excitement, I feel the approach of a phenomenon that I remember. It is the Policeman. He has stopped the music. He has frightened away the dark man and the lady with their music box. He seeks the admiration of my Nurse for his act. He walks away, his buttons shine, but far off I hear again the forbidden music. Delightful forbidden music!

IV.

The Lake.

Sated with adventure, my Nurse firmly pushes me on, and before I recover my balance I am face to face with new excitement. The land comes to an end, and there at my feet is the Lake. All my other sensations are joined in one. I see, I hear, I feel, the quiver of the little waves as they escape from the big ones and come rushing up over the sand. Their fear is pretended. They know the big waves are amiable, for they can see a thousand sunbeams dancing with impunity on their very backs. Waves and sunbeams! Waves and sunbeams! Blue water—white clouds—dancing, swinging! A white sea-gull floating in the air. That is *My Lake*!

V.

Dogs.

We pass on. Probably there is nothing more in the World. If there is, it is superfluous. *There* IS. It is Dogs! We come upon them without warning. Not *one* of them,—all of them. First, one by one; then in pairs; then in societies. Little dogs, with sisters; big dogs, with aged parents. Kind dogs, brigand dogs, sad dogs, and gay. They laugh, they fight, they run. And at last, in order to hold my interest, the very littlest brigand starts a game of "Follow the Leader," followed by all the others. It is tremendous!

VI.

Dreams.

Those dogs have gone! It is confusing, but it is Life! My mind grows numb. My cup is too full. I have a sudden conviction that it is well that I am not alone. That firm step behind reassures me. The wheels of my perambulator make a sound that quiets my nerves. I lie very still. I am quite content. In order to think more clearly, I close my eyes. My thoughts are absorbing. I deliberate upon my Mother. Most of the time my Mother and my Nurse have but one identity in my mind, but at night or when I close my eyes, I can easily tell them apart, for my Mother has the greater charm. I hear her voice quite plainly now, and feel the touch of her hand. It is pleasant to live over again the adventures of the day—the long blue waves curling in the sun, the Policeman who is bigger than my Father, the Music box and my friends, the Dogs. It is pleasant to lie quite still and close my eyes, and listen to the wheels of my perambulator. How very large the world is! How many things there are!

CARPENTER'S ANALYSIS

I. En Voiture. The first movement is in the nature of a short prologue, introducing the "principal characters," viz.: "My Nurse," "My Perambulator" and "Myself." The themes representing these ideas reappear constantly throughout the composition in varying form. "My Nurse" announces herself promptly at the beginning of the first movement by means of two violoncellos, soli. This soon is followed by the first appearance of the "Perambulator" motive in the celesta and strings, over which, almost immediately, the first flute announces the ingenuous idea, a descending scale, which stands for "Myself."

II. The Policeman. A few introductory measures, suggesting an interested and hurrying perambulator, are followed by the "Policeman," who makes himself known in flutes and clarinets over a pizzicato accompaniment. After a short development, this is followed by a sort of "Intermezzo" which is intended to suggest the conversation between the Policeman and the Nurse—the remarks of the former being voiced in a solo bassoon, and the responses of the latter in four solo violins, <u>divisi</u>. The conversation is interrupted by the "private signal" sounded by a muted trumpet <u>ff</u>, over an agitated suggestion of the perambulator theme in celesta and piano. The first part of the movement is then, in substance, repeated.

III. The Hurdy-Gurdy. There is no new material in this movement. Bits of familiar masterpieces are heard on the "Hurdy-Gurdy" (two xylophones and harp) with excited interjections by "Myself" and "Nurse." We all "dance together" to a little valse based on the "Perambulator" theme. The remainder of the movement requires no analysis.

IV. The Lake. The only themes necessary to mention, as belonging to this movement, are the first, suggesting the "little waves," allotted to the flute, and another, suggestive of the large and amiable ones, which is heard in the strings and the horns.

V. Dogs. The woodwind bear most of the burden of furnishing descriptions of dogs, in various themes and snatches of themes, which it would not be of interest to quote. "Ach Du Lieber Augustin" may be detected in the "melée" as well as "Where, Oh Where, Has My Little Dog Gone?" A variation of the last is used towards the end of the movement as the theme of a short fugue in the woodwind, suggesting dogs playing "Follow-the-Leader."

VI. Dreams. A résumé of all the preceding "excitements." It may be worth while simply to call attention to the softened and broadened version of the original "Nurse" theme, which here represents "My Mother," and also to the final "berceuse," which is made up in part of the "Child" theme over an accompaniment drawn from the "Perambulator" motive.

Alphabetical Index of Works

Chronological List of Works

Composed	Title	Published
1894	Love whom I have never seen	1894
	Minuet for orchestra	n.p.
	Minuet for piano	1894
	My sweetheart	1894
	Twilight reverie	1894
1896	Alas, how easily things go wrong	1896
	Branglebrink	1896
	In spring	1896
	Memory	1896
	Norse lullaby	1896, 1903
	Strawberry Night Festival Music	n.p.
1897	Flying Dutchman	1897
	Little John's song	1897
	Mistress mine	1897
	Piano sonata	n.p.
	Sicilian lullaby	1897
1898	Nocturne for piano	1898, 1906
1900	A little Dutch girl	1901
1901-02	Improving songs for anxious children	1904, 1907, 1913
1904	When little boys sing	1904, 1905
1905	Treat me nice	1918

1908	Berceuse for orchestra	n.p.
	The cock shall crow	1912
	The debutante	n.p.
	Go, lovely rose	1912
	May, the maiden	1912
1909	Green river	1912
	The heart's country	1912
	Little fly	1912
	Looking-glass river	1912
	Suite for orchestra	n.p.
1910	Chanson d'automne	1912
	Le ciel	1912
	Dansons la gigue!	1912
	En sourdine	1912
	Il pleur dans mon coeur	1912
1911	Bid me to live	1912
	A cradle song	1912
	Don't ceäre	1912
	Violin sonata	1913
1912	Fog Wraiths	1913
	Her voice	1913
	Polonaise americaine	1915
	Les silhouettes	1913
	To one unknown	1913
1913	Gitanjali	1914
	Impromptu for piano	1915
	Terre promise	n.p.
1914	Adventures in a perambulator	1917
	The day is no more	1915
	Gitanjali; arr.	n.p.
	The little prayer of I	n.p.
	Player queen	1915
	Wull ye come in eärly spring	1918
1915	Aged woman	n.p.
	Piano concertino	1920
1916	Little Indian	1918
	Spring joys	n.p.
	Water colors	1916
1917	The home road	1917
	Khaki Sammy	1917
	Land of mine	n.p.
	Little dancer	1918
	Sermons in stones	n.p.
1918	Berceuse de guerre	1918
	Birthday of the Infanta	n.p.
	The lawd is smilin' through the do'	1918
	Water colors; arr.	n.p.

1920	Pilgrim vision	n.p.
	Tango américain	1921
	Thoughts	n.p.
	Serenade	1921
	Slumber song	1921
1921	Krazy Kat	1922
1922	Les cheminées rouges	n.p.
1923	Diversions	1923
	Minuet for flute, violin, 'cello & piano	n.p.
	Le petit cimetière	n.p.
	O! Soeur divine	n.p.
1924	Skyscrapers	1926, 1927
	The Wrigley wriggle	n.p.
1925	A little bit of jazz	n.p.
1925-26	Jazz orchestra pieces	n.p.
1926	Four Negro songs	1927
	The little turtle	n.p.
	Mountain, mountain	n.p.
	Oil & vinegar	n.p.
1927	String quartet	1928
1928	America, the beautiful	n.p.
	The music doctor's blues	n.p.
1929	The hermit crab	n.p.
	Young man, chieftain!	1930
1931	Gentle Jesus, meek and mild	n.p.
	Song of faith	1932
1932	Birthday of the Infanta. Suite no.1	1932
	Patterns	n.p.
1933	Sea drift	1936
1934	Gitanjali; rev.	n.p.
	If	1938
	The little graveyard	n.p.
	The past walks here	n.p.
	Piano quintet	n.p.
	The pools of peace	1938
	Red chimneys	n.p.
	Rest	1934, 1936
	Worlds	1938
1935	Danza for piano	1947
	Danza; arr.	n.p.
	Morning fair	1936
1936	Song of faith; rev.	1939
	Violin concerto	1939
1937	Piano quintet; rev.	1937
	Song of faith; rev.	1939
1938	Birthday of the Infanta; rev.	n.p.
1940	Birthday of the Infanta. Suite no.1; rev.	n.p.

	Krazy Kat; rev.	1948
	Symphony no.1 (1940)	n.p.
1941	Adventures in a perambulator; rev.	n.p.
	Blue gal	n.p.
	A song for Illinois	n.p.
	Song of freedom	1942, 1943
	Symphony no.2 (1942)	n.p.
1943	Anxious bugler	n.p.
	Blue gal; arr.	n.p.
	Dance suite	n.p.
	Les silhouettes; arr.	n.p.
	Slumber song; arr.	n.p.
1944	Sea drift; rev.	n.p.
1945	Fanfarette-berceuse for Richard	n.p.
	Seven ages	n.p.
1946-47	Piano quintet; rev.	n.p.
1947	Piano concertino; rev.	n.p.
	Symphony no.2; rev.	n.p.
1948	Carmel concerto	n.p.
1949	Birthday of the Infanta. Suite no.2	n.p.

Undated Works

About my garden
Animato for piano
Bright truth is still our leader
Canterbury bells
Dawn in India
Dutch dance
Endlose Liebe
How to dance
Impromptu for violin and piano
Largo for piano
The marshes of Glynn
Midnight Nan
Miniature for violin and piano
Petite suite for piano
Prelude (and fugue) for piano
Schifferlied
Sehnsucht for piano
Serenade for piano
Triste était mon âme
Two little pieces Nr. I
Vier Jahreszeiten
War lullaby

General Index

About the Compiler

JOAN O'CONNOR is a Librarian at the San Francisco Conservatory of Music. She is interested in American and contemporary music.